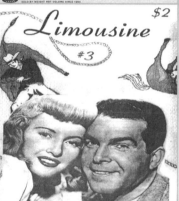

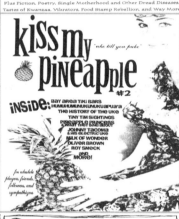

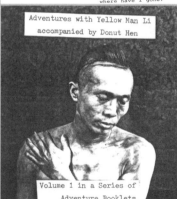

◆

PUBLISHER/EDITOR-IN-CHIEF: V. Vale
PUBLISHER/EDITOR: Marian Wallace
LAYOUT & ASSISTANT EDITING: Yimi Tong
GRAPHIC DESIGN: Matthew Petty
TEXT INTERNS: Anna Hsieh, Libby Lampert,
Jennifer Laskey
PHOTOGRAPHY: Robert Waldman, Olivier Robert
PRODUCTION CONSULTANTS: Andrea Reider, Valentine Wallace
PHOTOSHOP & SCANNING: Eric Rodenbeck, Thaddeus Croyle
COMPUTER CONSULTANTS: Mason Jones, Ron Klatchko
SENIOR EDITOR (NYC): Chris Trela
THANKS FOR SUPPORT: Scott Armst, Kyanne Breden,
Sharon Cheslow, Kris Lawson, Barbara
MacDonald, Jamie Miller, Greta Mudflap,
Molly Neuman, Teresa Piccolotti, Gregory
Pleshaw, Tiffanie Ragasa, Mary Ricci,
Seth Robson, Ken Sitz, Robin Takayama,
Stacy Wakefield, Catherine Wallace
FINANCIAL ADVISORS: Carol & Dennis Hamby
LAWYER: David S. Kahn, Esq.
WEB SITE: Jamie Lopez, Gentry Lane
http://www.vsearchmedia.com

◆

BOOKSTORE DISTRIBUTION: SUBCO, PO Box 160 or 265 South 5th, Monroe OR 97456
TEL: 800-274-7826 FAX: 503-847-6018
NON-BOOKSTORE DISTRIBUTION: LAST GASP, 777 Florida St, San Francisco CA 94110
TEL: 415-864-6636. FAX: 415-824-1836
U.K. DISTRIBUTION: AIRLIFT, #8 The Arena, Mollison Ave, Enfield, Middlesex U.K. EN3 7NJ
TEL: 181-804-0400. FAX: 181-804-0044

V/SEARCH
20 Romolo #B
San Francisco CA 94133
TEL: (415) 362-1465
FAX: (415) 362-0742
vsearch@vsearchmedia.com

*CALL, WRITE or E-MAIL for a
CURRENT CATALOG!*

Printed in Hong Kong by Colorcraft, Ltd.

10   9   8   7   6   5   4   3   2   1

Front cover: Photo of Toad (Revolutionary Knitting Circle) by V. Vale; Print by Dee, Colorarts
Back cover: Photo of Candi Strecker by Robert Waldman
Cover Design & Photoshop: Matt Petty

Table of Contents

4 ♦ Dishwasher Pete

22 ♦ Temp Slave

34 ♦ McJob

40 ♦ Revolutionary Knitting Circle

54 ♦ Aim Your Dick, Slant

66 ♦ Eight-track Mind

80 ♦ Tiki News

86 ♦ Arthur Cravan

90 ♦ Bruno Richard

96 ♦ International Mail Art

102 ♦ Candi Strecker

116 ♦ Murder Can Be Fun

134 ♦ Nico Ordway on Proletarian Novels

136 ♦ Zine Reviews

138 ♦ Zine Directory

141 ♦ Catalog

147 ♦ Index

One of the best-known zines in America is *Dishwasher*, published by "Dishwasher Pete," a modern-day blue-collar Ulysses roaming the continent investigating the true status of America's working class (or what's left of it). Famous for sending an imposter to appear on David Letterman's overrated TV spectacle, Pete is a low-key yet fervent social activist who is firsthandedly gaining perspective on the condition and outlook of workers everywhere, while attempting to envision how society might be improved. *Dishwasher* humorously and poignantly illuminates "Dishwasher Culture," which is far more complex than first meets the eye. Send $1 cash for the latest issue to PO Box 8213, Portland OR 97207.

♦ *VALE: When I first read* **Dishwasher,** *I immediately recalled George Orwell's description of working in a restaurant in* **Down and Out in Paris and London.** *Working a low-status job opens one's eyes to numerous inequities and class injustices. In your zine, you've managed to uncover and synthesize so many aspects of what might be called "Dishwasher Culture."*

I'm *addicted* to that feeling of quitting: walking out the door, yelling "Hurrah!"

♦ DISHWASHER PETE: I think it was always there, long before I stumbled upon it. I'm especially excited when I find references dating from the turn of the century. There's an attitude and appreciation for dishwashing that has always existed, and I can't take credit for that; I just make people aware of it.

There are thousands of dishwashers across the country who never thought they had a common *bond*. I get a lot of letters from people living in small towns who wash dishes and enjoy it, but they're surrounded by people who tell them it's "not good enough" and that they should find themselves a "career." It's great when they get hold of the zine and say, "Wow!" and suddenly they feel better about themselves. Their reaction justifies everything I'm doing. I'm glad *Dishwasher* has this effect on people.

Last night I visited a dishwasher friend at her job and found out she'd become a waitress. She shrugged her shoulders and said, "Sorry if you feel I've deserted the fold, but I gotta do what I gotta do to make this higher wage." I said, "Don't worry about me; I don't take it personally." This got me thinking about writing an article on tipping. There's a lot of public guilt over waiters and waitresses needing your money because they work so hard and don't get paid much. Meanwhile there's some guy in the kitchen with sweat dripping down his back working just as hard. But nobody's going into the kitchen saying, "Here's a dollar for you, too." All labor *should* be thought of as deserving equal pay.

♦ *V: I knew a pantry worker who voluntarily shared her money with the dishwashers . . . As a dishwasher, do you feel like people treat you as if you were imperceptible?*

♦ DP: Yes—the position is usually looked down upon; a lot of waiters and waitresses don't want to even associate with the dishwasher. Also, I'm extremely quiet at work; I'm nearly invisible . . . just a fly on the wall. You see the spoils raked in by the restaurant, but the dishwasher who goes home the most physically tired gets the least. You can't help but feel "socialist," even if you aren't familiar with the term—

♦ V: *—or the body of theory and literature that goes with the term . . . What's your background?*

♦ DP: I was born in 1966 and grew up in San Francisco. I was kicked out of school several times for having "a complete lack of respect for authority." Some boss told me that recently, so I guess I haven't changed much! That attitude didn't go over well in the educational field, but in the workplace it's fine. As a dishwasher you are in control, because even if the bosses don't like your attitude, they still need somebody to wash the dishes and keep the operation running. They may see you as existing at the bottom of the barrel, but you still hold a trump card: you can walk out at any moment!

♦ V: *In work, you discovered an unsuspected dimension of freedom—*

♦ DP: I'm *addicted* to that feeling of quitting: walking out the door, yelling "Hurrah!" and running through the streets. Maybe I need to have jobs in order to appreciate my free leisure time or just life in general.

People forget they don't have to put up with drudgery—that it's *voluntary*. I can say that because I don't have children to support, but I purposely kept my options open so I can walk out of a job on a moment's notice. I minimize the responsibilities on my shoulder that might be affected by such an act.

I don't know how young I was—maybe around ten—when I realized you can work all your life and still end up poor.

♦ V: *What are your parents' occupations?*

♦ DP: My mom's a teacher and my dad was a white-collar clerk working in the customs field. We were pretty poor, and throughout childhood we watched our dad lament about coming to America filled with visions of wealth, and how everybody was becoming rich except him. He struggled and worked well beyond the age of retirement and still never really got ahead. I don't know how young I was—maybe around ten—when I realized that you can work all your life and still end up poor. I'd rather not go chasing those rainbows and just be happy with what I have.

♦ V: *Where is your father from?*

Pete . . . dishwasher or enigma? Photo: Michelle Gienow; Photo collage: Eric Rodenbeck

♦ DP: He immigrated from Scotland. My mom came from Canada, which used to be a separate country before NAFTA annexed it to the United States.

♦ *V: So you grew up in San Francisco, a "liberal" city. It's expensive to live here, actually—*

♦ DP: Fortunately, we had a rent-controlled flat for about a quarter of a century. That helped, but eventually we were evicted because the landlord found a loophole in the law: an immediate relative can move in and take over a place. He kicked us out and had his son move in. Who knows how high the rent is now.

♦ *V: What happened to your parents?*

♦ DP: They had thought they were going to live there the rest of their lives. Fortunately, they were able to find a place in San Francisco that wasn't too expensive to buy. My brother had to co-sign the loan. My parents and brothers and sisters still live in San Francisco.

♦ *V: Do you have a big family?*

♦ DP: Two brothers and two sisters. I started traveling because I knew I'd never be able to afford living in San Francisco. It's rather unfortunate; it took me awhile to get used to that.

♦ *V: Was your initial impulse to flee to the suburbs?*

♦ DP: My dream was to live in the suburbs, away from the turbulence of the city. Now I've had my fill of suburban life, which I'm grateful for because it showed me everything wrong with that world. I lived

Cover of Dishwasher #4

in Walnut Creek [Bay Area]. It was difficult being around all these rich white people; this was not my world at all. I realized there wasn't a problem with me getting adjusted to it; it was just *unadjustable!* Now I could live the rest of my life without seeing another suburb—I *know* what's there. I might have liked living in a small town 40 years ago, when towns still had some character, but now the suburbs are just places where people can escape from the city once they've achieved a sufficiently high income. Then they can live in a bland world detached from their neighbors and be locked up in their houses on so-called "safe" streets.

> **Nowadays, I can't *believe* how personally employers take it when I quit. I think, "Did you expect me to grow old and die in your restaurant?"**

♦ *V: Did your parents encourage education?*

♦ DP: My parents read a lot. I've always liked to read; I guess that made me want to travel. When I lived in San Francisco I never really traveled; there were long periods when I never left the city limits. I started reading about regional dialects and folkways and decided to see, firsthand, places like Appalachia, the South, the Northeastern cities, the Midwest, etc.

I get excited just by a pronunciation or phrase that's different, or some peculiar product or tradition. But this is all disappearing under the influence of television which is bringing about the homogenization of the whole country, which in turn is homogenizing the whole planet into one "safe" culture. I'm still on the lookout for remnants of *difference,* where the "corporatization" of culture isn't so apparent. It would have been much more exciting to travel 70 or 80 years ago, when the regions were very different from each other, and the towns were all very unique.

♦ *V: As a dishwasher/sociologist you can travel all over the country with the freedom that hobos used to have. America used to be regularly criss-crossed by thousands of them hopping freight trains.*

♦ DP: There was a lot more demand for transient or itinerant workers who would follow the different harvests. Back then there was more acceptance for someone coming in, washing dishes for a week, and then leaving. Now there's this ethic about even crap work like washing dishes: you're supposed to be *loyal* to the job . . . and stick with it and "move up." Also, now you have to prove you're a legal resident just to get hired, whereas ten years ago nobody cared—especially about a dishwashing job. Of course, it's much more enjoyable to move fluidly between jobs.

♦ *V: So it has become much harder to work as a dishwasher?*

♦ DP: Nowadays, I can't *believe* how personally

employers take it when I quit. I think, "What did you expect? Did you expect me to grow old and die here in your restaurant?" There seems to be a growing obsession with job security, a feeling that if you have a job you'd better stick with it and "count your blessings."

♦ *V: Also, people who have been working jobs for 25 years are getting fired right and left—*

♦ DP: That's true. It used to be that if you had a job and wanted it for the rest of your life, then fine, it was there for you. But that's not an option anymore. At any moment your job can be pulled out from under you, so people are scared into sticking with the crappiest work situations.

♦ *V: What was your first job?*

♦ DP: I was eight years old when I started delivering the San Francisco *Chronicle*. Every morning I had to get up at 4 A.M. I had that job for seven years.

♦ *V: Did your parents have a strong work ethic?*

♦ DP: It wasn't them telling me to get a job so I could learn some moral lesson; it was me thinking, "If I want money to go to the movies, I better earn some." My parents didn't *have* any money to give me. All my brothers and sisters worked for their own money, so it wasn't any big deal to be working at that age and basically be supporting myself. Of course, my parents paid the rent and board and everything, but I never wanted to bother them with frivolous things like buying some candy for me.

In my neighborhood, a lot of my friends were Filipino. They told me it was customary for them to give half of their paper route money to their parents. This made me feel really shitty. Here I thought I was being so heroic by not pestering my parents for candy money, while these friends were matter-of-factly helping meet the family expenses. So then I tried to give my parents half of what I earned, but they wouldn't take it from me—I was eight or ten years old.

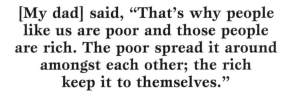

[My dad] said, "That's why people like us are poor and those people are rich. The poor spread it around amongst each other; the rich keep it to themselves."

I had a lot of other jobs, too, like passing out flyers around the neighborhood for local restaurants. It seemed like I was always being offered jobs without really looking for them. This made me feel uneasy: "Why are you picking on me? Why don't you ask someone else?"

♦ *V: What's the worst job you had back then?*

♦ DP: Some people on my paper route hired me to work in their yard. At first, there were some *bona fide* things to do, like uprooting some brush and weeds. But after I got everything cleared out, the only thing

Cover of *Dishwasher #13*

left was to clean up the dogshit . . . I became very conscious of being lower-class and cleaning up these rich people's dogshit. At ten years old I remember thinking, "Something's wrong," and quitting that job—it didn't seem right.

♦ *V: You began to critique work at the age of ten—*

♦ DP: Yeah. When I first got my paper route, I went around collecting the monthly bill. I thought I would get a big tip at the wealthiest-looking building (a big, grand four-story house). After I had given the old man his change, he asked if I had change for a quarter. I didn't understand why, but I gave him two dimes and a nickel. He held out the nickel and said (condescendingly), "Here you go—this is for *you.*" I let it sit in my palm thinking, "What—a nickel?" This was supposed to be my big payoff.

I went home and told my father, "Dad, the guy in that big house just gave me a nickel!" He said, "That's why people like us are poor and those people are rich. The poor spread it around amongst each other; the rich keep it to themselves." I remember one Christmas the very poorest family on my route—a single mother with six kids—gave me $20 for the holidays. This woman couldn't afford this, but she wanted to give it to me. I tried to give it back to her. I remember these two incidents very clearly.

♦ *V: That's classic.*

♦ DP: These stories may sound simplistic, but for an eight-year-old they made perfect sense. They showed me what I was heading towards as an adult. Now I work in restaurants where the owners constantly make money and are able to buy fine houses and cars. Meanwhile, after you've worked there for a year they want to give you a dime raise in "appreciation." I think, "Oh, thanks a lot! I hope that car I just bought you is doing pretty well! Your kid's braces sure look good."

♦ V: *The owners make money off your labor and just take it for granted . . . So you did the paper route until you were 15?*

♦ DP: Yeah. Then I was just like any other teenager in San Francisco trying to get a job—no luck. I still have a phobia about looking for work in S.F. because of that. I tried to join the Retail Clerks' Union as a bag boy—went down every week and kept my name active on the list. I forgot one week and had to start all over again with my name at the bottom of the list. I wasn't able to crack the union, no matter how hard I tried.

I got a job at a neighborhood Boys' Club as a lifeguard, even though I didn't know how to swim. I *told* them this but they said, "That's okay—if someone's drowning, just throw 'em a lifesaver!" I would sit in my street clothes near the pool and tell all the kids, "If you're drowning, I'm going to throw this to you. I'm

not jumping in, because then we'd *both* drown!" After awhile I got fired for sassing off to some adult, so they transferred me to the Arts and Crafts Department (one of those jobs created to "get kids off the street"). When that ended, the mayor's youth job program wouldn't hire me again—they thought I was "too much trouble."

♦ V: *Didn't you ever aspire to a middle-class career?*

♦ DP: It's in our society that we should all be working toward that. No matter how poor you are, you're expected to pretend that someday you'll be a doctor. Every year the nuns at our school would ask, "What are you going to be when you grow up?" Destitute kids would get up and crow about how they were going to be some great lawyer—this was what you were *supposed* to say. I would always say I wanted to be a house painter, because I remembered watching one with a paintbrush in one hand, a sandwich in another, his transistor radio playing while he sat on a plank brushing away in the sun. I thought, "That's the job for me—I could do that!" The nuns were never happy when they heard this: "A *house painter?!* Are you sure you don't want to be a doctor?" "No, ma'am." When I was about 20, I was sitting on a roof painting a chimney and had a flashback: "Hey! When I was a kid I wanted to be a house painter, and now here I am!" And I *still* enjoy that. The problem is: anybody you

Dishwasher Book Review

DOWN AND OUT IN PARIS AND LONDON
By George Orwell

I don't know if Orwell was simply "slumming" when he lived the experiences recounted in this book, or if he was actually floating along on the bottom, destitute and desperate. But he did indeed spend time in Paris as a "plongeur" (hey, that's French for "dishwasher"!)

After a long spell of not being able to find work (this was during the Depression), Orwell was overjoyed to be hired to labor 13 hours a day, six days a week, in the steamy basement of a hotel, slaving over the dishes. Though the job left him with little spare time to have a life, he was grateful to at least be eating. He was quickly horrified by his co-workers who'd been stuck in these conditions with no prospects of escaping. The meager pay provided them with barely enough to survive, while the hours were long enough to prevent them from having any time to seek any other employment.

Some experiences George included were the discovery that the management barred the dishwashers from having

mustaches (Yeah!); how the employees used a code on the hotel's bell system to warn others when a manager was approaching; how the dishwashers sold the leftover food to pigkeepers and split the proceeds; and how coffee and tea was the choice for dishwashers when it came to illicit pilfering. (Waiters were even attacked as wannabe snobs!)

A friend's tip on another job enabled Orwell to escape the hellish torment the hotel forced upon its hundreds of employees. Though his new dishdog job was in a small Russian restaurant, his hours were even longer and his pay even smaller. As was the case at the hotel, the sanitary conditions here thoroughly disgusted him. The food was nibbled on, spit on, sneezed on, infested, dropped, putrid, but always still happily served to the customers. His washing exploits here included drying the crockery with a borrowed pillow case, scrubbing copper pans with sand and chains, and not having enough time to give the dishes a proper washing so he simply wiped the grease from them with a table napkin (we all know how that is).

—Pete, from *Dishwasher #11*

Drawing from Dishwasher #12

work with is bound to be a raging alcoholic; all house painters are alcoholics.

♦ **V: *Someone told me it's because the fumes damage the nervous system—***

♦ DP: That's why I had to quit those jobs; I couldn't keep up with the drinking!

♦ **V: *What college did you attend?***

♦ DP: Saint Mary's College in Contra Costa County. It's quaint and pleasant. It used to be a liberal arts school, but now it caters to business majors because they're the ones who turn into rich alumnae (meanwhile, liberal arts students go on to become dishwashers or whatever and don't pump any money back into the school). I guess I didn't fit in there because they kicked me out. I had no idea what I was going to do with my life. I did different jobs then; I started washing dishes and was also a janitor at a church—that was interesting.

♦ **V: *How so?***

♦ DP: It was an Episcopal church but they hired me because I was Catholic—they didn't think an *Episcopalian* should have to do this! [laughs]

They gave me a list of chores that supposedly took 20 hours a week. The first week I did them all in 3 hours, and some of the volunteer ladies got mad: "Are you sure you're doing a good job?" One old guy told me, "Slow down, son—take it easy and stretch it out to 15 or 20 hours." So that gave me the green light to just sit around, take naps, try to learn how to play the organ, etc—nobody was around anyway. By the time I left, I estimated I had the job down to 20 minutes per week— all I *really* had to do was to empty the trash, because that was the only thing people could tell for sure was dirty or not. Churches stay pretty clean because everyone's on their "best behavior"; they're sure not having big parties and messin' the place up. They use it one day a week for a couple hours and that's *it.*

♦ **V: *What was your first dishwashing job?***

♦ DP: I got a job at a restaurant where the bosses originally wanted me to cook or be a cashier. There wasn't really a dishwasher—everybody traded off doing it but hated it. But after they asked *me* to do it, I realized, "Hey, this is great! I don't have to deal with customers or the pressures of cooking. I'm by myself in the back just washing dishes, and since nobody else is around, I've got kind of a free hand to screw around back here." So I started volunteering to do them because I realized I liked the job a lot.

♦ **V: *You discovered a dimension of freedom: freedom from bosses looking over your shoulder, and from having to be nice to customers—being Mr Politeness Man.***

♦ DP: Yeah—that was the last time I've ever dealt with "customers." Sometimes when I'm washing dishes and am publicly visible, customers will ask me questions. I do my best to ignore them—I'm being paid to *wash dishes,* not to answer to people. I don't have a very high opinion of customers—actually, it's

Cover of *Dishwasher #12*

more the customer/employee *relationship* I dislike. When I *am* a customer and go into a store, I'm immediately confronted with: "HI! HOW'S IT GOING? CAN I HELP YOU WITH ANYTHING?" "No, I just want to buy a pack of gum; leave me alone." "THAT PACK OF GUM, WOULD YOU LIKE ANYTHING ELSE WITH THAT?"

♦ **V: *They're trained like parrots to say these exact words which marketing studies have determined will sell more product—***

♦ DP: Yeah: "HOW ARE YOU TODAY?" I think, "What do *you* care?"

♦ **V: *Nowadays people are getting really low wages working in stores, yet even to get these jobs they have to undergo lengthy training in these creepy seminars—that never used to happen before. Years of market research are finally yielding results.***

♦ DP: There have been plenty of studies conducted as to the exact degree a smile should be when somebody walks into a store, or the exact wording of a greeting. I'm no fan of "customer relations." Even when I'm taken out to eat, I loathe having to give my order to the waiter—who's suddenly my *best friend*—I'd rather just get the food myself! What makes waiters even slimier is: they're not acting friendly because their bosses are forcing them to; they're doing it so you'll give them money. I always feel like saying, "Look, I'm

from *Dishwasher #12*

not going to give you a tip at all, so don't even bother smiling—we'll both be better off." It's disgusting how someone will give you an exaggeratedly cheerful treatment just because they want money from you.

I was thinking about this last night when I encountered the dishwasher-turned-waitress. When I was leaving the restaurant, a homeless guy opened the door for me and held out his hand. I wondered what was the difference between this guy holding the door for me and asking for change and a waitress carrying food ten feet and asking for change.

♦ *V: Nevertheless, a lot of waitresses depend on tips to pay their rent. Every waitress has stories about being stiffed for tips by obviously well-to-do people.*

♦ DP: My gripe is that the burden is put on the customer; the waiters and waitresses should be paid a living wage to begin with. This is something that the restaurant owner should be taking care of; instead it's thrown onto the waiters and the customers to work out some kind of deal.

♦ *V: In France, most menus say "service compris"—no tipping required. Tipping doesn't exist or is rare in other countries, that's why a lot of Europeans don't tip when they visit America. This seems to be a better system; there's a lot less anxiety when it comes to paying the bill.*

♦ DP: In Oregon, the Oregon Restaurant Association (of restaurant owners) keeps trying to pass a law to cut the minimum wage for waiters and waitresses in half. This already exists in some states where they get around two bucks an hour, on the theory that they'll make up for it in tips. The fact that restaurant owners are spending hundreds of thousands of dollars lobbying to cut their payrolls in half doesn't mean that menu prices will suddenly drop—it just means that owners will increase their profits. This illustrates the problem with tipping in a larger sense: "Okay, we're going to pay our workers even lousier, so could you please pony up? They're going to be even poorer, and it's not our fault. It's your problem now—*you* deal with it."

♦ *V: Perhaps restaurant owners should start planting suggestions in major media: "If you really enjoyed the service, you should leave a 25% tip."*

♦ DP: "Have you done your part this year? Have you left 25%?"

♦ *V: It's a real breakthrough that you discovered: you can travel around, always get a job, and quit whenever you want. You have all this freedom and you're able to form your own observations as to how society really works."*

♦ DP: I didn't plan this; it just happened. It's interesting to hear your evaluation—I would like to think that I write about washing dishes and just leave it at that. Any sociological observations I leave to others to point out.

♦ *V: You actually live what you write about. You're doing a critique of class and privilege from a unique viewpoint which preserves your personal freedom, self-esteem and well-being. That's at least partly due to the fact that you can quit at any time, and get an actual adrenalin rush from quitting—a feeling of joy or sudden freedom.*

♦ DP: I don't know *what* my observations would be like if I weren't in a position to quit. I just got a letter from a guy asking for advice because he's had the same dishwashing job for years, and is in a financial cycle where he can't quit because he has bills to pay, rent to pay. I don't know what to tell him. If I were writing from his point of view, I think I would have a different take on *everything.*

♦ *V: In a way, zine production is not only your "art form" but a way to "network" (I hate that word). When you travel, don't you stay with a lot of people you meet through your zine?*

♦ DP: That's true. I first started traveling because I wanted to see what was out there, but I was also taking the opportunity to visit friends as they moved to different parts of the country: "Hey, you moved to Smyrna, Georgia—can I come visit?" Where my friends were located at least partially determined where I would travel, and the more obscure the destination, the better.

You asked what kind of career goals I had in college. I remember telling people when they asked me what I was going to do when I left school: "I'll come sleep on your floor when you're a rich lawyer." I was *sort of* joking, but now it's true! [laughs]. I'm in an extremely fortunate position of having friends all over the country who invite me to come stay with them.

> **I loathe having to give my order to the waiter—who's suddenly my *best friend*—I'd rather just get the food myself!**

♦ *V: So how did you start publishing?*

♦ DP: I had been thinking about it for about four years before I put anything together. I would talk to other dishwashers and hear these great stories and think, "Wow, I should write that down." At first I imagined doing a one-shot deal; just one project. A lot of people promised to send me stories but they all turned out to be even lazier than I am. Then I realized that if I put out something myself, people would finally come around and contribute. Of all of the original dishwashers who inspired me to publish, I think only one has ever contributed something.

I've come to accept that "dishwasher culture" is much larger than what's actually in the pages of my zine, because of all the great stories I've heard that were never written down. I'm thinking of carrying around a tape recorder because there are a lot of people who tell great stories verbally.

♦ *V: Today you can get a recorder for $30 that does the job.*

♦ DP: I love to hear other dishwashers talk about their past: "One time I was washing dishes down in Texas and such and such happened . . ." I was always delighted by people who had washed dishes in different parts of the country. I always thought it would be neat to have a story for every state in the country, so if someone mentioned (for example) Tennessee, I could say, "Oh yeah, I washed dishes there once . . ." Then I decided to make that my goal: to wash dishes in all 50 states. I didn't think this was such a big deal, but it was funny to discover that this was what most people asked me about.

♦ V: *Hearing all these great stories—better than the ones you read in magazines—perhaps influenced you to publish and pass some of them along. The storytelling impulse must be the oldest form of cultural transmission; it's a human need to hear a story. This is completely ruined by our corporate culture that inundates us with oversimplified trash—*

♦ DP: It's like Hollywood telling the same story over and over. People seem to be addicted to happy endings—they have to know the movie will have a happy ending or they won't go.

There's a publication in Oregon for and by gas station attendants. By Oregon law, only gas station attendants can pump gas. I think this law was implemented when self-service gas began spreading across the country. People thought they were putting attendants out of work, and a law was passed to keep them employed. This publication is small (2"x3") and is circulated by workers sticking it in the little gas cap compartment. The car drives to another gas station, a different gas station attendant pulls out this publication, reads it and then sticks it in another car—that's how they're passed around. Meanwhile, car owners are completely unaware they're aiding and abetting a sort of workers' solidarity movement.

For a long time, as I traveled around the country, I would sneak into the back of restaurants and hand out copies of my zine to whoever was washing the dishes. I haven't done that lately, but hearing the story about the gas station attendants has inspired me to do it again. I wish there were a more covert way of going about it, but I guess just running into the back of a restaurant and running out again (before anybody knows what's going on) is fun in its own way.

♦ V: *Is self-expression your primary motive?*

♦ DP: Yeah. At first I just wanted to be the editor and not be responsible for the writing myself. Instead, I became very involved—the last issue and the next one have been nothing but my writing. By the way, there already are a couple of other dishwashing zines—

♦ V: *You're kidding!*

♦ DP: One was *The Dish Rag*, from Portland, Oregon. The woman who published it put on an event called The Dish Fest. I came up from California for it; there

were all sorts of contests and quiz games. Most of the audience were dishwashers; a couple of bands played whose members were dishwashers. She ended up getting me a job.

About seven years ago I heard about *The Dishwasher's Quarterly* and got very excited. I wrote the editor: "I've got all these dishwashing stories to send you." He wrote back: "I quit doing that." It turned out that it wasn't entirely about dishwashing, anyway; for him this was a "poetic" title. A lot of people send me their contributions and I can't use all of them, so it would be nice to see people starting their own—I'm still hoping there will be a whole new rash of dishwashing publications.

♦ V: *You must hear a range of stories—everything from "farmer's daughter" fables to sabotage-in-the-workplace ones—*

♦ DP: —which are my favorite. However, this morning a friend was telling me about her job; her boss told her not to use as much water as she does normally. I asked, "Were they bugging you all night about that?" (envisioning some great ongoing conflict). But she just said, "Oh no—the people I work for are *really nice.*" I realized that maybe I egg on some employers because I like big blowouts between employer and employee. I'm sort of at a loss when people tell me, "Oh yeah, me and my boss get along great." That's against the laws of nature!

THE DISHWASHER'S QUARTERLY

WHO KNOWS? HE'S A DORK!

WHATTA YA EXPECT, HE'S A DISHWASHER!

WHATS HE SMILING 'BOUT?

For years I slacked on getting this publication started. In the meantime, I was surprised to discover "The Dishwasher's Quarterly" - a zine a guy named Scott Bennett did for apparently only a couple issues. I figured my procrastinating problems were solved—I'd simply contribute to the Quarterly - but my enthusiastic letters weren't answered with the same energy. Scott had moved on from his dishwashing zine days so I started my own zine.

Now Dishwasher pays a tribute to The Dishwasher's Quarterly by reprinting this drawing from a cover of D.Q.

Cover of The Dishwasher's Quarterly

In one issue of *Dishwasher* I printed a story about this guy who was washing dishes in Little Rock, Arkansas. Hillary and Chelsea Clinton came in, so he made it a point to deposit one of his "boogers" in either Hillary's salad or sandwich. And yes, it was ingested. That kind of stuff happens all the time in restaurants—usually to the more irate customers.

♦ V: *Actually, I would much rather that had happened to Newt Gingrich—*

♦ DP: You have to take 'em where you can get 'em. I don't know what would happen if Newt Gingrich came into a place where I was working. It would be a mess, though.

A few years ago the National Restaurant Association (the nationwide restaurant owners' lobbying group) put their money on Newt Gingrich. They were thinking, "If this guy gets into power using our money, he's going to owe us big time." Sure enough, when he assumed the Speaker's position in the House of Representatives, the restaurant owners were first in line giving him their to-do lists. Their influence killed the national health care plan, because so many restaurant owners didn't want to provide healthcare for their employees. Owners try to make their employees disposable; if they're ill, just get rid of 'em and get another one. As long as the National Restaurant Association is in cahoots with Gingrich, there's no way the minimum wage will ever be raised to a "livable wage." It's frightening to think that my labor is helping to pay for their lobbying efforts. I would like to make restaurant workers more aware of the actions of the National Restaurant Association.

> ## It's amazing how millionaires in Washington, D.C. are debating whether or not I should get a nickel raise . . . saying, "the country just can't afford it."

I can't read or watch the news very often because it just gets my blood boiling. Not too long ago NPR (National Public Radio) did a segment on the National Restaurant Association's connection with Gingrich, and half an hour later they did a separate story on the minimum wage debate. I was yelling at the radio, "Doesn't anybody know how to put the pieces together?"

The minimum wage debate is crazy, because you can go back and read newspapers from any decade and the same arguments are used over and over again: "If the minimum wage gets raised, employers will have to lay off workers because they can't afford the increase." This has never happened; the unemployment rate has never gone up after a minimum wage increase. If anything, the increase gives poorer people better purchasing power and puts more money back into the economy. It's called "spreading the money around." The speedboat industry might feel a dip, but the grocery stores are probably selling more food to regular people.

That whole "logic" that connects raising the minimum wage with lay-offs always confounds me. Why don't the bosses *regress* the minimum wage and drag it down to a dollar an hour—that way they can hire four times as many employees, and unemployment as we know it would be gone! That's the stupidest argument: "If we raise the minimum wage to a livable wage, we would put poor people out of work, so we're going to leave them at a slave wage out of the kindness of our hearts."

As I travel around the country, I hear the same debates over and over. Millions of workers need to say, "Look, all of your arguments and predictions have been proven false." It's amazing how millionaires in Washington, D.C. are debating whether or not I should get a nickel raise . . . saying, "the country just can't afford it." Meanwhile, nobody cries out when restaurants raise their prices to keep up with inflation; everybody gets to keep up with inflation except for wage earners.

Phone Fun

Posing as eager 19-year-old "Pete Disher," a dishwasher interested in pursuing his profession in the military, I called some recruiters. I told them I didn't wanna be part of the "baby-killing stuff," just wanted to "wash dishes for my country." The response was varied though each branch did wish to sink their claws into this kid. After feeling out my character for 10 minutes—the air force guy finally broke down and admitted, "We're not hiring any dishwashers right now." The navy guy initially kept telling me I could wash dishes as much as I wanted to, but then switched his tone by continually bringing up the ill-received idea of eventually becoming a cook. The army was perfectly ready to suck me in with this "small potato dishwashing idea," but obviously had no plans to let the dream unfold as desired. I could almost hear him thinking, "I'll make a killer outta this dumb pansy."

It was the marine guy whom I had the best response from. He kept prodding me on and on about how I could be the best disher in the whole corps. While each of the other lowlifes made appointments for me to come to their offices to speak with them in person (I had made myself sound super-desirable according to my height, weight, age, health, police record, etc.)—it was the marine guy who wanted me to bring along my birth certificate, social security card, and driver's license. I think he already had the paperwork filled out and just needed me to sign.

After being on the phone with Mr Marine for 20 minutes, I asked him if I should bring condoms along to our meeting. He was stunned and asked why I would ask such a question. I told him I thought he had invited me to have sex with him, but assured him repeatedly to forget about it. He claimed he couldn't forget about it. When he reminded me of the military's discriminatory ways, I proclaimed I hadn't *done* anything wrong and acted more eager than ever to join up. He became hesitant, wanting to be enthusiastic about my enlistment but was now scared of me. I promised and promised I wasn't interested in having sex with him until he finally agreed he'd meet with me—the dumb fuck.

—Pete, from *Dishwasher #11*

♦ **V: It seems you've developed a way to live your life with as much freedom as possible, without having to play the games demanded by so many other "professions." Where do you get the money for printing?**

♦ DP: Fortunately, there are people in wage-slave positions at copy shops all around the country who don't mind subsidizing the zine at the expense of their employers. They're making up for that gap between what they get paid and what they *should* be getting paid. They're simply taking it out in copies for me. And I try to keep the zine cheap so that anybody can afford it—especially a minimum wage worker.

♦ **V: Your overhead is low—the articles are handwritten and everything is pasted down. You don't have to carry around a $3000 computer set-up.**

♦ DP: *Dishwasher* is very minimalist from top to bottom. [laughs]

♦ **V: Yet the message gets across. Where do you find your great graphics?**

♦ DP: Mostly just digging around in the library, looking up old stuff.

♦ **V: You go to libraries?**

♦ DP: Well, I don't spend money on anything but food and transportation. So I think that libraries are the greatest free resource in the world, for everything from reading to taking naps. [laughs] I go to university libraries rather than municipal libraries because they have better facilities and their bathrooms don't smell as bad.

♦ **V: You've got a minimum-income, information-rich lifestyle—**

♦ DP: The opportunities are always out there.

♦ **V: And you seem to be making the most of them. You travel a lot, have friends all over and have this "art form" with which to express your philosophy and point of view and be completely creative—**

It's not like I sat down and thought, "I'm going to critique American culture from the point of view of—let's see—*dishwashing*, that'll work!"

♦ DP: It's all unintentional [laughs]. Several professors have used *Dishwasher* in everything from sociology to English classes. They do deep "deconstructions" of various issues and all I can say is, "Well, I wash dishes and I write about it." Not that I'm a complete moron, but it's not like I sat down and thought, "I'm going to critique American culture from the point of view of—let's see—*dishwashing,* that'll work!" It happened backwards.

♦ **V: You're the scribe for dishwasher culture—**

♦ DP: I'm just one among many, telling my stories like

other dishwashers are; I just wanted a forum to facilitate that. I definitely enjoy getting all the letters and dishwashing stories; I have manila envelopes full of them. I never thought the audience for the zine would go beyond dishwashers themselves. It was disheartening to realize that the majority of readers *aren't* dishwashers, but I recognize that people are still getting something out of the zine. More people than you can imagine have been dishwashers at one point in their lives. It's a universal job, at least in this country.

♦ **V: How did David Letterman find out about you?**

♦ DP: I started getting letters from newspapers, magazines, and radio talk show hosts. I didn't have a whole lot of interest in dealing with them, but I felt that anybody who sat down and wrote me a letter at least deserved the common decency of a reply, even to say: "I'm not interested in having a story written about me, but thanks, anyway." Then, my relationship with the press started to sour when I explained to one journalist I didn't want to be interviewed because I didn't want any hype or publicity I had no control over surrounding the zine. You know: "Here's some guy who washes dishes—and he's *literate!*" I didn't want any part of this and didn't see the need for it.

Our society gives us the false impression that we're all supposed to clamor to be recognized—as if we're all movie stars that just haven't been discovered yet. Personally, I'm not comfortable being the focus of attention—it was flattering, but I didn't want to deal with it. When I gave this [aforementioned] journalist my explanation as to why I didn't want to be interviewed, he used it as his interview! He wrote up a sort of "Noble Giant" story and got it all backwards. He said I had "a seventh-grade writing style, but that someone with a doctorate could appreciate it"—thanks a lot!

Basically, I'm just not good with publicity. Nevertheless, all these major media representatives were trying to find me. It all bottomed out when a guy from CNN tracked down my *parents'* phone number and began calling them two or three times a week. Every time I called my parents, my dad would say, "*Call* this guy and tell him to stop phoning us."

♦ **V: How did the CNN journalist find you?**

♦ DP: From what I gathered, he noticed that one of my past addresses was in the college town of Arcata. He called the college and fed the registrar some story to get my address (I had attended school there for about three days). I didn't want to talk to him, but finally I did. And he was the slimiest reporter you can imagine. He kept trying to soothe my apprehensions by telling me that he used to be "down with the people"; he "didn't *always* belong to this huge media conglomerate." He assured me he knew what was what. It just confirmed my intuition that I didn't want anything to do with him, especially since television is one of the worst mediums to be on—your interview will be chopped up into one sentence and they will cut up your words to

illustrate any point they want to make about you.

When I talked to him again and told him I wasn't interested, he gave me this whole hard-luck story about how he wished he were out writing for himself and not having to work for CNN, but had a family to support and a mortgage to pay. I don't have many regrets in life but this is one of them: I wished I had tape recorded this conversation. He actually said he needed to put shoes on his kid's feet! [laughs] He made it sound as though my not doing the interview meant sending his kids off to school barefoot! That was when I hung up.

After that, if any envelope bearing an "official" letterhead from New York or Los Angeles arrived, I would hold it up to the light and if I couldn't see any dollar bills in it I would throw it away unopened. I don't even bother anymore with all these major media people. Nevertheless, several stories were written about me without the writers having had any contact. Once somebody writes a story, then they all need to tell their version of that story. Instead of going out and finding their own stories, they just repeat what everybody else says. And it goes in waves; I won't hear from anybody for about three months—then all of a sudden I'll get five requests from newspapers in one week and I'll realize that some newspaper somewhere had written something. It's rather sick how they feed off each other.

Dishwasher got reviewed in *Playboy* four years ago. The reviewer, Chip Rowe, later asked what response I got and I sort of embellished it: "Oh, about 18-25 people wrote me." He seemed disappointed. But the *real* number was less than five—being written about in the major media doesn't mean a whole lot. People who read *Playboy*—the last thing they're doing is copying down addresses and sending away for some dishwashing publication!

The David Letterman Show had shown interest in me but I had just thrown away the letter and hadn't given much thought to it. In the meantime, my friend Jess Hilliard had offered to appear on the show posing as me. The show contacted me again and Jess had been pestering me the whole time, and I thought it would be neat to try and pull it off. I told Jess to call them (posing as me). He forged some sort of identity that was partly my story, partly his and part pure fiction. I was already in New York, but Jess was flown out there from the Bay Area. He appeared on the show and it was pretty weird.

♦ V: *How did he dress?*

♦ DP: He usually wears thrift store suits and wide

ties, and when he showed up they were immediately concerned about his "joke" tie—they wanted to send him down to the wardrobe room. (What's funny is: that's what he wears all the time.) But they thought he was trying to look like a clown or something, and talked him into taking off the tie so that he appeared on TV in just a sports jacket and collar. Actually, they didn't want him to wear a suit at all; they had expected him to look more "blue-collar"—

♦ V: *—dressed like a "dishwasher" from Central Casting—*

♦ DP: Right. I accompanied him to the studio, pretending to be "just a friend." I dressed up in a suit as a disguise, but they kind of recognized me. We had purposely kept them from reading many of the back issues; we wouldn't send them because that would make Jess responsible for more material. Then they got frustrated and put a researcher on the case who spent a couple days doing nothing but dredging up articles by or about me, including a photo of me. We thought we'd be able to cover ourselves with alibis, but hadn't settled on a single one. So when we got to their studio and they pegged me, we were fumbling with our stories. Then they decided they just *didn't want to know,* because the show was about to be taped.

♦ V: *Your friend went on the show as you?*

♦ DP: Yeah. If I were watching that on TV, I would have thought it was *weird.* Those shows always have movie stars, rock stars and other people who are very savvy being in front of the camera, but my friend was nervous, sweating, and staring downward the whole time. It was perfect. I don't think Letterman really knew what to do with him. [laughs] Jess does this magic trick where he puts rubbing alcohol on his hand and lights it on fire, and beforehand he talked them into letting him do it. He tried to light Letterman's cigar with his hand and nearly scorched the guy's face—it was great.

By the next day they knew they'd been *had,* because people from all over were calling and faxing them. My acquaintances who didn't know what was going on thought someone had done this maliciously: "That wasn't Pete! Pete's a friend of mine—that's not him! Who was that?" The woman who booked us—her job was in jeopardy. For a comedy show, they didn't have much of a sense of humor about it . . .

Viewed as a prank, this was basically just a guy who makes ten million dollars a year being duped by two dishwashers. To them it didn't really matter; they just go on and on and on with their television bullshit,

one guy...fifty states...
lots of dishes
plenty of time

WASHINGTON
IDAHO

OREGON ✳ IDAHO
WASHINGTON

raking in the dough. For us, it was this huge inside joke among my friends and people they knew; word got around really quick. And it was at the expense of an obnoxious corporate entity: a television network.

♦ V: *Shows like Letterman are allegedly satisfying that true need for conversation that people feel; the need to live a thousand other lives. But they're just bullshit—*

♦ DP: What's funny is that shows like Letterman are so scripted. The ghostwriters supply Letterman with the questions, and then he's free to go off from there. So if he asks people if they've been to France lately, it's because he knows they've got some anecdote about being there. Since my friend wasn't a media star, his "conversation" was rehearsed in advance so he'd have some "answers" ready. But this so-called preparation actually made him *more* nervous.

♦ V: *The nervousness was the real truth of the situation. Interesting people should totally refuse to appear on shows like that.*

♦ DP: If anything, I hope I set a good precedent for anyone who's into publishing for their own needs and doesn't crave being a "media star." I've known a few people who went on talk shows. A friend's roommate pretended to have a crush on him, and they both concocted some story to get a free trip to New York, and it was a complete fraud. I thought that was pretty neat. But I can't imagine anything worse than going on TV as "yourself." That would have to be a *low point* in my life.

♦ V: *They don't give you any money, either—*

♦ DP: Actually, we got $500 altogether.

♦ V: *But that's nothing compared to all the money they're raking in—*

♦ DP: We were hoping it was going to be a lot more, because my friend's rent was due. They thought they could excite us by giving us free food, and the sad thing is: we *were* excited! [laughs]

♦ V: *One of my favorite Dishwasher stories was when you got a job at a restaurant where "the help" could eat anything they wanted. So for your first meal you sampled about 15 different dishes, plus all the juices and desserts on the menu. That story made total sense—especially if you hadn't worked or eaten much for awhile.*

♦ DP: You should never spend money on food when you're working around food. I love nothing more than getting as much free food as possible and also passing it

on to friends—especially if it's fancy restaurant food. Like I said, the only things I spend money on are food and transportation, so if I don't have to spend money on food, I have more money to spend on transportation. Yeah, I don't like spending money on food. [laughs]

Dishwashing and writing go hand in hand, because when you're washing dishes you're cut off from any social interaction and free to think the whole time. It's the best time for me to write. If I'm working every day, I'm usually thinking about the same topics. So it's basically already written by the time I get it down on paper.

Recently I've started revising what I write, and this is new to me because all of my earlier issues were first drafts. But after I printed up the copies, I'd read one and spot spelling errors, missing words or nonsensical sentences. Now I'm trying to be a little more responsible and not have the reader deal with that. I don't have it in me to write really "slick," but I no longer foist my rough drafts on people. Someday I'd like to rewrite everything I've already done, and fill in

Dishwasher 7″ 45, $3 ppd from Pete's PO box (see article intro)

all of the stories that were left out.

♦ V: *Nothing like self-improvement—*

♦ DP: Although . . . when washing dishes, *anybody* pretty much reaches their peak of ability after about half an hour. And I don't like to work hard or fast. This surprises people with whom I work with, or work for: "Aren't you supposed to be some great dishwasher? You're the slowest guy I've ever seen!" "I never said I was fast, I just said I did it. If you want some speed demon, you're barking up the wrong tree . . . Good luck if you ever find one!"

♦ V: *In San Francisco, most dishwashers aren't white. Is that true across the country?*

♦ DP: In New Orleans the dishwashers generally tend to be black and the wait staff white, so I had trouble finding a job there.

About eight years ago I was in San Diego and couldn't find a job dishwashing. I think the employers thought that since I was white, I was more apt to leave the job soon, or quit if I got any bullshit. Meanwhile they view somebody who just crossed the border as a worker who would be more apt to put up with bullshit because, as an "illegal" immigrant, they don't have many other options.

I wonder if people who immigrate to this country see my zine and think, "This guy wants to write about washing dishes? God, I'd love to fucking do anything *but* wash dishes. I was a doctor back in my old country." Which is true—I've washed dishes with people who are college-educated and even professional, but because they speak broken English they're looked down upon. Americans just *assume* that they're stupid, so they kind of play along. Since I work alongside them, they tell me how they had a profession in their old country, or that they never spoke English until six months ago. I'm thinking, "God, that's pretty good for six months." But to the waiters or bosses this guy is a moron who can barely speak English.

♦ **V: Are there ever problems working with people who barely speak English?**

♦ DP: I've been planning to learn Spanish for about a decade now. I was working with a guy from Mexico and we couldn't communicate all that well. But he liked to sit around as much as I did—that's the universal language of any workers of the world, I suppose!

♦ **V: Maximize the loafing potential of a job—**

♦ DP: I want to put out a Spanish language issue of *Dishwasher*, directed to that populace you mentioned. It would obviously be different, and would speak more directly to that audience about minimum wage issues, our rights as workers, etc. In San Francisco, if you go down to Army near Mission Street you'll see a big crowd of Latino males looking for day labor. Employers know they have cheap labor on their hands—workers who are basically disposable. Undocumented workers have no rights, so, "Throw 'em two or three bucks an hour, and what can they say? They're not going to go to the police or the labor relations board."

♦ **V: Some dishwashers have mouths to feed and work two jobs, 16 hours a day. I knew a pantry worker who worked with someone like this, and once in awhile she'd have to wake him up so he wouldn't get fired.**

♦ DP: In New York City I met some Ecuadoran guys who were getting just $2.50 an hour—in *New York City!* How can you live off that? That employer probably told them: "I know you can't get another job; you don't have the right papers. You'd better dance for me."

♦ **V: You travel more than anyone else I know—**

♦ DP: I grew up in San Francisco but I didn't even go to Berkeley [15 miles away] until I was 19 years old. But I always *wanted* to travel, and now it seems so easy . . . second nature. These days I'm envious of people who can stay in one place! I wish I could do that. I try, but every time I try I fail.

♦ **V: How can you do zine production on the road?**

♦ DP: Zine production is always going on in my head. When I go somewhere, just the new surroundings give me a new perspective on whatever I'm working on. Sometimes this is a hindrance, though—I've been working on one essay for awhile and I keep changing it, so it's still not done. The best way travel helps is to give me a deadline: "This guy's going to give me a ride

out of town on Friday so I have to get the zine done by then." That was just the case with my record. I was photocopying the inserts, folding, collating, stapling and stuffing 3000 copies of the record and had to get it all done in Reno before my ride left for San Francisco.

Now that I travel constantly, I see a lot of tourists and wonder if they ever think about what they're doing. When I was walking down 57th Street in New York City a few months ago, I saw lines upon lines at all these "theme" restaurants (that are opening up all over the world): the Hard Rock Cafe, Planet Hollywood, etc. I thought it was amazing that people would go to New York City and wait in line in the rain to eat at a restaurant that's just like one in L.A. or Chicago, when there are a million *unique* places to eat in New York. I guess in the tourism trade people are going for *safety:* they want to know in advance what they're going to get. So why bother traveling?

♦ **V: Right . . . By the way, how did your record come about?**

♦ DP: There's a history of that inside the record sleeve. It started four years ago—that's about the normal pace of my projects! Somebody showed me a song they'd written, "Born To Wash Dishes," and I thought, "Wow, I should put out a whole record of nothing but dishwashing songs!" I invited various bands to participate, and some bands hung in there with me a long time, and others have long since broken up. I'm pretty happy with the result—mostly because it's done! Hopefully there'll be a few more; there are already a couple of bands lined up. I'm completely musically inept but maybe I can write some decent lyrics for the next one.

♦ **V: What are some past songs which mention dishwashing?**

Gil Scott-Heron is famous for the line, "The Revolution will not be televised." But in a way the opposite has happened.

♦ DP: "Inner City Blues" by Gil Scott-Heron: "So you say you never heard of the Inner City Blues?/And what's more, you don't understand what the ghetto people mean when they say they're livin' behind walls?/Well, put on your best suit and white shirt and tie/and come on downtown and stand in line for a job washing dishes for which you may not qualify." That's a good song.

Gil Scott-Heron is famous for the line, "The Revolution will not be televised." But in a way the opposite has happened. Nothing's given a chance to brew and develop anymore, before the media takes hold of it and grinds it to death. Also, there's an instant commodification of everything that might develop into something "revolutionary." For a long time I liked the mystique of the Unabomber—I thought it would be great if he died and nobody ever knew who he was, leaving it to everyone's imagination. Then people would just have to read what he *wrote.* But now he'll be on the cover of the *National Enquirer* and there'll be TV movies made about him and his *message* will be long forgotten beneath the soap opera of his story.

♦ *V: The newspapers already tried to play up some bogus romance angle: "Failed Romance Linked to First Unabomber Bombing." Have you done any other collaborations?*

♦ DP: I've been collaborating on some comics. I can envision the story lines and layouts, but I just can't draw. The same thing with music: I can think of song lyrics, but I can't perform them. Collaboration is a great way to utilize everybody's talent. I know people who are good at writing tunes but horrible at coming up with lyrics; likewise, there are artists who can draw but are short on ideas for stories.

♦ *V: Any thoughts on e-zines vs. paper zines?*

♦ DP: Well, I've never read or seen an e-zine; they don't really interest me. E-zines just don't seem *necessary* for my life. The Powers That Be make pagers and e-mail all seem so essential, whereas ten years ago we were doing just fine without them. We didn't

---

Jess Hilliard on the David Letterman Show

♦ *VALE: You impersonated Dishwasher Pete on the David Letterman show—*

♦ JESS HILLIARD: Pete was with me when I showed up backstage. He was disguised as my friend "Jerry." The Letterman people were very condescending; I asked questions about the show and they were very vague about everything. They kept staring at us like hawks. It turned out that they had managed to obtain a photograph of Pete. When they confronted Pete about this, I spoke up: "No, no, that's my friend Jerry. I always send *his* picture out as a joke, because I don't like to use my own photo." But they weren't buying it. They were mad, and this was five minutes before showtime. The last thing I heard before walking onstage was [sarcastic tone], "Well, you *seemed* to have your story straight."

♦ *V: They treat people like cattle—*

♦ JH: Especially people who are not celebrities. I showed up in one of my best thrift store suits—fergodsake, I wanted to look *nice* on TV! It's a once-in-a-lifetime experience; my mom was watching. The first thing they asked was, "Can we re-dress you? You don't really look the part." I said, "But this is not a *part!*" (Did they expect me to appear wearing an apron?) They wanted to redo my hair and I said, "Don't *touch* my hair!" So right away there was friction. They did talk me into taking off my wide tie, because (as it turned out) it might have upstaged the flashy tie that Letterman was wearing.

The woman who booked me was skimpily dressed and wearing a micro mini-skirt. She was kind of attractive, and very flirtatious while being overbearing, constantly invading my personal space trying to elicit information from me. She was sitting higher than me and kept crossing and uncrossing her legs (which were eye-level with me, less than a foot away) and touching me, while trying to get me to admit I wasn't the "real" Dishwasher Pete. I wish I had a video of this woman

Jess Hilliard. Photo: V. Vale, collage: Yimi Tong

talking to me; she was all over me like an animal. It was one of the most intimidating experiences I've ever had. Now I know the ugliness behind all those "live" TV shows.

The next day it was all over the Internet how Letterman had been duped. Two weeks later, I called them collect to ask when I could expect the $500 that had been promised, and got the woman who had booked me. She started screaming about how I had tried to ruin the show, and that there might be a lawsuit. She said, "I *know* this isn't Dishwasher Pete. I hope you realize that I'm losing my job over this." That was probably a lie, but if she does, she deserves it because she was the rudest, most manipulative person I've ever met in my life. Then she hung up on me.

Apparently, on the Internet you can look up all the guests that have appeared on Letterman's show. A friend told me that when you try to look up "Dishwasher Pete" it says, "Access Denied." Another thing—they could have paid us $5,000 and it would have been just a drop in the bucket to them. It's pathetic that they pay such a small amount. And when the limousine picked me up at the New York airport and took me to the hotel, the desk clerk asked for a $100 deposit. I had no money or credit card, and he had to call the Letterman people to vouch for me. They had the nerve to get mad at me: "You mean you don't have *any* money?" Were they seriously expecting this homeless guy who washes dishes for a living to have $100 on him or a credit card—like, "he's just slumming it"?

When you consider the fact that "Pete Dishwasher" isn't his real name, and that I've written articles for the magazine, too, maybe I'm the part of the magazine that would be on TV and Pete's the guy who does the traveling and dishwashing. It's just a loose interpretation of who this character may really be . . . Ⅴ

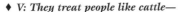

need to put zines on computers.

♦ **V: Well, people in foreign countries really appreciate e-zines. But they're having to settle for a greatly reduced quality of communication, with fewer graphics and no stickers or inserts or notes (the "perks" that often come with a hand-made paper zine). Plus, the most radical zines just aren't on the Internet. Personally, as a human being equipped with hands and a sense of touch, I like zines that are real and palpable; I like the soiled pages of a zine that has been crumpled traveling through the mail.**

♦ DP: There's not much about the aesthetic of reading things on the computer that is very appealing. I actually do a lot of my reading outdoors, or if it's indoors, it's in bed or lying on a couch. You can't take a computer with you outdoors; it's just not the same as having something crumpled up in your pocket that you can read whenever you want. Plus, simply looking at computer screens gives me a headache.

♦ **V: One of the alleged "advantages" of e-zines is the ability to put your work on the Internet and have people read it instantly and send you feedback. Then again, there's that instant gratification syndrome—**

♦ DP: In the last few years, with the rise of the Internet and all that, I've noticed that people are becoming so much more impatient. Nobody used to ever complain about me taking months to get a zine to them; now, it's like, "I sent money to you last week. Where is it?"

♦ **V: What are your favorite small towns?**

♦ DP: I'm going to Mentone, Alabama, which I'm curious about. I like a lot of the small towns in the South—

♦ **V: Really? What about all those white racists?**

♦ DP: They're there, but there are also people who aren't racist *or* white. After the Civil War, many states in the South divided themselves into hundreds of counties as a way to defeat the power of the new black vote. Hundreds of small towns are county seats with a courthouse and jail smack in the middle of town. Power is very decentralized, and this seems to have helped preserve the local color.

♦ **V: In many of these towns, it feels like time has stood still. There are lots of dilapidated buildings with old '50s signs still in the windows—**

♦ DP: Yeah; that's why I like 'em. But like everywhere else, Walmarts are creeping in on the edge of town. In my quest to see as many small towns as possible, I feel like I'm racing against time. I'm planning to walk from Alabama to North Carolina.

♦ **V: You're going to walk?**

♦ DP: The original plan was to bike it, but then I started thinking about the fact that I would need to *get* a bike—not to mention having to learn how to repair it—

♦ **V: You can visit all those old juke joints—**

♦ DP: There are bars in Mississippi where the bathroom consists of four walls and a hole in the corner. I went in one once and thought, "Where do you go to the bathroom?" Then some guy walked in behind me and started peeing on the wall. I thought, "Oh—okay!" I love that quirky backwardness of the South—not the *racism,* but the lack of homogenization. In other parts of the country, it seems like everyone just wants to be cosmopolitan, and because they watch television they think they're an expert on everything. Not so in the South.

In my quest to see as many small towns as possible, I feel like I'm racing against time.

♦ **V: Have you ever been to the Appalachians or the Ozarks?**

♦ DP: I was passing through the Ozarks and was offered a job on a blueberry farm. All the workers were either Mexican migrant workers or local teenagers. One morning the foreman didn't show up, and the owner asked me if I wanted to work. I had considered picking blueberries but since it was 95 degrees and extremely humid, I decided not to. The owner said, "No, I don't want you to pick; I want you to be the *foreman.* You don't have to *do* anything—just sit in the shade and make sure all these people are picking." I was trying to figure out why I (of all people) was somehow qualified to do this, and realized it was because I wasn't Mexican and wasn't a teenager. I couldn't accept the job; it seemed too weird.

♦ **V: You chose to reject your privilege . . . Being on the road a lot, you probably get offered a wide variety of cooking—**

♦ DP: Yeah. I didn't grow up exposed to a vast range of "cuisines," so I had to learn. I've purposely worked my way through entire menus at restaurants, never eating the same dish twice, just to expose (and acclimate) myself to as many different foods as possible. Similarly, I've also tried to condition myself so I can sleep in any possible place and position at any time. If I have an opportunity to sleep in a bed, I try not to get too used to it! Because I know that the next night I'll be sleeping on a floor, or in the backseat of a car.

The same necessity for "flexibility" applies to employment now. Periodically there are news reports about some guy who was once an accountant or something, but because of hard times he's now washing dishes. *So what*—there are a million people out there washing dishes now—why not run stories on *them?* Why just talk about a guy who happened to be doing another job before he did this job?

♦ **V: What's the worst job you've ever had?**

♦ DP: If a job's *that* bad, I quit. I've had jobs that lasted only half an hour! Two or three times I've gotten a

THE DISHWASHER by Jim Seymour

In The Hobo's Hornbook, *George Milburn wrote that Jim Seymour, a frequenter of "Bughouse Square" (Newberry Square) in Chicago, was one of the hobo's favorite poets. Seymour's poem, "The Dishwasher," which first appeared in the IWW press in the* Industrial Worker *(May 1, 1913) has been frequently reprinted in IWW publications at the request of readers.*

Alone in the kitchen, in grease-laden steam,
I pause for a moment, a moment to dream,
For even a dishwasher thinks of a day
Wherein will be leisure for rest and for play;
And now that I pause o'er the transom there floats
A stream of the Traumerei's soul-stirring notes,
Engulfed in a blending of sorrow and glee
I wonder that music can reach even me.

For now I am thinking, my brain has been stirred,
The voice of a master the lowly has heard,
The heart-breaking sob of the sad violin
Arouses the thoughts of the sweet "might have been";
Had men been born equal the use of the brain
Would shield them from poverty, free them from pain,
Nor would I have sunk in the black social mire
Because of poor judgment in choosing a sire.

But now I am only a slave of the mill
That plies and remodels me just as it will,
That makes me a dullard in brain-burning heat
That looks at rich viands, not daring to eat;
That lives with its red, blistered hands ever stuck
Down deep in the foul indescribable muck
Where dishes are plunged, seventeen at a time,
And washt!–in a tubful of sickening slime!

But on with the clatter, no more must I shirk,
The world is to me but a nightmare of work;
For me not the music and laughter and song,
No toiler is welcomed amid the gay throng;
For me not the smiles of the ladies who dine,
No warm, clinging kisses begotten of wine;
For me but the venting of low, sweated groans
That twelve hours a night have installed in my bones.
The music has ceased, but the havoc it wrought

Within the poor brain it awakened to thought
Shall cease not at all, but continue to spread
Till all of my fellows are thinking or dead.
The havoc it wrought? 'Twill be havoc to those
Whose joys would be nil were it not for my woes.
Keep on with your gorging, your laughter and jest,
But never forget that the last laugh is best.

You leeches who live on the fat of the land,
You overfed parasites, look at my hand;
You laugh at it now, it is blistered and coarse,
But such are the hands quite familiar with force;
And such are the hands that have furnished your drink,
The hands of the slaves who are learning to think,
And hands that have fed you can crush you as well
And cast your damned carcasses clear into hell!

Go on with the arrogance born of your gold,
As now are your hearts will your bodies be cold;
Go on with your airs, you creators of hates,
Eat well, while the dishwasher spits on the plates;
But while at your feast let the orchestra play
The life-giving strains of the dear Marseillaise
That red revolution be placed on the throne
Till those who produce have come into their own.

But scorn me tonight, on the morn you shall learn
That those whom you loathe can despise you in turn,
The dishwasher vows that his fellows shall know
That only their ignorance keeps them below.
Your music was potent, your music hath charms,
It hardened the muscles that strengthen my arms,
It painted a vision of freedom, of life–
Tomorrow I strive for an ending of strife.

—from *Dishwasher* #11

dishwashing job and the boss came up and asked, "You're not that guy that goes around the country washing dishes, are you?" I'd usually reply, "Oh, no no no." One time I admitted I was, and asked the owner how he knew. He said, "I dunno—guy named 'Pete' washing dishes; it seemed like you *had* to be him!"

The thing about publishing *Dishwasher* that makes me happy is the fact that a pretty large cross-section of people read it, including older people and people of various races and social standing. At first I hoped only dishwashers would read it, and got disheartened when that turned out to be incorrect—I felt I was failing, somehow. Then I realized the zine had an impact

on people *regardless* of occupation. People would write letters: "I never washed dishes before in my life, but you made me think about things in a different way."

One advantage of traveling is the fact that I can't be easily reached. The complaints I hear involve just that: "It's so hard to get hold of you." But I always say, "Just drop a letter in the mailbox and it'll reach me within three weeks." There's so much *instant communication-gratification* now, what with pagers, cellular phones and e-mail, that it seems ludicrous—soon we'll all have communication implants in our brains: "Hey, I was thinking about you at 4 o'clock;

why didn't you think back?" I get my mail every three weeks and that works *fine.*

♦ *V: By documenting this occupation, it's like you're going undercover to expose class dynamics—*

♦ DP: I'm not pretending to be anybody but myself. Even if I weren't writing about it, I'd still be experiencing all of this just the same. I really liked the book *Rivethead.* The author worked on an auto assembly line for ten years until he had a nervous breakdown, and he wrote all about this. There should be entire libraries of books like that: people writing from their own experiences and in their own words.

After I finish my walk I plan to do more research on dishwashing unions early in the 20th century. Cooks and waiters had unions at the time, but they wouldn't allow dishwashers in, let alone women or minorities. So a couple of different unions, some affiliated with the IWW (International Workers of the World) or communists, sprang up in New York City during the 1910s and '20s. I plan to read old labor newspapers of the time.

♦ *V: Did you initially get interested in labor history by doing a zine?*

♦ DP: I've always been interested in labor history, especially material on the IWW. They were the ones who figured out that if the waiter's union went on strike, the bosses would make the dishwashers fill in for the waiters. It didn't help the waiters to be pitted against the dishwashers, and the IWW said, "You know we're all in this together, so let's all be in one union. We need to stick together and walk out together."

One of the outstanding examples of workers' solidarity was the 1934 San Francisco general strike. San Francisco had an extremely high percentage of unionized restaurants, so most of the restaurants shut down. Unfortunately, this general strike only lasted a few days. Since I grew up in San Francisco, I would read about these events when they were written up in the newspapers on their anniversaries. Even Herb Caen [columnist] would devote a column to this, saying, "I remember when . . ." Listening to old timers' tales about Harry Bridges made me want to find out the full story behind the labor rights' movement. It seemed like this was always part of my consciousness.

♦ *V: Wasn't the general strike notable because it was one of the first times people from different unions united? (That's why it was called a "general strike.")*

♦ DP: In Europe, general strikes were more common. In Britain during the '20s a general strike that really

THE LITTLE RED SONG BOOK

IWW Songbook International Edition

TO FAN THE FLAMES OF DISCONTENT

paralyzed the country occurred. The only examples in the United States were in San Francisco, Minneapolis and Seattle around the same time. But again, none of them lasted more than a few days. They didn't end very nicely for the labor groups, either. As exciting as they seem, on the scale of truly inspiring achievements they're still pretty tame. I actually joined the IWW for awhile, but then I got annoyed with them—there was so much bickering about ideology going on.

♦ *V: Where do you do your research?*

♦ DP: The Tamimant Library in New York. It's located within (but is not actually part of) the NYU (New York University) Library. Actually, a way to sneak into the NYU Library is to say that you're going to the Tamimant. However, librarians there constantly refer me to the Wayne State Library in Michigan. It's supposed to be *the* place for labor archives.

♦ *V: Are dishwashers usually male?*

♦ DP: Just as I've had bosses who said they would never hire a white person to wash dishes, so I've had bosses who said they would never hire a woman. I knew a waitress who insisted that she wanted to wash dishes, so the boss had her do the most strenuous, heinous kind of work just to "break" her, like some kind of a drill sergeant. But she was determined. It was hilarious, every day they tried to outdo each other. He'd say, "Go lift that 100 pound box," and she'd lift it. She did everything he asked, but after a few days she got tired of jumping through his hoops and went back to waitressing. Despite the prejudices of many bosses, I have known and met many great female dishwashers.

♦ *V: Besides washing dishes in all 50 states, do you have any other goals?*

♦ DP: There were all these working-class novels produced in the years during the Depression, and I'm trying to track them all down. They're full of colorful language, vivid characters and real-life situations about trying to survive in a thoroughly unjust economy—to me they seem *completely* up-to-date. I think there's about a hundred of these "great proletarian novels," including Michael Gold's *Jews Without Money,* Tom Kromer's *Waiting for Nothing* (one of the best) and Jack Conroy's *The Disinherited.* That last title sums up the real condition of our existence now . . . V

See page 134 for related reading list/article by Nico Ordway

Temp Slave

Temp Slave is an ongoing, black-humor critique of work published by Keffo, now in its 10th issue. Other one-shot zines he has produced include *East of Cali* and *Welcome to the World of Insurance*. For the latest issue of *Temp Slave* send $3 cash (or $1 for a catalog) to Keffo, POB 8284, Madison WI 53708-8284.

♦ *VALE: What's your job history? Did you start mowing lawns at the age of 12?*

♦ KEFFO: [laughs] Probably. I know that by the time I was 15 I had started working. I'm 36 years old and have had about 40 jobs—most of them temporary. Recently I got a "real" job working for a monster petrochemical company, but I don't know how long that'll last. My attitude toward work is: *I'd rather not.*

♦ *V: Where did you grow up?*

♦ K: I grew up in the Lehigh Valley in Pennsylvania, 50 miles north of Philadelphia. Formerly a heavy manufacturing/industrial area, it had a speedy decline when most businesses moved to the South or just died. It was a pretty desperate place to grow up. As long as I can remember, my dad worked at least four jobs: as a civil servant for the state liquor control board, a maintenance person for the post office, a naval reservist, and a neighborhood odd-job handyman. I think he was driven to make sure we had a roof over our heads by the *fear factor*—his parents had been very poor.

I'm 36 years old and have had about 40 jobs . . . My attitude toward work is: *I'd rather not!*

I didn't know who my father really was because he was never home. We had this relationship through little notes we'd leave each other: "How are you doing?" "Fine." Then he died at the age of 50. This may sound cold, but his death didn't affect me because I had no emotional connection to him. Part of my attitude toward work is a direct result of witnessing the way he lived.

♦ *V: What was your first regular job?*

♦ K: I worked for a clam-bake catering service. On weekends people would rent it out, get rip-roaring drunk, go nuts and vandalize the place. I was 15 years old and couldn't believe my eyes, watching all these *grown-ups* being drunk for eight hours straight.

♦ *V: It sounds like your first job opened your eyes and undercut the authoritarianism of "adult role models." What's your educational background?*

♦ K: After high school, I got a student loan and went to Kutztown University in Pennsylvania. I wrote for the school newspaper; I had visions of being a journalist. Politically, I was geared toward causing trouble for the administration rather than holding any socialist or Trotskyite ideas. I liked to spread weird rumors; I'd go to parties and whisper that the dean of the school was having an affair with a Catholic priest in the belltower. A few weeks later, I'd overhear someone telling the same story. [laughs]

♦ *V: How did you come to publish* Temp Slave?

♦ K: Basically, I like to write. I had done some freelance journalism and was getting frustrated with the whole "submission" process. I had a temp job working in the mail room of an insurance company that was promising me full-time employment. I thought, "Hey—this will be good. I can deal with this work: it's easy, I get benefits, I get a regular paycheck . . ." Then they reneged and said they were bringing in someone from another department to take over my job. Anger

All work and no play makes Keffo a very dull boy. Portrait collage: Eric Rodenbeck, based on cartoon by Clay Butler.

TEMP SLAVE!

WORK! WORK!

ISSUE 1

Cover of *Temp Slave #1*

and access to paper and copiers motivated me to produce the first issue—everything coalesced at once.

I printed 25 copies and just started handing them out. I had assumed that only younger workers would be receptive, but 60-year-old grandmothers were coming up to me with smiles on their faces, asking for copies. Since I was the mail person, I could go all over the company handing it out to people. I was getting fired anyway, so I didn't care if the bosses found out.

The first issue had a cover featuring a big, fat businessman with a whip; the image came from a clip art book. I wrote an editorial ranting about how temp work is a losing proposition, and that you have nothing to lose by showing a bad attitude, sabotaging the place and stealing things. I wrote most of the articles myself under assumed names. The first issue is very rough, but it didn't occur to me that I might do a whole series—I was just *mad,* so making the zine was a blast. The intention was to make other company workers laugh. I didn't have any other expectations—at that time I didn't know about the "zine scene," and wasn't doing it for the "workers' movement."

♦ **V: But you had a consciousness about "workers' rights"—**

♦ K: Right, and in 1990 I became involved with the I.W.W. [Industrial Workers of the World] for a couple years. Did you know they had an office on Market Street in San Francisco? The I.W.W. introduced me to mentors with more political experience, who showed me how to do street actions and how to use the local newspapers to our advantage, etc. Of course, watching my dad work himself to death had already made me sympathetic toward working-class issues. But I couldn't stay with the I.W.W. because I had a falling out with some of the members.

♦ **V: What made you interested in the I.W.W.?**

♦ K: I found a copy of *Rebel Voices: An I.W.W. Anthology,* edited by Joyce Kornbluh—those old "Wobblies" had a lot to say! This inspired me to contact the union. However, I soon found out that the new Wobblies are a helluva lot different from the old ones. The new members are just keepers of the flame, without a true working-class base. There are now about 500 members nationwide, but at the beginning of this century there were thousands upon thousands. The government had to crack down on them and literally crack their heads; they were a serious threat. Many I.W.W. leaders were jailed or deported. One of the great figures in American labor history, Big Bill Haywood (the leader of the I.W.W.), was threatened with prosecution and forced to flee to the Soviet Union, where he died.

Today's I.W.W. feels more like a historical society living in the past and celebrating the martyrdom of Joe Hill. There *are* members who are involved in issues like Earth First! and Food Not Bombs, but it seems more like a trendy thing—especially for younger people. They get these little red cards that say they're "Wobblies" and this nice little red pin. But you have to remember that many of today's Wobblies are volunteering their time and efforts to an idea of a better world. So, although their effectiveness is limited, their hearts are in the right place.

♦ **V: The I.W.W. songbook is still available—**

♦ K: The I.W.W. had a whole cultural history producing pamphlets (early zines), songs, posters, etc. They used to take the piss out of bosses through their graphics and their songs. The Wobblies were one of the first political groups in this country that had a keen eye for turning mainstream messages upside down and right side up! Their art, songs and organizing efforts touched working people on a level that has not been accomplished since then. Their efforts gave people hope.

> **. . . everything under the sun is sacrificed toward one goal: the greatest possible profits. No one is guaranteed anything.**

♦ **V: Didn't you write that "These days, all jobs are temp jobs"?**

♦ K: [laughs] In *Temp Slave,* a lot of stories concern temp jobs under the guise of regular jobs. Today, no one is safe because of the changing nature of work, the general economic situation and the way corporations operate, where everything under the sun is sacrificed toward one goal: the greatest possible profits. No one is guaranteed anything.

♦ **V: Before you did Temp Slave, did you have any experience doing layout?**

♦ K: I had worked on newsletters for the I.W.W. branch I was involved with. Basically, all you do is paste everything down on sheets of paper; you learn as you go along. I'm definitely more interested in design and graphics, although content is still Number One. In my first issue I printed articles like "Reasons to Call in Sick to Work," and included weird paste-ups. I once photocopied a doughnut and underneath wrote, "This is what working people really *love:* DOUGHNUTS!"

The whole star system of America denies the fact that this country was built by nameless and faceless people with hopes and dreams.

♦ *V: You were making fun of clichés about working people—*

♦ K: Yeah. I make fun of temp agencies and bosses but I also make fun of the pretensions held dearly by workers, as well as the concept of work itself. A lot of people have the wrong idea: that I'm *just* pushing theft and sabotage. But I'm also asking people to consider what they're doing, why they're doing it, and what the alternatives are. *Temp Slave* gives people an opportunity to spout off; a lot of people who want to write about work don't have a forum to do so. In the media you only read about the accomplishments of the elite: so-and-so made this amount of money or won this award. The whole star system of America denies the fact that this country was built by nameless and faceless people with hopes and dreams. *Temp Slave* is about recognizing these people.

♦ *V: Did you distribute the first issue outside your workplace?*

♦ K: Yeah; I found out about *Factsheet Five* and mailed them a copy, but it was four months later. A friend, without my knowledge, sent a copy to *Labor Notes,* which reports on militant labor actions. It's a small publication but every major media source in the country reads it. At the time, nobody else seemed to be doing a publication on the issue of temp work and temp agencies. Then suddenly the mass media began featuring dozens of stories about this. I got a few mentions, and all of a sudden I started getting a lot of orders—not just from young radicals, but people in every age group.

Some people like it for the humor, some just want to read it, some mainly like the graphics, and a few are genuinely interested in union movements. Others are out-and-out crazies who love to read insane stories. And *everyone* has a bad work story. You can walk up to anybody on the street and they'll say, "Ohmigod! Today at work . . ."

♦ *V: That's true; the issue of employment cuts across all barriers that separate people—*

♦ K: Exactly. There are all kinds of people, but the one thing we all have in common is *work.* It's a common thread. How do Americans introduce themselves? "Hello. What do *you do?*" I've been in Ireland, Germany, etc and it seems that the people I've met aren't so interested in that. They'll eventually get around to asking, but it's not like in this country where your job is your identity.

♦ *V: Temp Slave has a great deal of emotional vehemence behind it—*

♦ K: Well, I have a lot of anger and bitterness about things that have happened to me and treatment I've received. One of my first eye-opening experiences was when I graduated from high school and got a job working for the Kraft Foods factory. At that point, I was one of those clueless people who wanted to "do my best," and I worked like a dog for four months, expecting a future with the company. One night the boss came up and said, "At the end of the shift, you're through. We just don't need you anymore." After he left, I got so furious that I let all the margarine just roll off the conveyor belt—*Splat! Splat!*—and soon there was this giant mess. [laughs] I just stood there with my arms crossed and the boss ran up and screamed, "*You*—get the hell out *now!*"

♦ *V: You didn't get any advance notice?*

♦ K: Right. That was in 1978 when the company was paying most of its factory workers something like $7 an hour. There were people 30–40 years old trying to support families on that.

Another miserable job I had was on a concrete construction crew. I worked with these guys who

Cover of Temp Slave #8

harassed me all day long. They just didn't like me; I guess it was because I wasn't "hard-working enough." Our job was to set up forms and pour concrete to make septic tanks. We were supposed to install these other little forms to create compartments, and when I got pissed off, I would "forget" to do this. The concrete would be poured and there would be this big, hulking mess of concrete with me standing there going, "Oops—I forgot." [laughs] I would get this profane tongue-lashing from the bosses, but what could they do? They'd have to bring in a truck with a crane, lift up the tank and take it somewhere and dump it. All the while I'd be standing there laughing inside.

This brings to mind the issue of responsibility, and I feel I'm as responsible as the next person—I'm just not responsible toward bosses or work! Don't get me wrong—I've done things deliberately, but I've also made stupid mistakes. [laughs] In college, I had a job projecting movies, and once in a while I would forget to set up the next reel change correctly and the film would fall off and roll down the aisle. Hundreds of people would be in an uproar.

Another time, my job was to turn on the lights after some audio-visual presentation. It was dark and I was feeling the walls for the switch. I felt something and pulled it and it was the fire alarm. [laughs] I looked out the window and the entire building—a girls' dorm—had emptied into the street! I had to talk to the campus cops, and they looked at me like, "Boy, you are the stupidest person we've ever met." [laughs]

The easiest costs to cut involve workers—especially those who expect a "living wage"!

♦ V: *Why do you think labor unions have diminished in this country?*
♦ K: The union movement has done a lot of good for this country; however, they face an enemy—a corporate structure that is well-financed. Not only do the corporations have money, they spend time understanding the tactics of unions. So when a situation gets heavy, they know how to deal with it. There are also historical aspects to consider. Labor unions came to power using some very radical tactics, but they were also aided by a mafioso element. Take the Teamsters, for example. They used mafia henchmen as their thugs, to make people "see reason."

In the '30s, the government passed the Wagner Act which gave working people the ability to form unions. Previously you had to fight tooth-and-nail to be recognized as a union, but under the Wagner Act a long list of procedures was established to file grievances, etc. In one sense that was a good thing, but it was also bad because it took away the *energy* behind the original union-forming crusades. The Wagner Act effectively undercut the original class foundation, replacing it with a heavily bureaucratic organization.

Then during World War II, pacts were formed between government, big businesses and labor to "cooperate for the war effort." By the '50s, America was one of the few relatively prosperous countries. There was an unspoken agreement that continued between the different factions: "You do the production, we'll legislate it, and then you can profit."

But with the rise of international competition, American corporations decided they were no longer willing to play this game. I'm no economist, but obviously businesses look at their bottom line and try to figure out where to cut costs. Companies have been out-sourcing their jobs (going to foreign countries), hiring temps, cutting back, and doing anything they can to raise profits. The easiest costs to cut involve workers—especially those who expect a "living wage!"

Unions have declined because of the bureaucracy which has developed within them. The head honchos are very male, white and older, and a lot of young people don't see any relevance. Besides, most unions are corrupt. The pretense is that unions are for working people, but some of the presidents and vice-presidents make $150,000 to $300,000 a year. What does that person have in common with somebody like me, or a guy working in a factory?

Another cause is the working class itself, which in this country is basically conservative. Most of the people I've worked alongside with just want to have a job

Illustration this page from *Temp Slave!* #3 opposite page from *Temp Slave!* #6 and support their families; they're also narrow-mindedly patriotic. If I started talking about Marxist or Anarchist ideas, they'd probably get out their baseball bats and run me out of town. Or they'd go, "What the fuck is this guy talking about?" People base their views on what they see in the mainstream media; their minds are saturated with news stories about people who have pet pigs—you know, stories that are irrelevant and don't help people *think*. So it's very difficult for someone to come in and change a whole mindset. There are all kinds of issues.

People base their views on what they see in mainstream media . . . you know, stories that are irrelevant and don't help people *think*.

Even though I'm involved with work problems, I don't believe that any kind of change in this country is going to come through union movements (unless some radically new kind of movement develops that I can't presently envision). I don't know *where* change is going to come from, but it's not going to come from labor unions because there's no energy there.

♦ **V: There are a handful of companies that refuse to go to other countries for labor. Some even do profit-sharing and have an emphasis on quality control—**

♦ K: A trendy business buzzword is "quality management," which attempts to involve workers in the whole process of being a company. Right now I work for this paternalistic corporation that pays me a half-decent amount of money, but we're constantly in "meetings" to evaluate our performance. This is a new form of oppression.

Another form of business tomfoolery is the "team" concept. Basically, companies want their employees to come up with solutions to problems within a workplace. *Isn't that nice:* they "care" about what I think. Of course they care about what I think—it saves them money. Instead of hiring a high-priced consultant, they tap the brainpower of their employees. What they are doing is stealing the intellectual property of their employees. How's that for "team work": you do the work and we make the money! It's all bullshit . . . just another friendly form of fascism. American corporations slay me. Even though everyone calls them "capitalist," through tax breaks, theft and phoniness they practice a perverted form of socialism: socialism for the rich.

♦ **V: It's just new jargon for the same old work-related oppression. In Zines! Vol. One, *Paul Lukas* said that America is swiftly becoming a service-based economy rather than a manufacturing economy.**

Fuck Shit Up

1. Always come to work a few minutes late.
2. Never admit to mistakes.
3. Use the restroom on company time.
4. Always use the company copier for personal projects.
5. Mislabel computer disks.
6. Make personal calls on the company phone.
7. Steal company letterhead to make up phony memos.
8. Arrange phony meetings for bosses.
9. Learn access codes to computers. Fuck up the works.
10. Use company mailing system for free postage.
11. Place "Out of Order" signs on copiers.
12. "Lose" important paperwork.
13. Rearrange or steal paperwork from boss's desk.
14. Glue locks on company cars.
15. Make personal labels on company equipment.
16. Always take long lunch breaks.
17. Go to the water fountain frequently.
18. Walk around your workplace with paper in your hands. (Bosses think you are busy.)
19. Spread rumors.
20. Sabotage equipment. The lowly paper clip is a wonderful tool.
21. Steal supplies.
22. Never volunteer for a job.
23. Find a hiding place and disappear.
24. Start a union organizing effort.
25. Have a nice day and don't get caught!

—from Keffo's zine, *Welcome to the World of Insurance: An Introduction to Corporate Hell*

♦ K: I guess I'm one of the lucky ones (if you want to call it "lucky"): I work in a manufacturing plant. I've been trained and have acquired real skills. Now I can probably get a job anywhere in this country. Although most of what America still manufactures is crappy consumer goods that people don't need, like tanks—

♦ V: *Not even that many, anymore—*

♦ K: Yeah. [laughs] I liked that *Saturday Night Live* skit where someone is pretending to be Lee Iacocca. He says, "This car is American-made." Someone comes up and says, "No, the body's made in Japan." Lee says, "Well, uh, the seats are made in America." "No, the seats are made in Mexico." Eventually you find out that the only part of the car that's made in America is the floor mats. [laughs] But at the same time I'm not one of those idiots screaming: "American jobs first!" *I'm not for jobs at all.* [laughs] But I don't look down my nose at people who do work.

♦ V: *Don't people send you a lot of stories about pranks on the job?*

♦ K: Sabotage and pranks are a touchy subject. I know every trick in the book. I've either read about it, done it, or heard about it. I feel that workers should be like poker players: you don't put your cards on the table, you keep the authority freaks guessing. I try not to reveal everything I know because the bosses have to be kept off guard. What people read in *Temp Slave* is radical, but there's so much more involved.

There are a lot of run-of-the-mill acts, like people stealing the place blind or sending out phony faxes. At

1001 Ways To Reward Employees

Just to prove how godawful and ignorant bosses are, here are some tidbits from a newly released book titled 1001 Ways to Reward Employees *by some schmo named Bob Nelson. I was reading this stuff and needed to rub my eyes just to make sure that it was real. Unfortunately, it's all too real. So I add my own comments to the mix . . .*

1. Bag the dough—the green variety, anyway. To really motivate, throw a pizza party for that nose-to-the-grindstone, outstanding employee who landed a tough contract. It's a fun, public way to say thank you for a job well done. In return, for what amounts to a gold star, Nelson contends, the employee will double his or her effort to do well again—eager to earn another sweet. (At the party or picnic smash the boss in the face with a pie!)

2. Nelson contends: money isn't everything: the rank and file want praise. He quoted a recent survey of workers and said that 63% of the respondents ranked "a pat on the back" as a meaningful incentive. (Touch me, bossman, and you're dead!)

3. Here's some more Nelson nuggets: Write at least five personal Thank You's on Post-It notes and hide them among an employee's papers. Name a space after a worthy worker, such as the "Sally Jones Corridor." Splurge and offer to pay a really excellent employee's mortgage for a month. Bring an employee a week's worth of bagged lunches; pay for house-cleaning services; give a day off to go to the beach; pay for a magazine subscription; allow workers to bring their pets to work on Fridays. (Put a Post-It note in the boss's paperwork saying "Fuck off!" Name a toilet stall after your boss. Bring your boss a bag of insects. Pay vandals to spraypaint "ASSHOLE" on the boss's garage door. Send 100 magazine subscriptions in the boss's name to his home. Order your dog to attack your boss.)

4. Nelson informs us that, "At the Advanta Corp., one manager treats his women employees to lunchtime manicures or throws the department a surprise picnic in a local park." (Get your fingernails and hair dyed bright neon green.)

5. Nelson again: "If you receive a $500 award, what are you going to do with that money? Probably use it to make a house or car payment, and poof it's gone. But if you get a nice gift like a widescreen TV, every time you turn it on, you'll probably remember where it came from and why you got it." (Honey, the TV picture is rolling again!)

6. One executive rewarded a salesman with a new suit. (Salvation Army special, I presume.)

7. At the Philadelphia-based Bell Atlantic cellular phone division, "cell sites," where transmission towers are located, have been named after top employees. (Hey, imagine that—THE TOWER OF KEFFO!!)

8. Nelson remarks about the do-gooder President of WordPerfect who promises vacations in Hawaii if production doubles: "I can only imagine how exciting it was to work there. People must come to work, saying, 'Thank God it's Monday.'" (Yes, 51 weeks of drudgery and pain for a week in Hawaii.)

9. Nelson enthuses: "Every employee has at least a $50,000 idea—if we give him the opportunity to get it out." (Then, once out, we'll give him a pizza and make millions off his idea!)

10. Nelson the moralist: "My fear is that we are losing humaness in the workplace. We're spending more time doing what's urgent than what's important." (You should know, Big Bob!)

—Keffo, from *Temp Slave #4*

one place my job was to catalogue files, and I started moving them all over the place so the person in charge could not figure out where the hell they were. I've been sent stories about computer workers deleting files, programs and back-up disks on their last day at work—little things like that. But truly extraordinary tales of sabotage are rare.

Some people really like messing with customers—they complain about them, make fun of them, scream at them and rant at them. People also steal time by going to work late, going home early, taking long lunch breaks, walking down the hallways carrying things but not really doing anything, etc. But I haven't really heard of any massive acts of sabotage because most people are not going to admit it. Anyway, I'm geared toward a more humorous approach to the workplace, like taking a company's symbols and rearranging them. It's more of a Situationist approach to propaganda-making. The book *Sabotage in the Workplace* contains all kinds of hilarious examples of disruption, and they can be found in *Temp Slave* as well.

There are a thousand ways to break up the typical work day. Have you seen those nun hand-puppets with boxing gloves? I took one to work and delivered mail with it and people were just blown away. In this sterile environment, they saw this nut coming toward them with a puppet on his hand.

One time I met a copier repair salesman. He told me he got a call from a law firm that was up in arms because every time they tried to copy legal documents, an image of a pen would show up on random copies. These people were having "shit fits"—they believed that a pen had fallen into the copier. Finally, the salesman realized there was no pen. Apparently a disgruntled worker had made photocopies of a pen, inserted these sheets randomly into all the reams of blank paper, and then resealed them. Someone else would come along and load up the copier. I thought this was a brilliant illustration of pranking.

I'm not one of those idiots screaming: "American jobs first!" I'm not for jobs at all.

♦ *V: One step beyond most people's thinking . . . Are you familiar with* **Processed World**?
♦ K: Yes, they've been publishing since the early '80s, although I didn't find out about them until 1992. Some people have compared *Temp Slave* with *Processed World,* but they didn't really influence me because I wasn't aware of them when I began my zine. I throw around words like "Situationist," but I'm not all that well-read in Situationist theory—I guess I'm just a wise-ass at heart. The juvenile delinquent is still in me.

Cover of *Temp Slave #9*

Processed World was like a revelation to me—I had no idea that other people were thinking and acting along the same lines that I was. I wound up writing a story for them. I think *Processed World* was written by more intellectual kinds of people. However, it didn't "talk down" to anyone; *PW* crossed a lot of barriers that separate working people from intellectuals. For that, they will always have my respect.

♦ *V: Have you ever been in jail?*
♦ K: Cops really like me! I mean, I've been busted for the usual array of minor offenses like underage drinking, disorderly conduct and traffic violations. Once I know I'm going to be busted, there's no use being nice to them. On countless occasions, they take a look at me, listen to me, and within minutes I'm sitting in the back of a cop car in cuffs. And this is for minor dust-ups! But thankfully, I've mellowed.

As for jail, yes, I've been put in cells to cool out. But I've never done time for political raps. I won't sit down in an orchestrated political display, get herded into a bus with a bunch of other "rads" and go to the pokey. I think that's useless. I don't need to earn my prison stripes that way; if I'm going to go, it's going to be big time!

♦ *V: Do you make any profit off* **Temp Slave**?
♦ K: It doesn't even break even; the last issue cost a dollar to print and a dollar to mail. I'm interested in cartooning and graphics, so I actually pay the cover artists. *Temp Slave* is a zine; I have no intention of it becoming a glossy national magazine or having ad pages throughout to finance it. I don't think many people would want to advertise in it, anyway. [laughs] I'll be damned if I'm going to call up companies and

say, "Hello, this is Keffo from *Temp Slave* zine, and I've got a hot readership. My demographics are . . ." I feel this is the one kind of work that should not make you money. At the same time, I don't look down my nose at people and say, "Just because I'm doing it this way, you should too." I do include a few ads, but they're all free.

That's just the financial aspects of doing *Temp Slave* There's another cost to doing a zine and that's the personal part of it. I live in a small apartment. My zine has taken over my life. I come home from work and zines and bits of paper with addresses and phone numbers on them are scattered everywhere. People from all over the world write me; I get calls from people I'll never meet. Fred Woodworth of the *Match,* a great zine, once wrote me, "Some of my subscribers think I work for them." I had to laugh because it's the truth. I'm finding it extremely difficult to relate to non-zine people. Of course, when I'm around zine people it's just as bad. It's like one big huge dysfunctional family circus.

♦ **V: Do you trade for other zines?**
♦ K: Yes. I get a lot of zines that I consider crappy, but I give people the benefit of the doubt because maybe they'll improve as they keep doing it. I'm not into the gossipy aspect of analyzing what people do in the "zine scene," even though some people are dead serious about it.

I'm not into that gossipy element of analyzing what people do in the "zine scene" . . .

♦ **V: What's your critique of straight journalism?**
♦ K: When I hear mainstream journalists talk about "objectivity" I want to go for my gun: "What the fuck are you people talking about?" I have written some straight journalistic pieces for the local newspaper—I can *do* that kind of journalism, but I detest it. It's a boring formula: open with a quote, give some back-

THE HIDDEN MEANING OF CORPORATE LOGOS!

WE FUCK WITH YOU

WE ARE ALWAYS WATCHING YOU

BOSSES ARE ASSHOLES

WE'RE ALL BULLSHIT

TREADMILL

CORPORATE PEOPLE ARE CLOWNS

SMILE! YOU ARE BEING ZAPPED BY RADIATION

KEFFO

ground, then descriptive information, and end with another quote or some witty statement. If you write for a straight publication, you already know what kind of story you're expected to do. When you interview someone, you make them fit the preconceived notions that the publication already has. So in a way it's impossible to be really truthful. You're never given enough space to go in-depth, anyway.

♦ **V: What kind of critical feedback have you received?**
♦ K: Occasionally, I'll get hate mail—there are a lot of crazies out there! Sometimes I'll get well-reasoned arguments against what I'm doing, like [sacrosanct tone], "I believe that if you're hired to do a job, you should do it the best way you can." [laughs]

When I first started publishing, I appropriated graphics here and there in the Situationist tradition. I made the mistake of using a cartoon from a nearby paper, and the artist got hold of my phone number and screamed at me for half an hour. He called me a hypocrite: "You're talking about exploitation, but *you're* exploiting people!" I was thinking, "What? In comparison to a major corporation that makes billions of dollars exploiting people in third world countries? What are you talking about?" Finally I said, "Okay, I made a mistake. Let's make amends. I want to pay you and I'd like to meet you face-to-face so we can discuss this whole matter." The guy said, "No—fuck no!" I was shocked that he wouldn't take any money; I guess he just wanted to vent some spleen. That incident made me realize that I had to start playing by some kind of rules, and I started paying almost every contributor. So now, I'm accused of being a hypocrite.

I went to a party and met a woman who said, "I saw one of your *Temp Slave* stories in a mainstream glossy magazine. How much did you get paid for that?" I said, "Nothing." She said, "You're a fucking idiot. It's people like you who are harming us *serious* aspiring writers." She took this high tone with me. So on the one hand I'm accused of being a hypocrite, and on the other hand I'm a fucking idiot.

I'm pretty sure that temp agencies read my zine. They have a lobbying group and they probably order it. I can't tell; if somebody sends me money in the mail, how am I supposed to know who I'm sending it to?

♦ **V: You've featured some funny cartoons and art work in your zine—**

♦ K: Yes, cartoons and graphics are a hallmark of *Temp Slave.* I prefer to do cut-and-paste, Situationist-style graphics because, while I'm capable of drawing, I'd rather leave it up to people who can draw better. I'm the kind of person who believes that visuals are more forceful than text. While there's a lot of text in *Temp Slave,* I try to make sure that every page has something of interest graphically.

> **I still have hopes that more and more people will figure out that the present concepts of work are a dead end.**

I love cartoonists and cartoons. Once I knew I was going to do *Temp Slave* for the long haul, I made damn sure that the cartoonists were paid for their work. People in the zine scene think I'm crazy when I tell them what I pay for a cover. As far as I'm concerned, it's worth every cent.

♦ **V: What's your vision of how society can function without work?**

♦ K: I really don't know, but the way things are going now, it's going to be a work-less society. [laughs] The handwriting is definitely on the wall; there are no jobs anymore! Whether people like it or not, that's the way it's going to be. The country only needs a certain number of people with technical knowledge to keep functioning; for the rest of us, it's like, "Good luck!"

What people should seriously start thinking about is how they can interact with and meet other people to find creative ways to avoid this doom-and-gloom, No-

Future scenario. Food Not Bombs, where people are learning how to organize to feed themselves, may be an indicator.

I've begun looking into alternative ways of living. Every once in a while I'll go to Dream Time Talking Village in West Lima, Wisconsin, run by a group of people came into ownership of half of a small town. They're developing radical horticulture, dumpster-diving for building materials, and holding workshops on how to actually do things. I look at those kinds of living experiences and I'm drawn to them because it's like, as the old Wobblies used to say, "Building a new society in the shell of the old." Plus, I'm constantly inspired by what I read in the zine *Bummers & Gummers,* written by a group of people who live on an Oregon farm and publish information on self-sufficiency. It's all about something real that you can touch, and forces you to pose questions about how you live.

These are examples of people trying to work things out. However, there are lots of people who just say, "Why bother? Why work to begin with?!" That "enlightened" statement is usually rattled off by parasitic types who have little to offer other than their smart-ass "wisdom." Some people have to work for a living—hell, I have to work!

I suppose there really isn't much chance of society

Cartoon from *Temp Slave #10* by Clay Butler

functioning without work—not mainstream society, anyway. But I still have hopes that more and more people will figure out that the present concepts of work are a dead end.

♦ **V: People can't go out and apply for jobs anymore; they have to create their own.**

♦ K: Yeah. There might be a pretty heavy re-emphasis on entrepreneurship: people producing crafts and running small shops. That was a big thing in America at one time before mall culture took over and wiped out a lot of that individuality. There are at least two models of the future: people could really hone the do-it-yourself kind of self-sufficiency, or the elites in power will just have to pay people to keep quiet while they get on with their business at hand (like bread and circuses in the last days of Rome). The latter would be a reversal of the attitude that people have now: "Throw the bums off welfare and into the street!"

Once you're on the street for awhile, you have no way to keep yourself clean regularly, so how are you going to get a job? The homeless are a very visible result of what's going on economically. But what isn't seen are the families struggling to keep a roof over their heads. They're ashamed and embarrassed because they've projected all these feelings of failure onto themselves. I don't have any pie-in-the-sky attitude about the future. I've always known that I was going to butt my noggin up against the rest of the world; I knew that no one was ever going to give me a helping hand. Sure, there are political groups out there trying to make a change, but they're so miniscule. People really have nowhere to turn.

You read these stories about people who grab a gun,

go out and "off" 30 people. Everyone asks, "Why is this happening?" Well, it's because these people are completely gonzo; they don't have anything in their lives and they're depressed. I'm surprised this doesn't happen more often. Anyone can get a gun and go to a street corner and start mowing down everyone in sight.

Anyone can get a gun and go to a street corner and start mowing down everyone in sight.

I saw this show on *48 Hours* about workers who kill their bosses. They interviewed a grieving family: "Well, this guy came to work and killed my husband and wiped out the rest of the work floor." Then they interviewed one of the killers: "They treated me like shit while promising better wages in the future. Then all of a sudden they fired me. I got drunk, went back and took care of business." Yet these clueless broadcasters can't figure out why people are doing this; it's treated like a freak accident. Nobody performs the most elementary analysis, like, "Maybe this job meant something to this guy, and when it was taken away, his life had no meaning anymore. He wanted justice and he took matters into his own hands by shooting people who had wronged him." Although, granted—this is a pretty intense way of taking care of business! I've noticed that companies have increased their security measures. Everyone is afraid of someone going off.

♦ **V: The behavioral archetype has been disseminated.**

♦ K: I'll give you a prime example. I did a zine titled *Welcome to the World of Insurance: An Introduction to Corporate Hell.* Most of the visuals were lifted from company manuals—I just reworded the captions. I included a story about this employee who worked at the same insurance company as me. He'd sit in his little cubicle mumbling to himself, and periodically would tell people that he was waiting for a spaceship to take him away. Once he brought a pistol to work and whipped it out during a meeting, and they didn't fire him! Finally the bosses called him on the carpet: "Your work performance has gone down. We'll give you some severance pay and a good recommendation, but we have to let you go." He accepted this without protest and went home, but then something snapped and he returned and *BOOM! BOOM! BOOM!* got three of his bosses.

It was fun producing *Welcome to the World of Insurance.* Do you remember James Brady? He was the fall guy that got whacked in the head with a bullet during the Reagan assassination attempt. The insurance company I worked for would periodically mail out an ad with a photo of Brady sitting in a chair looking like a vegetable, his wife Sarah standing behind him. The caption testified as to how the insurance company had

Cover of Temp Slave #10

Mr. Dickman the Boss

helped them through tough times. I used the photo, but substituted my own caption: "Hi, I'm Sarah Brady and this is my husband Jim. Jim was stupid enough to take a bullet for Ronnie. Look at him now. I can't even trust him around matches—he'll burn the place down. But thank god for our insurance company . . ."

I managed to include 300 copies of my Brady photo flyer in a company mailout. Shortly thereafter my job ended. A couple months later I called an acquaintance who was still working at the company, and he whispered, "If the boss found out that I'm even *talking* to you, I could lose my job! Do you know how many people called up the company angry about that Brady ad? The management finally figured out that it must have been you who did it—after putting me and everybody else through the wringer!"

♦ **V: *Physically, you fit the archetype of a working-class American—***

♦ K: Recently I was at the anarchist book fair, and looking around at everybody else, I must have looked like an FBI agent. But I'm probably crazier than the vast majority of the people there. I have a clean-cut look, but it's like I'm undercover. I definitely identify with where I've come from: "This is what I do and this is who I am. I've never had an easy job; I've done a lot of work with my hands. I've been a carpenter's helper, a construction worker, a factory employee, etc. At my current job I have to start up equipment that requires 75 steps from start to finish to operate. If you saw some of the people I worked with . . . some of them are out-and-out gorillas! They like me because I have a sense of humor, but they have a sneaking suspicion that there's something *else* happening with me. [laughs]

Having said I identify with my working-class roots, I also feel that I'm not really connected to *anything.* When I try to explain the technical aspects of my regular job, people give me a blank look, because it's so outside the realm of their experience. Most people I meet are waiters, cooks, clerks, etc, and they don't even know the kind of work I do exists.

At the same time, I do a zine, but I hate that whole fanboy and fangirl kind of thing—I don't want to be a part of the whole *zine-ocracy.* If other zinesters don't like me or don't understand my motives—well, I don't base my self-worth on the zine I do.

On another level, what I think and what I do as a writer puts me into conflict with working-class people, because our interests are different. My attempt to

think sets me apart! My view of the world is counter to the usual stereotypical working-class view. But I can bullshit with the best of 'em; I go to their bars, parties and weddings and still I know I don't fit in.

I can't be a part of the political scene because I get bored to death listening to people babble about theory. I move in and out of different worlds, never remaining in one for very long. Yeah, I look the part but I don't think the part!

♦ **V: *But you're trying to do something to make a better world, by illuminating oppressive systems of hierarchy, or work situations—***

♦ K: *Temp Slave* is trying to raise people's consciousness without telling them what to do or directing them toward a specific political action or group. All workers, especially those not making a lot of money, have shared interests.

I manage to produce about two issues a year. Some of my distributors suck; they just don't pay. I'm not like, "This thing's a zine—let's turn it into a *business!*" It's a constant worry to come up with money for the next issue—only one issue ever broke even, and that was because the printer accidentally gave me an extra 500 copies. I do all the stapling and collating myself, too. I'll keep *Temp Slave* going for awhile because it's good for my sanity and it's fun to get it out there and see people's reactions.

♦ **V: *How many do you normally print?***

> **Temp Slave is trying to raise people's consciousness without . . . directing them toward a specific political group.**

♦ K: About 2,500 copies. I could probably turn *Temp Slave* into a big-time publishing effort; the media and the attention are there. I've gotten offers from advertisers, and distributors always want more than I have on hand. But this is not a typical publishing effort. I do everything wrong, yet circulation keeps growing. I've been contacted by the *New York Times* and every other major media, and to the dismay of people who want that kind of attention, I blow 'em off! [laughs]

Temp Slave helps other people, but it really helps me the most by letting me work out my anger and frustration. **V**

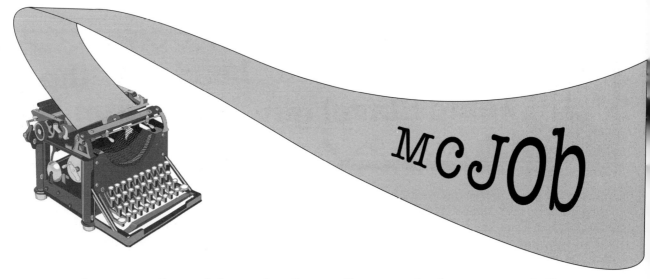

McJob

A seasoned participant in the mail art and zine scenes, Julie Peasley publishes *McJob,* an incendiary, humorous critique of daily work. She also produces numerous other art projects, ranging from gun earrings to her UFO Museum Tour mini-zine (contains color photos; $2). Send $2 cash for a copy of *McJob,* and for a catalog send $1 to PO Box 11794, Berkeley CA 94712-2794.

♦ *VALE: What do you do to make money?*

♦ JULIE PEASLEY: I'll be honest—right now, I like my job! [laughs] At least, as compared to other jobs I've had. So I'm not going to be spitting venom too much. But I can.

I've actually found work I can tolerate: at a custom photo lab doing machine prints which aren't really custom, but since this lab has a more professional clientele, there's more potential for *fun.* My main concern was no contact with the public [laughs] and I got it. I sit there by myself and work, which is just how I like it—independent!

♦ *V: What was your least favorite job?*

♦ JP: The jobs I disliked the most were the ones I wrote about in *McJob*—that's why I put out the zine. Before I put out the first issue I was looking for a job and not finding one. There was nothing but crap in the classifieds. I thought about all the jobs I'd had and realized how bad they were; I had really sad, sad memories.

I've worked a lot in photo labs. Customer service is the worst—photography is so subjective that you're *destined* to get into arguments with people. It's really stressful and not fun. A lot of the time I can sympathize with the customers, but the technology just isn't there. So you either have to lie, or wimp out and say, "That's the best we can do"—then nobody's really happy. You come up with a million little white lies in customer service jobs.

One horrible job I had was working as a maid for $3.75 an hour at a convention center in 1989–1990 while in college. There were some interesting co-workers: demented old women who would talk about their latest stomach ulcers or other medical problems. I can't believe I tolerated wearing the uniform, which was pastel polyester—you were supposed to keep it ironed. I got into trouble because I didn't *have* an iron. Little details like that made the job pretty creepy.

The main problem was the compensation—it's hard to believe how little we got paid—and when we finally got a raise, it was up to a whopping $3.95. Some maids get pretty good tips, but at this place people rarely stayed longer than a night or two, so there was no reason for them to tip. Since we worked in teams, when we *did* get a tip we'd have to split it among three people, so once in a while I'd take home a dollar—big deal.

What I hated the most were customers who obviously have never had to work a low-paying job . . . people born with a silver spoon in their mouth who are incapable of any empathy. People who are used to being waited on just can't understand what it's like to be on "The Other Side."

♦ *V: What other projects, besides producing a zine, have you worked on?*

♦ JP: I made an art car out of a Toyota hatchback, but I don't have it anymore because it died. I had seen one art car in Denver and photographed it, and that was

Illustration from *McJob #2*

my inspiration. I was 16, had just gotten my first car and I was having that identity crisis as a teenager where you *have* to be different—I think that's why I did it. I stenciled all these designs on the outside and had people draw all over the inside, grafitti style.

Then when I got to college, I made another art car because the first one was long gone. I was going to decorate this car with plastic flowers all over the outside, but I ended up just covering the upholstery with astro-turf and gluing little things all over the inside. Recently I saw another car with astro-turf upholstery and I couldn't believe somebody else had the same idea. But that was *all* they did, though—maybe they did it for easy cleaning and it wasn't an "art" thing. [laughs]

There are a lot of art cars here in the Bay Area; they're a whole subculture. Did you see the film *Wild Wheels?* That's an amazing and inspiring documentary. It was made by Harrod Blank, who lives in Berkeley.

♦ V: *Where did you find the astro-turf?*

♦ JP: Good hardware stores will have it; it comes in big rolls. Fun projects will just *leap* out at you when you go to the hardware store. [laughs] If you're lacking ideas and need an art project, just go there—you'll find *something.*

♦ V: *When did you start self-publishing?*

♦ JP: I think it was 1989. My first zine was called *No Poetry* because I hated all the poetry I saw in zines—I thought it was all really crappy bullshit. This was when I was a sophomore at college in Boulder, Colorado. Actually, my "make-a-zine" impulse got jump-started by seeing *Factsheet Five.*

Also, I got involved with self-publishing because all my friends in college were doing it. I had one friend who would go to Kinko's and make his own stickers and flyers and zines, and I thought, "I can do this, too." I did it also as a backlash against the art department—being an art student, I wanted to do something more graphic and accessible than the people who were making all these huge paintings.

Fun projects will just *leap* out at you when you go to the hardware store.

♦ V: *What was in the first issue?*

♦ JP: The content was graphic design and clipped images, no writing. Part of my motivation was realizing that as a woman I was getting paid less—all my male friends were getting paid more at their jobs. So I made a graphic that said, "The difference between making $6 an hour and $4 an hour." Under the $6 was a penis, and under the $4, a vagina. [laughs] That was my first political statement in a zine.

I remember spending a lot of time at the library and going crazy doing research. A lot of the pictures in my zine came from the library. I was on a mad hunt for deformed animals and, of course, went through the diseased body phase and a total fascination with death. That's passed a little, now that I'm getting older. [laughs]

♦ *V: Pathology, sickness and death have become so over-the-top trendy, on a Beavis-and-Butthead level—*

♦ JP: Yeah, they really have. Serial killers are so *passé!* [laughs] For a time, it was pretty deviant to be interested in that, but now it's just completely banal.

♦ *V: I think it all got translated into some weird macho-ism, like "I can take more than you." People were trying to out-gross each other with little details from books they read—like* "shock one-upmanship." *You know it's all so normal when Time-Life publishes coffee-table books on serial killers . . .*

♦ JP: It still has the power of shock value, but we're so saturated with those images and stories that it's just not shocking anymore. It's *really* hard to find shocking things today.

I guess my initiation into forensic pathology

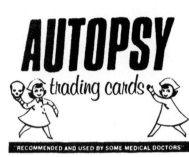

imagery took place when I got a job working at a photo lab that had the police department's account. This was in Boulder. It was weird because we were this photo lab staffed by high school kids and college students—you wouldn't think the police department would bring *us* their negatives to print, but they did. I guess they didn't have their own photo lab. I saw hundreds of crime scenes involving suicides, murders, drunk driving accidents—there were a lot of really gory close-ups. These photos were always up-to-the-minute; I would see the crimes before they were written up in the newspaper the next day. Seeing that every day kind of sobers you up!

It's strange because you don't think of Boulder as having much crime, but there was a lot that went unreported. I know, because I saw the photos.

♦ *V: Didn't you publish some autopsy trading cards back in 1990?*

♦ JP: My friend Mark got the idea to design those, and I ended up publishing them. The photos came from a library book on police forensic pathology that was published in the '60s. At the time the book seemed like a gold mine, because we had never seen pictures like those before.

♦ *V: In your mail order catalog, you offer a whole variety of "products." How did that happen?*

Top Five Shittiest Jobs I've Had

1. **Maid:**

It was 1990. I had limited marketable skills. I was a poor college student. I was a maid at the College Inn, a hotel leased to the university for conferences, conventions, football players, etc, but still a hotel in a sense that there were pubic hairs on the toilet seat.

2. **University Cafeteria Food Server:**

I worked in four different cafeterias at the University of Colorado during my early college years. At first glance, this appears to have maggot-level status, but in reality could play a significant part in helping kids pay for college. Starting wage was $4.50/hr—competitive at that time.

3. **Newspaper Delivery:**

Aahh yes, the trademark job of 13-year-olds. I guess I must have been reclaiming my lost youth because I started newspaper delivery one month after college graduation at age 22. They will hire *anybody*. They're *desperate*. Beware jobs that require only that you be a homo sapien with opposable thumbs. In fact, they're so desperate and they know what a shitty job it is, that they make you sign a contract saying you'll give 30 days notice if you decide to quit. Well, as soon as you start working, it becomes apparent not *if* you're going to quit, but *when*. In my case, I gave the notice after three days, so they had me for 33 days total.

And what hell those 33 days were! Compounded with the depression of working alongside high school graduates after I just graduated from college, I was living with my parents, sleeping on their couch, and had all my belongings in self-storage. Suffice it to say, I now look back at this chapter of my life as the *lowest* point thus far.

4. **Lehrer's Flowers:**

Simultaneous with the aforementioned shittiest job imaginable, I enlisted a two-week temp position with Lehrer's Flowers ("the one who cares calls Lehrer's") for $4.50/hr during the Valentine rush. I worked there 9–6 and delivered newspapers 2 AM–4:30 AM, so I was basically hating life for two weeks. All I remember doing when not working or sleeping was watching the winter Olympics and the "Smells Like Teen Spirit" video on MTV.

5. **T-Shirt Seller:**

Somehow, the jobs that always advertise the biggest potential for cash are always some sort of sales job. Let me tell you, I am no salesman. I don't even push my own DYSLEXIC products on people, much less someone else's wares. If I'm going to sell it, I really have to *believe* in it. Otherwise, selling is merely an acting job, better served by theater and drama majors.

—Julie Peasley, from *McJob #1*

McJOB®1

em·ploy·ee or em·ploye \im-,plȯ(i)-'ē, (,)em-; im-'plȯ(i)-,ē, em-\ n
: one employed by another usu. for wages or salary and in a position below the executive level

em·ploy·ee (em ploi'ē, em'ploi ē'), n. a person working
for another person or a business firm for pay; worker.
Also, em·ploy'e, em·ploy'é. [< F *employé* employed, ptp.
of *employer* to EMPLOY]

BAD JOBS!
GOOD JOBS!
BOOB JOBS!

STAN HEDDEN
Meat Plant
6 years

PETE BACA
Meat Plant
20 years

50% Off on
Fresh Sausage
Made by King Soopers Own
Sausage Makers

this issue is dedicated to Pete Baca, King Soopers Meat Plant worker for
20 years. let Pete be an inspiration to us all. or not.

| THE McJOB EXPERIENCE | HOW TO BE AN OVEREDUCATED AND UNDERPAID COLLEGE STUDENT/GRADUATE IN THE McJOB WORKPLACE | $2 |

Cover of McJob #1

♦ JP: That sprang from my mail art activity. *Factsheet Five* used to print an "Envelope Exchanges" section—they stopped including that years ago. You were supposed to throw a bunch of cool stuff into an envelope and send it to the people listed, and they would reciprocate. Back then that was totally new and different to me, so I started doing that and got to know a lot of people through the mail. I would make photos at work and laminate them, and make homemade postcards. It was kind of like zine activity; it went against the art world and was a cheap, fun activity that wasn't based on some structured art world format.

Since I worked a lot in photo labs, I started doing weird projects with photos that eventually ended up in my catalog. I produced them in large quantities and glued them into little booklets, like "Julie's UFO Tour." I did that just before the whole UFO craze ignited. I went to Roswell, New Mexico in 1994 and visited the two UFO museums there (that's where a supposed alien crash occurred in 1947). Today Roswell is inundated with gawkers and tourists, whereas previously it was a sleepy little town in a remote area. I wasn't really into UFOs, but after going there I really got into them. Now I have a project in the works: a compilation of people's personal UFO stories. At this point I have about 60, ranging from people who've been abducted to those who have seen weird lights. The museums were pretty convincing, but maybe I'm just a gullible person!

♦ ***V: You're just trying to give unconventional ideas a chance.***

♦ JP: I want to publish this in a slick book format with color reproductions.

♦ ***V: What's your early background?***

♦ JP: I was born in 1969 in Chicago but raised in Denver, Colorado by a single mom—my parents split up before I could even walk. I'm friends with my dad now, and I can see both sides—he was too young and he wanted to travel around the world, which he did. He's pretty eccentric. As an only child I stayed home a lot and did drawings and other indoor introverted activities. I didn't go out and play sports with other kids, which was the typical scenario.

My parents were both hippies, but they had jobs. My mom worked as a teacher and then became a "high-level secretary." One of her boyfriends lived with us for four years and he became a surrogate "dad." He was a doctor and facilitated me getting into photography when I was twelve. Later on, he helped me buy a car and go to college. My mom always "came through" with generous boyfriends!

I went to the University of Colorado at Boulder and got a B.F.A. in art. I did paintings throughout college but I never strived to become a "painter"; I thought that was ridiculous. After graduating, I started doing mail art and zines in earnest, as creative expression.

♦ ***V: Describe more about what's in your mail order catalog—***

♦ JP: I found a huge pile of tiny little plastic guns at a toy store in the suburbs. I attached earring hooks and offered them for sale, and a lot of people ordered them. A sixty-year-old nun from St. Mary's Convent ordered

Cover of McJob #2

McJOB®2

HOW TO BE AN
OVEREDUCATED AND
UNDERPAID COLLEGE
STUDENT/GRADUATE IN THE
McJOB WORKPLACE

OUR MOTTO:
Call in
SICK!

AD OF THE MONTH ➧

MORE PAGES!
SAME LOW
PRICE! $2

Part-time
SAUSAGE PLANT
Looking for exp. person to tie, hang,
cut & pack sausages. M-Thurs.,
8am-2pm. Call Continental Sausage,

some, and I had a lengthy correspondence with her. She was pretty liberal. She of course had never had sex in her life, and I asked her how she felt about that. She was totally happy with who she was.

I also offered "Nails from Jesus' Cross"—they were just nails dipped in red paint. I don't know if they were nine inches, but they were pretty big. They turned out to be too heavy to mail conveniently, so I raised the price to $10 and nobody ordered them anymore. They're a coffee-table novelty item. I sold chapbooks, which aren't zincs because they're not serial. Most of them contained clip art collages. I also sold skull tacks (little plaster skulls that I painted and glued onto tacks) but they were too much work to produce, so I dropped them. Everything was ridiculously underpriced and eventually I dropped a lot of items.

♦ **V:** *How did you start self-publishing?*

♦ JP: Probably the major impetus to start self-publishing was a friend who worked at a large copy chain, and let's just say he helped me out a lot. I probably would have done collage projects for myself anyway, but I had very little money and it would have been very difficult to publish a lot of copies. Even now, if I get $2.00 for a zine, the xeroxing costs me $1.10, the postage costs 55 cents, and I've got like a quarter left over—*yea!* [laughs]

In college my main creative outlet was mail art, and I put on a show which had 200 participants. My favorite mail art project was: sending out postcards to 100 of my correspondents asking them to list their five most hated foods. I got a lot of great answers—people drew comics, etc. I compiled them into a chapbook

with a color cover. The number one most hated food was organ meats (kidney, liver, heart, tripe, tongue, brains). Number two was fish and seafood. Three was sauerkraut—personally, I like it! Number four was Spam. There's a Spam museum now.

Most of my chapbooks had *frustration* as their basis. I kept the "politics" pretty subliminal by just using images rather than writing—I thought people's attention spans were really short. I know *I* wouldn't read anything past a couple sentences unless I was really interested in it.

Everybody I've come into contact with has a job trauma or horror story.

Through zines I've met a lot of great people, especially in San Francisco since there's a lot more going on here than in Denver, although it's picking up everywhere around the country. That's how I contributed to Johnny Brewton's *X-Ray.* If you ever close out a checking account, here's what you can do with the leftover checks: make art out of them! I took these checks and made them out to "Greed," and rubber stamped them with ominous messages. I glued them onto 250 sheets of paper which Johnny bound into an issue of *X-Ray.*

♦ **V:** *I just threw out a bunch of useless checks; wish I'd thought of that. Everyone needs to have a mail-art project just for recycling—*

♦ JP: Totally. I save up odds and ends just to mail out. Once I wrote an address on a mannequin head, pasted some stamps on it and sent it. I used to take clear plastic boxes and put miscellaneous things inside and send them to people. Now the new phase of my art is producing *McJob.*

It started out as a one-time project, but I got a lot of good feedback. I would say that *everybody* I've come into contact with has a job trauma or horror story. And everybody knows somebody else with one, too. Now there seems to be a whole sub-genre of zines: the *work-zine.* Work is a topic that a lot of people seem interested in reading about now.

♦ **V:** *Getting the wherewithal to pay for rent or food is a critical concern—*

♦ JP: People I exchanged mail art with did the widest variety of work to pay the rent: laying down linoleum in rich people's houses, phone sex, telemarketing, etc. *McJob* started out just as a way to vent frustration, but I got so many stories in the mail that I decided to continue publishing. As far as jobs go, there will *always* be something to write about! I've gotten more into the writing, away from images. A lot of people have sent in comics to illustrate their job situations.

♦ **V:** *The future seems to hold nothing but lousier jobs, worse pay, fewer benefits and longer hours—*

The Devil Walks Among Us

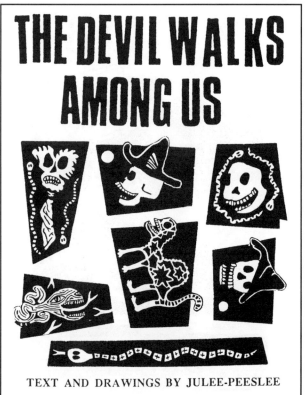

THE DEVIL WALKS AMONG US

TEXT AND DRAWINGS BY JULEE-PEESLEE

Julie's UFO Tour

Sonny and I headed to Roswell, NM (pop. 39,000) to see the two UFO museums there. Besides being interested in roadside attractions, we are totally interested in UFO phenomena, and had high hopes of being abducted or at least spotting a spacecraft out there in New Mexico. If you don't for some reason already believe in UFOs, you *will* after visiting these museums. Photos from around the world, personal stories, videos, books, top secret documents indicating government cover-up, magazines, wall displays and even 3-D life-size dioramas make these museums worth the drive. Best of all is the gift shop where you can buy magnets, stickers, patches, postcards of the little alien dude, books, T-shirts, coffee mugs, hats and copies of the original newspaper article on the 1947 crash at Roswell. Although the museums focus on UFOs around the world, the crash at Roswell is their main emphasis. At the Research Center (Museum #1), a mini one-room library houses the most extensive, definitive international collection of books and periodicals on UFOs. Hey! While we were at the second museum (Enigma), we were interviewed by a Lubbock TV station for a story on UFOs (due to our being the sole museum patrons at the time).

Julie stoops to alien's level. Self-portrait.

In 1947, an alien spacecraft crash-landed a few miles northwest of Roswell. Although many witnessed it and handled the debris, the government still insists it was a "weather balloon" and has been covering it up ever since. Retired military personnel know about the crash and the supposed four alien bodies (one was still living but soon died). A movie was even made about it (called "ROSWELL") starring Kyle MacLachlan and Martin Sheen, but the film just skims the surface and comes off like a made-for-TV after-school special. It's a good introduction, nonetheless. The fact is, over 350 people saw *something*.

I believe in UFOs and can only hope that one day I, too, will be lucky enough to see one.

Both museums are on the same street, easy to find and about six miles apart: Enigma UFO Museum, 6108 S. Main, Roswell NM 88202; the International UFO Museum and Research Center, 400-402 N. Main, Roswell NM 88202.

♦ JP: I don't see how that's going to turn around. Everybody's scrambling to learn Photoshop and QuarkXpress so they can get high-paying temp jobs, but soon there'll be so many experts that the pay will drop a lot. In the future, you'll be poor—but you'll have a computer!

Jobs are getting more casual— you can be a waiter with a million piercings and tattoos now.

♦ *V: Employers think, "It's just fine if you don't want to join the corporate gravy train, because you can be exploited better working at home—you're not organized or unionized. We don't have to pay benefits and we can terminate you anytime we want. If you don't like working for ten dollars an hour, there are millions of other people who will."*

♦ JP: Right. But it seems there's more leniency now in the workplace, at least in major cities in California. Jobs are getting more casual—you can be a waiter with a million piercings and tattoos now.

♦ *V: But there's not more leniency in the salary-paying department!*

♦ JP: Of course . . . As the population explodes, I think there will be more and more weird niches of specialized zines, like *Tiki News*—you probably wouldn't have seen that seven years ago. Zines will continue to be more widespread and diverse.

♦ *V: What are your hopes for the future?*

♦ JP: To be able to work for myself and make enough money to survive—hopefully, more than enough. To be able to do just what I want to do. Having to work for somebody else can really make you depressed on a daily basis! **V**

For Julie's zine reviews
see page 136–137

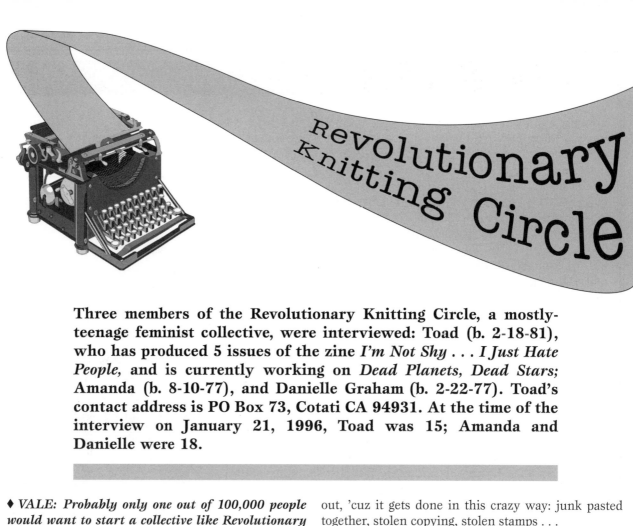

Revolutionary Knitting Circle

Three members of the Revolutionary Knitting Circle, a mostly-teenage feminist collective, were interviewed: Toad (b. 2-18-81), who has produced 5 issues of the zine *I'm Not Shy . . . I Just Hate People,* and is currently working on *Dead Planets, Dead Stars;* Amanda (b. 8-10-77), and Danielle Graham (b. 2-22-77). Toad's contact address is PO Box 73, Cotati CA 94931. At the time of the interview on January 21, 1996, Toad was 15; Amanda and Danielle were 18.

♦ *VALE: Probably only one out of 100,000 people would want to start a collective like Revolutionary Knitting Circle—*

♦ TOAD: —but those people find each other. *That's* what's strange.

Zines spread information to people who are isolated. The suburbs are so desolate—they're scary. The suburbs have driven me crazy. Probably the reason I'm the way I am now is because I grew up in them. I can't even deal with most of the people in this town; their ways are so strange—their "normalcy."

I get letters from people who live in the middle of Nebraska or Tennessee and have no friends—everyone hates them in their town; they get beat up. And they're so amazed to find people who feel the way they do; they think they're the "only one." That's what suburbs and small towns do to people.

♦ *V: How did your zine get to Nebraska?*

♦ T: I don't know; it passes through people. I don't really sell my zine or advertise it. About two years ago I gave my first zine to my friends—*hesitantly;* I was embarrassed. But they said, "Oh, this is really good!" Next thing I knew, someone wrote about it in their zine, and someone else wrote about it, and it spread; zines I've never heard of printed advertisements for it.

♦ *V: It's great that people advertise it who have no vested interest and nothing to gain; they simply like what you published—*

♦ T: I don't have the masters, either—I have to copy *other* people's copies. It's amazing that it ever comes

out, 'cuz it gets done in this crazy way: junk pasted together, stolen copying, stolen stamps . . .

♦ *V: All you need is paper, pen, scissors and glue—*

♦ T: That's why they call it the "Photocopy Revolution," because all you need is a copy machine.

♦ *V: Whose house is this?*

♦ T: It's my parents' house. I sleep here sometimes, but mostly I consider my home, like, *everywhere.* Friends often stay here because a lot of them are homeless, and I'm just lucky enough to have parents that let them.

♦ *V: Were your parents "1960's counterculture"?*

♦ T: Definitely. When I was a little kid it bothered me—I was *embarrassed,* but now I'm so happy, because I couldn't deal with having "normal" parents. When my parents met, I think my mom worked as a muralist and my dad was just some crazy hippie.

♦ *V: What does your dad do now?*

♦ T: I think that just through chance, looking through newspaper ads, he got a job in the lumber industry. My mom's an artist. My early childhood was mostly spent in Oakland. When I was a little kid they'd take me to Haight Street. In fourth grade, we moved to Sonoma County and have lived here ever since.

For awhile, I was struggling to be popular. I had long hair that was hairspray-styled, all pouffy and fluffy. I had all the right clothes and tried really hard to fit in. In junior high, I was even voted "Best Looking" in the yearbook. But in the seventh grade, something happened. I always had this weird sensitivity to things that other people don't have—I guess you could call it an "artist's sensitivity" to the world. And I started seeing through people. It hurt me when I realized that people didn't even like their own friends—especially amongst the so-called "popular" people. I saw such cruelty toward others, and couldn't play the game anymore. So I went really inward.

The suburbs are so desolate—they're scary. The suburbs have driven me crazy.

I was going crazy, going to therapists—it was bad. They wanted to give me anti-depressants, but I didn't take them and I'm very glad for that. Principals sent me to counseling because they thought, "You have a problem." (They didn't tell me that the *environment* was the problem.) Maybe one counselor helped me.

The whole time I thought I was inferior to everyone else—not in terms of social class, but inside I felt *defective*. Everyone else seemed to get along well in life, but I couldn't smile all the time the way they could. Little did I know that *everyone's* that way—they're just really good at covering it up!

♦ **V: This was in the 7th grade. That's the onslaught of puberty—**

♦ T: Definitely; I was a little precocious. I decided, "I was going to kill myself anyway. So I might as well just run away and have an adventure, and see what *could* have happened." Late one night I locked myself in this gas station bathroom and cut off all my hair (this sounds totally cheesy) and ran away to a place called "Humboldt House." It felt like I had found a place where I finally belonged.

Humboldt House was a communal house in Santa Rosa. All kinds of people were living in it. Everything was falling apart; the stairs were rickety, there were broken windows patched with duct tape and graffiti all over the walls. It was really nice! It was an old Victorian house with a good spirit to it. I met most of my friends through that time I ran away from home.

♦ **V: That was only two years ago—**

♦ T: Yeah; I've gone through a lot since then. I saved the newspaper article from when everybody got kicked out.

When Humboldt House got the eviction notice, everyone had lived there for so long and under such bad conditions that they decided, "We're not going to leave here without a fight." So they tore down the walls. We were having so much fun burning fires in the backyard and breaking all the windows. But pretty soon the cops came and gave a two-day notice to leave. I guess they came in and busted everyone—I wasn't there, I just heard about that. Everyone got kicked out of the house and because they had nowhere

Toad.

Amanda.

your depression)?

♦ T: I ran away from home and found this community that for the first time accepted me, even if I said things that were strange or if I looked kind of funny. But as it turns out, punk is like any other community. So my ideals are kind of *crushed.* But I still have them.

I've been able to isolate myself from society and stick with my own friends, because I was in an independent studies program at home. But through a glitch in the system I was sent back to high school for a month. It gave me a taste of reality as to what "normal" kids my age were going through. They were talking about dances and who's going out with whom. It was so crazy that I felt I was going to go insane all over again.

[Amanda arrives]

♦ AMANDA: But think about what punks talk about: the show, and who's been fucking who, and who gave scabies to who. There's a parallel right there.

♦ T: Once a family starts turning into a social scene, things get fucked up. It shouldn't be such a social scene; it should be more like a *community.*

♦ *V: What's the difference between a social scene and a community?*

♦ A: A community is more of a common bond and support for each other, whereas a social scene is a gathering on a more superficial level. Seeing a band is a social scene; hanging out and talking at Toad's house is "community."

A community is more of a common bond and support for each other, whereas a social scene is a gathering on a more superficial level.

♦ T: There's a song, "A Hundred Punks Rule," which is based on the theory that communal living gets corrupted after more than a hundred people get involved. The group is no longer tightly-knit; there are just too many people, and different cliques develop. Instead of holding onto each other for dear life, everyone becomes weird.

♦ A: When humans are around too many other humans, they become desensitized, because you can only acknowledge so many people. In certain African tribes, you greet each person you encounter; every person is important. In New York City, every person

---

to go, most of them became homeless and still are.

♦ *V: And these are kids, right?*

♦ T: Most were teenagers ranging from 16–20; a couple were older. They were college students, artists and musicians. It was a "rad" house.

♦ *V: Can you backtrack to when you were suicidal—what were the reasons?*

♦ T: It's like Siddhartha Gautama—I was sheltered most of my life and suddenly started realizing that the world is not a beautiful garden—there are people dying, people sick, people getting beat up. And it's not just that; it's the weird mental games people play that are the most cruel.

♦ *V: They say depression is caused by feelings of powerlessness to change anything—*

♦ T: That's why for a long time I was seriously suicidal. But that gave me a perspective you can't get except when you're right at the brink of going over the edge—that point where you can come back and say, "Well, I could have died last night, but instead I'm alive today, so therefore I can do anything."

♦ *V: And now you do a zine—*

♦ T: And sometimes you send them in the mail and they fall apart and the post office returns 'em in a plastic baggie, all destroyed.

♦ *V: You don't profit; the zine is like a "cause"—*

♦ T: It's definitely a cause. I've never made any money off my zine, ever. I don't even worry about it. I don't think you should charge someone for access to information—especially for art. It's not fair for someone to have to pay six dollars to go into a museum—it's just not right. *All* people should have access to art, even if they have no money.

♦ *V: How did you turn your life around (from*

can't be important or you'd go insane. So you become desensitized. There was a study conducted [Desmond Morris, *The Human Animal*] in a small town where a man lay on the ground and didn't move. Within ten minutes somebody had come up and was asking him what was wrong. They did this same study in New York City, where there are a lot more people on the sidewalks, and it took 45 minutes before anyone even *stopped.* Everybody kept walking by him like, "Trees in the forest, trees in the forest—oh, look at that log that fell. Trees in the forest, trees in the forest . . ." In a city you only recognize people from your own smaller community. It's like the difference between the telephone book and your address book.

♦ T: With my zine, it's gotten to the point where I get so many letters that I can't deal with people as *individuals;* I can't write each person a really long letter and have a good relationship through the mail. I'd rather have ten people write to me whom I know really well, than a hundred people who just write, "Send zine." When things get too big, everything gets lost.

♦ A: I play guitar and sing, and when I play *small* shows, people are totally emotional; some of them are even crying. However, I also like big shows because it's fun to socialize; I like chatting it up sometimes.

♦ *V: Amanda, where were you born?*

♦ A: I was almost born on the Golden Gate bridge, but my parents made it to the hospital—goddamit! It would have made such a good story. But then again, I almost died when I was born, so I guess that would have been bad. I had so much snot in my lungs that the doctors were worried they couldn't suck it all out—I was turning blue, dying from my own phlegm. My mom thinks it might have been due to gasoline fumes; something was wrong with our car.

♦ *V It's lucky you're alive—*

♦ A: I probably would have been anyway. I'm a survivor, dammit! I'm burly. I'm tough. I'm strong.

♦ T: I know kids whose parents are abusive and I say to them, "You know, you should run away from home!" This might seem like I'm being a bad influence, but I think I'm helping them out.

♦ A: I don't know—running away if you have abusive parents is one thing, but stealing and drinking

Robitussin . . .

♦ T: But I can see how people turn to drugs and alcohol, especially if they get to a point where they realize what the world really *is* behind all the media lies.

♦ A: But drinking is too easy of an escape.

♦ T: It's the easiest way out, because you can't deal with anything if you're drunk. You can't make a difference or change anything; you just sit back and go, "Whatever . . ."

♦ A: After awhile, you lose track of what's important.

♦ T: I was never really into drugs, but I remember a period when I would go drinking at least every other day. Actually, I think I got a lot of writing done because I was having so many experiences. It's weird: alcohol and writing almost go hand-in-hand. I guess it's because feelings are experienced so passionately with alcohol.

♦ A: Because it is "emo."

♦ *V: How do you define "emo"?*

♦ A: It means "emotional," like, "I got helluva *emo*—I cried all over the place." [laughs] . . . Support systems are necessary, especially in our culture where there are so few.

♦ T: Yeah, like the RKC. We started the Revolutionary Knitting Circle for girls in the Santa Rosa area—

♦ A: —it was started by Danielle, Melissa, Lani, me, and some other people. We needed a support network for women since the only time we saw each other was when we were drunk, or if we were mad because someone was fucking a guy we wanted to see. Instead of unifying over our common bonds, we were battling each other. We needed a group where we could sober up and talk about issues that concern us. RKC has been going on for two years.

♦ T: The people have changed. Some of the founders never show up anymore, but there are always new people who are amazed that they've found an arena to be able to talk in.

♦ A: It's especially good for younger girls in the community because they're able to come into a welcoming environment. We went through a couple of names; for awhile we were going to be the Weaver Beavers.

♦ *V: What's the message behind the name?*

♦ A: We wanted to be a knitting circle, like the ones in the past. Historically, they were one of the few forums

Cover of Toad's zine *I'm Not Shy . . . I Just Hate People #1*

About The Revolutionary Knitting Circle

The Revolutionary Knitting Circle has met weekly since October of 1994. All women and girls are free to attend our meetings. We ask that members be sober at meetings because we feel sobriety is necessary for our group to really communicate. It is also important that members keep what we share at meetings confidential. Confidentiality is important in our group because it builds trust and makes members feel safe.

We have no set style for R.K.C. meetings. Sometimes we sit together and talk about ourselves or share opinions and information on issues. We sometimes share literature or flyers and discuss them. We also have made flyers, stickers, shirts, and a zine together. We've gone on trips to places such as a rally and a self-defense show. Also, we've just had fun doing things such as bowling and exploring.

Over the past year, the R.K.C. has really helped its members. Through the group, some of us have learned to trust and be friends with women; some have realized that their problems are shared by many women. Each R.K.C. member benefits from the group differently, but we all benefit personally and/or politically.

ABOUT THE

REVOLUTIONARY

KNITTING

CIRCLE

★ ★ ★ ★ ★ ★

GIRLS' GROUP

SOME QUESTIONS MEMBERS OF THE R.K.C. ARE OFTEN ASKED:

Why do you have a girl's group?

To many R.K.C. members, the punk scene offers an alternative way to approach life. However, the punk scene is still male dominated and we need an alternative to this. We also think the R.K.C. helps us be friends with other girls instead of competing with them. The group gives us a space where we can reassure each other that we all face similar problems relating to our gender and offer each other support. At meetings, we help each other stand up for ourselves and our opinions. R.K.C. meetings also give us a place to have fun and meet people.

Why not have a co-ed group to deal with gender issues instead of excluding men?

Men and women have different issues regarding gender; we deal with women's problems. Also, women in our society are taught to compete with each other for men. When we are together without men, there isn't so much competition and it's easier for us to build solidarity. A women's only group allows us to step outside the roles we play relating to men and take a look at them. We are not opposed to co-ed groups, we just choose not to be one. If you want to start a co-ed group, tell us about it! I'm sure many R.K.C. members would be interested in it.

Are you lesbians?

Just because we choose to gather without men doesn't mean we're gay. Members of R.K.C. are accepted whatever their sexual preference, but we are not a lesbian group.

Don't you male-bash at R.K.C. meetings?

The R.K.C. doesn't exist to bash men. We spend our time becoming friends, building female solidarity, and discussing problems and our lives. We have a lot more to talk about than just men: ourselves. We have lives outside of relationships to men, and there are women's issues beyond how women relate to men. Also, concern for women's issues is not synonymous with hating men.

Are you feminists?

As a group, we are against the oppression of women. We consider this to be feminism. Whether or not you consider us feminists depends on your definition of feminism.

Are you Riot Grrrls?

Riot Grrrls are free to join the R.K.C., but we choose, as a group, not to be connccted with Riot Grrrl or any other organization.

women had to in order to get together and talk. Women had to meet under different pretenses.

For instance, women can hang out together when they're knitting, when they're preparing a meal, or at a baby shower. But they can't just get together to *be* together—to be women. Men always ask, "Why aren't *we* involved? You're a Feminazi; you hate men!"

♦ T: Or they'll assume that you're a lesbian—

♦ A: We have girls in the group whose fathers think, "Oh, girls hanging out together . . . well, *obviously* you're lesbians, then." *No,* we're just trying to create a support system and a community because there isn't one.

♦ T: We need places that have a zine library, and where people can listen to records for free, so that everyone has accessibility to information—it's so expensive to buy. We also need places for bands to practice and where people can play musical instruments, even if they don't own any.

♦ *V: Amanda, you're in a band?*

♦ A: Well, I play guitar and sing. [laughs] I always thought, "I'm never gonna have a band. I'm never gonna play; no one's ever going to hear my music." Finally I just said, "Fuck that—I'll be my own band. I'll play my guitar and sing, and they'll just deal with it." Now people want to play with me and I tell them, "Dude, I'm a solo act."

♦ T: One of the underlying philosophies of punk is "D.I.Y." (Do It Yourself). When I was a little kid I wanted to be a writer, and my mom would tell me to write to publishers and see if I could get something published. I would say, "No, I'm not doing that so they can rape it for all it's worth!"

♦ *V: That's why the zine revolution started. You can put something out and say what you want to say, without anyone else interfering.*

♦ T: I think it would be rad if people on my street—everyone—made zines. Everybody has multi-faceted lives that they want to talk about; they just don't have a forum, except for television. And television wrecks things. Everything ends up becoming a media object; it's like pornography. Everything becomes trivialized and distorted. If you want information you have to know people, write letters, read, and all this has dignity to it. With television, information is being spoonfed to you without work, without criticism, and with unthinking acceptance.

Danielle. Photo: Trent Gaylord

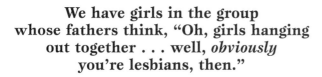

We have girls in the group whose fathers think, "Oh, girls hanging out together . . . well, *obviously* you're lesbians, then."

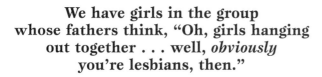

[Danielle arrives]

♦ *V: We're talking about the Do-It-Yourself spirit that zines embody, and about community.*

♦ DANIELLE: The whole tribal idea of working as a group, and also thinking *cyclically* rather than linearly, has been stripped from us. So, all of these independent projects face a dilemma because this culture socializes us to not promote that tribal way of acting or living.

♦ T: I think it's a combination of too much drinking and too much to hope for. I have so many ideas, but it's not hard to lose sight of them.

♦ D: A friend of mine calls alcohol "the opiate of the masses." I totally agree. We were talking about what a different world we would have if there were no media, cigarettes, alcohol—all these things that keep us sedated on so many levels: the political, the personal, etc.

♦ T: I have to confess that alcohol helped get me through a difficult time in my life. It was like therapy, because when I was drunk I would realize exactly what was hurting me.

♦ A: But the problem is: the alcohol disables you from *doing* anything about it.

♦ D: We're so rootless and stripped of our souls that the root of the problem is never finding the root of the problem! We're taught to be distracted by minor issues.

♦ A: When problem-solving, I often can't find a meeting ground between my emotions and my reason.

♦ D: Descartes' model of the "disembodied intellect" is about how we have separated our intellect from our emotion. In our culture, emotions are seen negatively.

♦ A: And it makes it really difficult to solve problems, especially emotional ones, when you don't know how to fit the two together to make a solution.

♦ T: Machines don't have emotions—that's one of the main reasons that they're so limited—

♦ *V: Their only goal is to get a job done—*

♦ A: And why do we want to get things done? To make somebody money. And *whose* money are we making?

♦ D: We make more money so we can buy more stuff, so we can make more money so we can buy more stuff . . . then, are we humans anymore?

♦ A: We're consuming machines!

♦ D: This whole culture is dehumanizing. Look at the way women are objectified in the media, especially

with the "waif" look. The media is promoting sickly, frail, emaciated women as beautiful—

♦ **V: *Like Kate Moss—***

♦ D: Exactly. The weak, child-like look.

♦ A: It's because you can control children; they're weak and vulnerable.

♦ T: This image is the antithesis of early examples of beauty, like the Venus of Willendorf with her big hips and big droopy breasts.

remembering failure with a smile

Cover of I'm Not Shy . . . I Just Hate People #3

♦ D: That's like the Madonna/whore dichotomy: you're either the mother or you're the sex symbol. If you don't fit into one of these roles, what do you have as a role model?

♦ **V: *We're just left with the nuclear family model. There are no grandparents or extended families like there used to be.***

♦ T: Children should be raised in a tribe where every adult in the community is responsible for helping to raise each and every child.

♦ D: We've been raised in this huge isolating culture of urbanization—

♦ **V: *And sub-urbanization, particularly. In Spain, many cities have a park—a kind of community gathering center—every few blocks, where all generations regularly hang out. These cities seem far less alienating than the suburbs.***

♦ T: I was told that Rohnert Park is actually the second "designed" city in the country. If you look at it on a map, there's no core. The closest it has to a downtown is a strip that has two shopping centers facing each other. There are no sidewalks, and the nearest you get to a downtown square is the parking lot. But you're not allowed to stand around and talk, so you get shuffled into stores. Once they figure out you're not buying anything, a security guard is there to tell you to move along. It's very exclusionary.

When you live in Rohnert Park, the TV is practically your only company.

♦ **V: *A lot of social change efforts just don't last— why not?***

♦ T: There are plenty of good movements, but then the media distorts and turns them into something entirely different. Everything gets trivialized.

♦ D: The hippie revolution is a good example of that. Once it became a media show, it was all over. Look at the punk scene—

♦ A: It's being trivialized again through Green Day and Rancid. It's becoming a fashion-pop statement.

♦ D: The media strips out the essence from the ideas of any movement. The original message might be, "We're in pain. We're crying out for help. We need something. We want social change," then the media takes that and cashes in on it.

♦ T: They make it "cute."

♦ A: That totally degrades it; then we feel even more powerless.

♦ T: That's why I feel hurt when I see some band (that I used to like) on television. It's not so much about them selling out personally, but about having what they sincerely believe in, become something objectified.

♦ **V: *That's the entire process of being in the media: regardless of your personal ideas, you become an object. You rationalize, "I'm just trying to get my message to a larger audience—"***

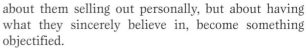

There are plenty of good movements, but then the media distorts and turns them into something entirely different.

♦ A: The main problem that arises from something being objectified is that it immediately loses its power. Like when women are objectified: they're not on TV to say anything meaningful or to be heard; they're viewed as a "thing."

♦ T: What I picked up from the punk community is that you have to question everything to the root of your being. Everything you've ever been taught— everything in the world—you need to think about, and question why.

♦ D: You can't consider yourself "alive" if you simply accept things and are not thinking and questioning.

♦ A: But I do that all the time: forget to question

things. We're not taught to question. It's so hard to be alert every single minute because everything that happens to you, you need to question.

♦ D: There are people who spend their whole lives questioning—researchers, for example. Noam Chomsky researches all of the time and he still feels like his work is never done. One of the things he advocates is starting the spread of information on a *community* level—

♦ T: It's like when you go to another city, you can just walk up to someone who looks punk and most of the time they'll be nice to you and you can get a lot of really good information out of them, like where you can stay. Whereas Yuppies can't do that. A lot of stuff is really word-of-mouth. Punk is the only community that I know of where you can do that.

♦ D: The punk scene is great, but it's also very male-dominated. In some ways it's just a mini-replica of society: people consuming drugs and alcohol; it's male-dominated and hierarchical.

♦ A: Most of my problems in school dealt with the hierarchy of how popular you were. Unfortunately, I was stuck really low on that chain. Sometimes I still feel like I need a man to be okay because the popular girl *always* had a boyfriend—somehow that made her okay. What happened in school still affects me today. The way I interact with men and women, and the way I interact with *myself* in the mirror, all relates to early incidents.

♦ D: These days it's culture and media doing the child-rearing. We don't really have parents to look to as guides anymore. Our roles have become so unclear and confusing. Media does everything it can to strip us of ourselves. To become this media model—to be a part of it—women lose themselves and create a false self that acts and looks the way that men want us to, while our real selves cry out for help.

Cartoon from *I'm Not Shy . . . I Just Hate People #1*

Women are supposed to be like *this,* or they're supposed to be like *that:* "You have to be sexy, but you can't be a sexual being because then you're a slut." There are so many different standards to live up to.

♦ T: You can't win. It's just like the lyrics in that Crass song, "Honesty is by no means a way of survival." People should just be honest about things that aren't necessarily pretty about their own bodies, and maybe they could finally be honest with themselves. That's the first primal step. Women should admit that their boobs are droopy because it's normal for them to be that way.

♦ A: I often battle with myself as to who I am. I'm still a virgin. I consider myself a very sexual person, but I'm still "the virgin." I'm surrounded by people having far too much indiscriminate, drunken sex, and I refuse to participate in that. I don't *want* to have sex with lots of people!

People still find it difficult to discuss *menstruation.*

♦ D: People still find it difficult to discuss *menstruation.* It's because "Women are bad; women are gross. They menstruate, and that's disgusting!" Human bodies can't be real, they have to be Barbie dolls. I'm not allowed to have cramps, I have to be "sick." I have cramps, I'm bleeding everywhere—fuck you!

♦ A: My mother would tell me, "Men don't want to hear about your menstruation. Why should you burden them?" "I'm so sorry, I don't mean to tell you this, but my uterus hurts and I'm bleeding profusely. Yes, that's right, I'm having a problem." As if you had a headache you wouldn't tell someone, "I have a headache."

♦ D: It's scary how we stuff toxic tampons made of bleached rayon up our bodies. We risk getting toxic shock syndrome so people won't know we're bleeding.

♦ T: Where in history did something basic like menstruation get so warped and perverted?

♦ D: [whispering] Christianity. The followers of Christianity have traditionally hated women. Women were too powerful; once goddesses controlled the cycles of life.

♦ A: It was important for a woman to bleed; it meant she was fertile.

♦ D: It became necessary to pull women down, to control them. So, women became disgusting and corrupt. If they were powerful, they were witches.

♦ T: The classic Christian paradox is that women are supposed to be both virgins and mothers. That is so fucked up!

♦ A: I act the way I do because I feel censored. Instead of saying, "I'm bleeding," I say, [forcefully] "I'M BLEEDING! ANYBODY WANT TO STAND UP TO THAT? COME ON, TAKE ME ON! I'VE GOT

CRAMPS! HEY, I ALSO MASTURBATE WITH PILLOWS; I DON'T USE MY HANDS!"

I thought I was deformed because of the way I masturbated. I also thought my nipples were deformed. Once this girl saw my breasts and said, [gasp] "You have the weirdest nipples I've ever seen!" But they are so normal; I just have big aureoles.

♦ D: The issue of masturbation was a liberating point in my life. A friend mentioned detachable shower heads and I said, "I love those!" She said, "Ohmigod! Those are the best things in the world!" After that I just began talking about masturbation. I realized, "I can't believe I've been keeping quiet about this just because I hate my body."

♦ A: A friend bought me a book on women and sexuality, the *Hite Report*. This was a turning point in my life. I looked up "masturbation" and it listed the most common ways women do it. The first most common way was lying on your back using a finger, and the second was on your stomach using a finger. Then I got to the third most common way women masturbate: using an object. The book quoted this woman saying, "I *straddle pillows* and I *hump* them." That's exactly what I do!

♦ T: I remember for months you kept telling everyone, "I have the third most common way of masturbating!"

♦ A: There are so many things that we are not allowed to say; if we only just fucking screamed them and made people hear them, then it would become okay.

♦ T: It's like taking the ugliest detail and amplifying it 500 times—that way everybody gets used to it.

♦ D: "What if I don't want to be pretty? What if I want to be a human being?"

♦ T: When we had a Revolutionary Knitting Circle slumber party, we had dye and curlers in our hair and were wearing avocado masks—just to be traditional. We had on ugly pajamas or ugly underwear and were just sitting around being normal. I think that's a really root girl-bonding experience: being ugly in front of each other and being truthful about it.

Ugliness is really how you choose to define it—for instance, like body hair. I was sitting in the shower one day and I had a realization: "I gotta shave—no, I don't; this is *cute*. Fuck that!" If you really want to shave, go ahead. But consider why you want to.

♦ A: The only reason I ever shaved was for men. I was afraid a man was going to see my armpit hair and say, "Ugh, gross," or feel my leg and go, "Ugh, *gristly.*"

♦ D: I know. I remember one time a male friend was talking about this girl: "Oh, and she waxed her legs all the way up to her hips and it felt so good and smooth." Do you know how many ingrown hairs the poor girl is going to have?

♦ T: That's sick. That's like weird medieval self-torture.

♦ A: Well, look at the things we do that are torture: acid face washes, boob jobs, nose jobs—come on, you can manipulate your body to look good for *whom*?

♦ T: Do you know what the *Iron Maiden* was? It was this big box shaped like a woman with spikes inside. In the Middle Ages, it was used to torture women accused of witchcraft. All these people casually having surgery to alter their bodies is like putting themselves in the Iron Maiden. If your hips are too big, just *buzzzzzzzz!* [makes chainsaw noise]. It's a disgusting metaphor, but I think it's true: slicing off bits of yourself that you think are unappealing and unwanted. That's very unhealthy.

The issue of masturbation was a liberating point in my life. A friend mentioned detachable shower heads and I said, "I love those!"

♦ D: If you were happy with yourself, why would you do that? Obviously, there's something wrong.

♦ T: If you watch bad movies and bad TV, you'll notice they all have the same basic roles for women. Especially in movies involving rape. There's always the generic business woman-type walking to her car,

Illustration from a Revolutionary Knitting Circle flyer

and an unknown dark man comes out and attacks her by the car. I've seen this image so many times. You can break it down by using Freudian dream analysis: the car equals daily life, the woman who carries the briefcase has only gained economic power through her job, but she's still being raped every day in her daily life because the dark man who waits in our subconscious, attacks her.

♦ A: The sickest thing I ever saw was this tits-and-ass movie. This girl was wearing a skimpy little outfit and dancing around while a cartoon character (resembling a Tasmanian devil) watches her from the corner. The woman is real; she's dancing around, and you see the cartoon character's eyes bulge out. Then the cartoon character starts *raping* the woman; I couldn't believe it. And you know there's somebody watching this somewhere with a beer and a hard-on, laughing. Are we supposed to laugh? It made no sense.

♦ D: The scary thing is that the media and movies help set the standards for what our lives are like, so most people go: "I guess that's normal. I guess it's okay to look at women that way."

♦ A: I think zines are bringing back storytelling: "This is what I've done and this is my experience. Do you identify with this? Let's share our stories."

♦ T: That's what's really amazing when you read a zine for the first time—depending on which kind you read, of course. I remember thinking: "This is so real." I felt I was reading about universal experiences that weren't being acknowledged on television. Most mass media lack truth and passion.

We should start a commune. A new colony where we can be free from the social stigmas of the past.

♦ D: There was this guy who wanted to find a completely uninhabited place with no remnants of human machinery. He wanted to get as far from civilization as he possibly could; he didn't want planes, engine sounds, or any human-produced noise. So he went to Africa and tried to record just five minutes of absolutely no sound, and couldn't do it. He couldn't find a place people hadn't somehow penetrated with their noises.

♦ A: I think I have the answer. I read about these pirates who took garbage barges, put soil on them and were able to grow plants. They sailed out into international waters where no one can touch you. If we could get enough barges with soil, we could make an island! It would be the garbage barge commune.

♦ D: The kind of commune that me and my friends have been talking about is one where we grow our own food and are self-sufficient. Anything we might need from the outside world would be obtained through barter. Other than that, we would completely disconnect ourselves from the outside world and its hierarchies. Would it work? I don't know.

♦ T: I'd rather sail off and at least *try* to live on a commune and be happy than say, "Oh well, fuck it. I'll just keep on living the way I've been living."

♦ A: When I have a conversation like this, I talk to someone else and two days later I hear them saying what I said to another person—it branches out.

♦ D: I recently went to see the play, *Three Sisters,* by Chekhov. The three sisters are intellectuals in this horrible small town. Their goal was to work for the future, always preparing for it: "People will remember us. They'll look back on us and be happy." In every era, everyone sees themselves as significant. Everybody wants to be remembered and have their ideas spread.

♦ **V: That's the wonderful thing about zines: they migrate all over the world.**

♦ D: I'm not an existentialist and I'm not as cynical as Chekhov, but there's a jarring truth about how things change all the time, yet in every era we continue to be dissatisfied, always yearning for what's just out of reach.

♦ T: I don't think that's necessarily bad.

♦ A: Things will probably keep going the way they have always gone. What's important is trying to improve yourself and affect others, trying to spread ideas among those you know and care about. If the whole world doesn't change tomorrow, if I never live on a garbage barge in international waters, I'm not going to be terribly crushed. As long as I have my community which supports me, I'll be okay.

♦ D: I feel I need more than that. Tolstoy talks about the need to bridge the infinite and the finite. We bridge our finite existence with something like religion because we need to feel we're part of something greater and larger than our short existence. Otherwise, what's the point of living?

That was what Chekhov captured in this play. In every single era, each individual person is the most important person in the world, and they will be for all time. That's what they need to think to stay alive.

♦ A: Also, we always think, "Migod, it's us against the world." I'm going to affect the one-millionth of one percent of people that I can. That's my small community support system; the people I care about. You can't

R.K.C. SEZ: SMASH THE PATRIARCHY !!!

change the entire world, it's impossible.

♦ T: Hitler didn't think so. People don't necessarily *want* to be changed; maybe our views are fucked up and we don't realize it.

♦ *V: Some people aren't receptive to new ideas. You can't convert people. Concern yourself with your own changes, even if other people are the ones who need changing.*

♦ D: We shouldn't try to change other people. Women are already so selfless, everything becomes "trying to change other people."

♦ A: Women are taught not to feel anger. I feel guilty about being angry. Recently I had a traumatic situation with a boy and was crying all day. I thought, "But I have to look pretty for my show tonight, or no one's going to like me." I ended up repeating in front of the bathroom mirror for fifteen minutes: "You're strong, you're pretty. You're a strong, pretty girl; pretty girl; you're so strong." It was time for Amanda to be the strong, composed woman.

Women are getting a taste of freedom and are learning to group and to fight back against centuries of oppression.

♦ T: But this isn't the first time in history that women have gathered together. It's just not mentioned in history books. They'll talk about Rome forever, but that's just a return of patriarchy.

♦ D: I wish there was an accessible way for us to learn about all of this lost or hidden history. How have things gotten this way?

THE BLOODY KOTEX WASTEBASKET THAT IS MY LIFE.

I'm going to affect the one-millionth of one percent of people that I can.

♦ *V: Why is there a myth that only men have the will power to do a zine for 20 years? And why are there so many more zines by men than by women?*

♦ D: In order for women to present their work it has to be extremely good. That's the reason why I haven't put out a zine yet.

♦ T: That's why I almost didn't. The trouble is, you might never do it. There is never going to be the perfect time, perfect place, perfect circumstances or perfect subject. So, you might as well put out whatever you have.

♦ *V: That's the wonderful aspect about zines: it's*

"normal" to publish your immediate feelings and thoughts—anything that comes straight out of your mind or emotions—

♦ D: You're right—I feel more resolute; I'm definitely going to do my zine. I've been waiting for years, and what especially makes me want to do one is to hear that there are stacks of zines by men, and so few by women.

♦   ♦   ♦

Toad ran away from home again and had more adventures, then returned to her parents' house. What follows is a brief phone interview on May 23, 1996

♦   ♦   ♦

♦ TOAD: I'm glad I'm back living with my parents because I just finished another zine, I've been painting, I'm also working on a film and a band. People who live on the streets are permanently in check by not having food and shelter, and they can't accomplish things within the world and themselves. It's terrible because there are all these people with wonderful lives and memories who are withering away, without being able to have anybody listen to their stories.

♦ *VALE: Why don't you write down the stories you heard? It's like giving a gift to those people who passed through your life, and it's doubtful they would have the means to tell their own tales.*

♦ T: I was just thinking about that today when I was answering my mail. I get these zines mailed to me that are done by alienated teenagers in the Midwest. They have cutouts from magazines of pictures of models with notes here and there, but they're basically rehashing things they've read in magazines and seen on TV. It's hard to find something real or substantial in them.

I was originally drawn to zines because people were coming from a level that was brutally honest. It's not really that way anymore, and I think it's making all of the original zine writers jaded and sick of it all. Zines are getting absorbed into the mass media. The kind of lingo used in the media is just soundbites and bullshit, and it makes me sad to look at zines that just recycle this. But there are always people who never change and continue to produce things from the heart.

I ran away to Portland and was living on the streets. The streets become a black hole that sucks you in; you can't get out. All you can think about is how you're going to eat and where you're going to sleep. Once I walked around at night, cold and miserable, and passed a health club window where all these people were walking on treadmills. I thought, "Migod! They're spending money to walk around, while I *have* to walk around all night because I have no money!" I'm sure some of them were on diets, too, and I would have been *glad* to eat all the food they were refusing. It's so ironic. Living on the streets can show you what's really important in life: mainly, to just enjoy living, and to take care of yourself and your friends.

♦ *V: You're in a position now where you can record your memories and give them a life of their own.*

I was originally drawn to zines because people were coming from a level that was brutally honest.

♦ T: That's what made me want to write a novel. I wanted to write about things that I'd seen, but I was afraid of what might happen if my friends read it. I'd have to do what Sylvia Plath did and write it under a different name and publish it in a different country.

♦ *V: Don't worry about anyone; just write it!*

♦ T: Yeah. I'm sort of secretly writing this novel, but I'm always changing the names and twisting things around. I have some pretty good stories to tell, but it's not quite finished yet. I think I need to live for at least

another ten years. [laughs] I always feel like I've lived this long life, but I've only been exploring and traveling and really living for two or three years. My childhood is this gray area that is kind of foggy until age 13, when I feel my life really began.

♦ *V: Maybe you're an old soul.*

♦ T: I've been told that. But my mom once said, "Maybe you're a *new* soul, maybe this is your first incarnation on this plane of existence. Maybe *that's* why everything seems so strange to you." This world is so strange to me and everybody seems to take it as normal and day-to-day. When I look at it, it's seems like the craziest place. I just can't believe the stuff that I hear people talking about, and they say it with such a straight face! It's so bizarre! [laughs]

♦ *V: You haven't been on the planet long enough to be painting a lot—how do you get your ideas?*

♦ T: With anything I do, I just sort of do it. The inspiration comes from somewhere beyond me and I don't really understand it; I just see the end results.

My mom was a painter and I just found some of her old paints in the closet. I used some old particleboards as canvases. It always turns out good.

For all the things that I do, whether painting or writing or music, I invent my own way of doing it. I've tried before to do things like they were *supposed* to be done, but I've always ended up making a fool of myself. You just have to go ahead and invent your own way of doing it—then it looks like you know what you're doing, because it's your own style.

When Your Hair Is Purple, You're Free

I saw them lost under wash-out hair dye . . . The more they try to stand out, the closer they blur together, a sea of magenta and scared eyes in high schools everywhere. Rebels for a day, who are they trying to shock anyway? They're easy to hate, scoring low on the punk scale, they live at home and buy Rancid T-shirts at the mall. They let you feel superior for once, "I've seen it all . . . I was here first . . ." I'm not naive . . . I'm not naive . . . This is where punk turns into an exclusive yacht club. Where talk of community and equality seem to get forgotten and the pecking order comes in. It's the same old social hierarchy only with pierces and patches and half-understood political ideas. So fucking junior-high cliquish.

I saw myself eyeing suburban punk refugees with disdain, but wait, was I not one of them just a year or two ago? I swallowed my stupid pride and forced myself to talk with them.

Sure enough, I came across some pretty rad people, aside from their cheesy Nordstrom's punk get-up. But I've seen the way other punks looked at them differently, especially at shows in the city. The way you'd stare out at us from streetcorners as we'd walk by.

This glare of "What are *you* doing *here?*" and this stance of YOU ARE NOT ONE OF US. Just because their clothes weren't shabby enough or their hair wasn't punk enough, there are two more minds in the world you'll never meet.

People have this compulsion to label things, to corner the unknown and stick it in a jar under its title. We do this to ourselves. We always seem to have to define ourselves in relation to others. We build barriers amongst humanity in this way; we're punks, they're jocks; we're hard-core, they're poseurs . . . Us vs. Them . . . Ours vs. Theirs . . . Our identification in isolation? Our domination in subordination? A matter of Punk or Not, PunkOrNot, Punkernaut . . . So many of you fucking *punkernauts!!*

Guard yourself from superficiality. One of the most cruelest things is to be trivialized, misunderstood. Don't set rules for who you can talk to or who you can befriend. If they're willing to accept you, you should do the same. Open your arms to open minds . . . even those whose hair is coated in manufactured insolence.

—Toad,
from *I'm Not Shy . . . I Just Hate People #3*

◆ **V: One good thing about not having a huge amount of money: you're forced to make do with what you have.**

◆ T: I'm one of those people who always walks with their head down, looking in the gutter for strange pieces of trash. There's something really great about making use of whatever you find in your surroundings. There are all these rich-kid bands and zines and they have all the means and all of the best equipment, but they put out the worst stuff you could ever imagine. They lack any kind of substance.

It all comes back to the people who have some sort of real vision who can put together something with anything they can find, and then everybody else ends up copying their makeshift ideas. The commercial videos on MTV are all trying to have this sloppy style with frazzled edges. They're attempting to copy the look of poor art students trying to put a movie together. People always end up doing that. [laughs]

◆ **V: It seems kind of backwards.**

◆ T: It's really backwards because they don't know what they're doing. They just focus on the superficial aspects of form and don't know what's underlying.

Some slick "Generation X" magazine (the kind with models wearing vinyl) wrote and asked me to contribute something to their publication. They were totally flaunting the fact that they're distributed by chains like Barnes & Noble, as if that would be really appealing to me. They kept saying, "We're the best alternative mainstream source for music and fashion." And I'm thinking, "*Alternative* mainstream? What do they take me for?" They come from a totally different attitude than the people who do zines. Zines are all about being independent.

> **They kept saying, "We're the best alternative mainstream source for music and fashion." And I'm thinking, "*Alternative* mainstream? What do they take me for?"**

It's just like going to shows—you can instantly tell who the record industry people are, just like if you're a shoplifter you can tell who the undercover store security are. These "talent scouts" are wearing a freshly silkscreened T-shirt of some new punk band, and they're kind of middle-aged with a really crisp, squeaky-clean leather jacket. You know they're thinking, "I sure look good tonight with my bondage bracelet." [laughs]

◆ **V: What's happening with the Revolutionary Knitting Circle?**

◆ T: We used have meetings in this communal house. Different girls, mostly from the punk scene, would come. In the beginning we would just talk and people would end up crying and holding each other. But after awhile, it turned into a bunch of high school girls who just wanted to make stickers and work on T-shirts. It's good because it's community action, but it felt terribly impersonal because many of us didn't get to know each other. It's sad: the people who were originally in it mostly still feel the same about things and want to meet, but we've all gone our separate ways. We need to start over with a clean slate.

◆ **V: It's a lot easier to start something than to continue doing anything over a period of time.**

> **I believe that once you're a punk, you're always a punk . . . Once you've arrived at that state of mind, you can never leave or forget it.**

◆ T: I think the most important thing is that people try and continue to care. I see my friends who used to feel so passionately and fight against things, but now they don't really seem to care, or are preoccupied.

I can't decide if the worst evil is getting a job or drinking too much. We used to have so much fun, have the greatest adventures, and talk about revolution and politics. Now, I'll stop by their house and they're drinking the same kind of beer every night, in the same living room, watching movies, smoking a lot of cigarettes, and not really talking but laying on the couch with their eyes half-closed. That's what happens when you stop caring. That's what's so scary about alcoholism.

◆ **V: No wonder some people became straight-edge.**

◆ T: Yeah. I think everyone saw their friends do that. It's like those people died. What's the point of living if you don't care anymore and don't feel that kind of magic about things anymore? You're basically dead.

That's also what happens when people get caught up in jobs and working, and other day-to-day stuff. After awhile, the things that once seemed so important now seem like "just a phase." Whereas I believe that once you're a punk, you're always a punk—even if you don't choose to label yourself with that term. Once you've arrived at that state of mind, you can never leave or forget it.

◆ **V: Certain ideas and principles seem to endure—**

◆ T: Yeah. I remember being kind of sad, thinking about how now no one wants anything to do with "Riot Grrrl." But the beliefs that went along with it are worth holding on to. People might not be writing about it, but I think that anyone who came into contact with it still carries it with them. I know that when I walk down the street, I'm facing the world with things that have made me stronger: Riot Grrrl, punk, etc. I'm a fuckin' feminist! It's weird when you talk to other girls and they don't want to have anything to do with it. But they are; they're feminists, they're Riot Grrrls.

COMMUNAL CRASH PAD VANDALIZED

Hangout for SR youths closing

By EILEEN CLEGG
Staff Writer

Dozens of young people were rousted from a well-known communal home near Santa Rosa Junior College on Tuesday, a day after four tenants were arrested on charges of vandalizing the home.

Police said the arrests were based on complaints from the property management firm that tenants broke windows, sprayed the front with graffiti and damaged the porch of the house at 714 Humboldt St.

The tenants were apparently angry that they were being evicted in mid June, according to the management firm.

But the four people who were arrested say they just happened to be at the home and were not responsible for the vandalism, which could have been committed by any one of a large group of youths who pass through the home.

"For some of them, it's the only home they know. Sometimes when people get freaked out, they get violent," said Heather McCausland, who said she was wrongly arrested.

McCausland said she did not condone the vandalism, but understood the anger of those who had no place else to go and would now be homeless.

Santa Rosa police admit they still need to find witnesses to the vandalism and are continuing their investigation.

"Unless we find someone who witnessed it, we do not have a case," said Sgt. Mike Steen.

On Tuesday, Prospect Property Management officials were accompanied by private security guards as the youths were allowed into the home to retrieve their belongings.

The old three-bedroom, two-story home is owned by Edwin Sampson. Prospect spokesman David Schwiesow said his firm has managed the house for the past year.

For years, the house has been a center of what residents describe as a "community" for punk artists and social activists, as well as a crash pad for travelers and homeless youths.

"It probably looks filthy to people who go to malls and don't understand communities," said Gabriel Sanchez, 18, an Arkansas resident who was passing through Santa Rosa when he heard about the home. "But it's one of the happiest places these kids have ever had."

Some residents were students, some had jobs and some were teen-agers who had been kicked out of their homes without

JOHN BURGESS/PRESS DEMOCRAT

Young people evicted from a Humboldt Street home in Santa Rosa hug and say their goodbyes Tuesday. Four tenants on Monday were arrested for allegedly vandalizing the home.

A ripped poster from the movie 'It's a Wonderful Life' is among belongings packed in a shopping cart by young people evicted from a house at 714 Humboldt St.

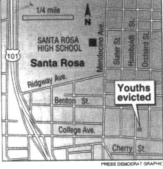

PRESS DEMOCRAT GRAPHIC

money or a place to live. The residents said they pooled money to pay the rent, shared food and held weekly meetings to divvy up the household responsibilities.

Estimates about the number of residents living there have varied from 8 to 30.

Police said the house has been a source of neighborhood problems for years because

of noise and disruption from the ever-changing and growing population of tenants.

Schwiesow said last month Prospect Property Management issued a 30-day notice after receiving complaints from neighbors and discovering how many people were living in the house.

Tenants said they were originally given until June 15 to move out. But on Monday, Santa Rosa police responded to a vandalism complaint from the management company about the damage to the house and the tenants were given three days to leave.

An article about the Humboldt House eviction that appeared in the Santa Rosa *Press Democrat Empire News*, May 31, 1995. Contributed by Toad.

♦ **V: *Again, Riot Grrrl was just feminist principles plus Do-It-Yourself punk principles. Doing something like stickers, fliers, or zines can never be belittled as a "phase." You can do them forever because they're fast, cheap and easy. You can crank out a sticker or flyer overnight and plaster the town with them and get quick results.***

♦ T: I was thinking about people who deface billboards and

change the messages conveyed on them. I really admire that, and wish I had some comrades who are daring enough to do it with me. But a lot of my friends are getting older: "I'm over 18, I could get arrested. You're young and would be let go." They're just getting old and I hate it. That must sound pretty crazy, huh? There are some things that I'm smart enough not to try, but for the most part, I can still live without fear of consequences . . . **V**

slant

For several years Mimi Nguyen volunteered at San Francisco's Epicenter Zone, a non-profit, collectively-run punk performance space, resource library and zine/record/T-shirt outlet. She published the punk-feminist zine *Aim Your Dick* and the personal zine *Slant* while receiving a B.A. in Women's Studies from U.C. Berkeley and an M.A. in American Studies from N.Y.U. Currently, she is working on a compilation zine for and by people of color, tentatively titled *Race Riot*. Mimi may be contacted c/o V/Search.

♦ *VALE: In* **Aim Your Dick** *and* **Slant,** *you critiqued sexism in the punk rock scene—*

♦ MIMI NGUYEN: The intersection of racism and sexism has always been an issue with me. In *Aim Your Dick* #2 I wrote about how somebody had jokingly asked me about "Oriental sex secrets." I really went off on that one. It's such a ridiculous myth—do white people honestly think that my mom sat me down at the kitchen table when I turned 13 and passed on all this secret sexual knowledge? *NO!* I get really mad about that kind of bizarre nonsense, but I can't say that I'm surprised anymore.

♦ *V: What kind of feedback did you get from your zines?*

♦ MN: I got so many letters that I couldn't answer them all. Most were really positive, but I got a few pieces of hate mail. This amazed me because I didn't consider my zine as that big of a deal. But apparently it filled a void, discussing topics that weren't generally being dealt with. I was very angry and let it all out: "I hate this and I hate that!" A friend told me that he read my zine before he met me and thought I'd be this screaming, red-eyed "demon woman." I didn't realize I came off that way, but I was kind of glad. It's *nice* to be thought of as intimidating!

In retrospect, though, I'm a little wary of the reception the zine got. How much was I just feeding into punk rock's self-congratulating "radicalism"? I mean—how much was I just a *token:* a foul-mouthed Asian feminist anarchist?

♦ *V: How did you begin your first zine,* **Aim Your Dick?**

♦ MN: I had done some little zine-type projects in high school, and had seen zines like *Assault With Intent to Free* which were a big influence on me. I was inspired by the idea of self-publishing and being able to bitch about anything I wanted. When I came to U.C. Berkeley, I met my friend Marike in a cultural anthropology class; we hit it off because we were the only punks in the class. I had pink hair; her hair was purple and swaggered. It was love at first sight!

We decided to do a zine. After rejecting ridiculous titles like *Vaginal Discharge,* we chose *Aim Your Dick* because Marike had a male roommate who didn't aim when he went to the bathroom. His urine got all over the wall; it was pretty nasty. From there it blossomed into the horror story that it was. [laughs]

♦ *V: Meeting your friend was a catalyst for doing a zine—*

♦ MN: We fed off each other's energy for that first issue. We included material that got us in trouble with the local Berkeley anarchists. It was about the time that this young white woman named Rosebud broke into the U.C. chancellor's house with a machete; she was killed by the cops. She had hung out at Peoples' Park [famous '60s protest site in Berkeley], and broke in to protest the university's installation of volleyball courts there.

Mimi Nguyen: Not the punk she used to be! Photo: V.Vale; Collage: Eric Rodenbeck

It was sad that this woman died for the nostalgic re-staging of the Park's heyday, encouraged by older activists who wouldn't take responsibility for this afterwards. They martyrized her and wrote editorials about "the golden-haired, warrior-spirited young woman who ventured into the belly of the beast." This was offensive because they weren't recognizing or acknowledging their complicity in her death. And they were totally dismissive of some mental health issues she had.

In our zine I wrote an article explaining why I thought their attitudes were "problematic," and Marike wrote about how the People's Park cause was a dead end, distracting activists from more contemporary issues. We received a letter from a white hippie anarchist about how he was going to be at the next demo we were at with a brick aimed at our heads. Marike went and confronted him and he left town—Marike can be pretty intimidating when she wants to be. [laughs]

♦ *V: Why did you start* **Slant**?

♦ MN: I wanted to do a zine to network with people of color, because it's important to recognize that Asians and other people of color are in the punk scene struggling with identity issues. But we're *struggling by ourselves,* so it would be nice to have a support system just for *us;* a network.

I have a friend, Iraya, who's half-Filipina, half-Italian. We've had long conversations and found that we had both gone through similar processes of "decolonization" as we became progressively more aware of our problems with the punk scene. We realized that our identification with punk was only *partial,* and

Cover of Aim Your Dick #4

that there was a lot of contradiction and loss involved for us as queer-identified "colored" girls. We entered that "ex-punker subcultural limbo," and are now trying to define who our ideal audience would be. It's a kind of balancing act, doing this compilation zine for kids of color, *Race Riot,* and then airing my personal frustations in my other zine, *Slant.* The title refers to the most famous anti-Asian-female slur: that Asian women have slanted pussies.

♦ *V: How do you define "exoticism"?*

♦ MN: "Exoticism" has everything to do with histories of colonialism and the belief that the world's "other" cultures and peoples exist for the West to *collect.* Exoticism deprives indigenous people of agency and multi-dimensionality, reducing them to *objects.* "Otherness" falsely reinforces the "superiority" of Western imperial ideology.

Slant. **The title refers to the most famous anti-Asian female slur: that Asian women have slanted pussies.**

For instance, Asian women are fetishized as being docile and submissive, yet possessing amazing sexual prowess. In media representations (e.g., Madame Butterfly, Miss Saigon, etc), Asian women fulfill a diversionary purpose as heart-of-gold prostitutes or anti-revolutionaries. They then conveniently die, so that the white man (in these narratives) can return to the path of glorious "whiteness" (preferably with a white woman on his arm), and move on to reproduce whatever Western nation he came from.

Japanese women have to deal with the whole geisha stereotype, while similar representations about Korean, Filipina and Vietnamese women emerge from 20th-century white imperialist invasions. Wherever the U.S. military is present throughout Asia, thousands of Asian women are forced into the sex industry from economic need (or whatever). They have no access to decent health care or legal assistance if they're raped or even killed. Like I said, Asian women usually get to end up dead.

♦ *V: How does the media represent Asian men?*

♦ MN: In conjunction with these representations of Asian women, Western ideology either effeminizes or demonizes Asian men. Asian nations are typecast as weak, feminized and morally corrupt, so it's the white man's "burden" (or in contemporary lingo, the democratic duty of "free" nations) to set these "bad little natives" straight. And, it isn't just militaristic, it's cultural as well. Historically, third world cultures have been commodified and used to decorate white people's living rooms and provide them with exoticism in their lives. You know, it's like "adding a little bit of color" or "spicing up your rice." bell hooks addresses this in an essay, "Eating the Other."

A Chicano male anthropologist, Renato Rosaldo, calls culture-collecting and exoticism "imperialist nostalgia." After destroying a culture, the West then wants what it has destroyed, so it puts surviving cultural remnants in museums, or buys copies of antiques churned out for less than minimum wage, or makes movies romanticizing the colonizing experience (like *Out of Africa*).

♦ *V: Cibo Matto got major U.S. press. Is that another example of exoticism?*

♦ MN: I don't think they're responsible for that. *All* things Asian are becoming popular nowadays. To the U.S. music media, they're the next cute Japanese girl band, right after Shonen Knife. [laughs] It's all a marketing ploy . . . a happy-shiny global village notion, like "world music."

♦ *V: There aren't many Asian-female role models in American music or movies—*

♦ MN: I'm a big fan of Anna May Wong. She's amazing. When she worked in movies she knew she was being exoticized, but what else could she do? If she wanted an acting career, she had to deal with this as best she could. I saw an interview filmed when she was in her sixties; the interviewers were trying to get her to exoticize herself and she wouldn't cooperate. She was very stubborn, and obviously annoyed.

♦ *V: Are both your parents Vietnamese?*

♦ MN: Yes. My parents were from the Northern part of the country. They left for the South when Ho Chi Minh declared North Vietnam communist in 1954. Having fought against the French when they tried to re-colonize Vietnam, my dad did fight with the nationalist Viet Minh, but he didn't join the communist party.

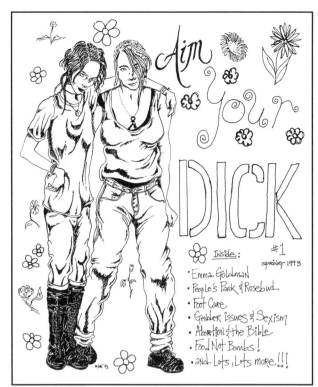

Cover of *Aim Your Dick #1*

Historically, third world cultures have been commodified and used to decorate white people's living rooms and provide them with exoticism in their lives.

I was born in Saigon in 1974. My dad was a professor of pharmaceutical biology, but since scholars (even of medicine) were considered bourgeois and "the class enemy," we had to leave in 1975 when Saigon "fell," otherwise he would have been thrown in the "re-education camps." My dad had a brother-in-law who worked for the Department of Defense, so we were part of the fortunate first wave of refugees that got out on a plane. I was 10 months old when I left the country. That's the story in a nutshell, without the complicated political context.

We bounced around various refugee camps and ended up at Camp Pendleton in July of '75. Catholic Charities were having parishioners sponsor refugees and we were sponsored by a white family in Minnesota, so that's where we ended up. They helped us to "adjust."

♦ *V: Did your parents speak English when they first got here?*

♦ MN: They knew French because they had grown up under French colonialism, but their English was kind of "iffy." They took classes, but it's like taking a language class in high school. Even though they've been here over 20 years, their English is still not great. Sometimes I'm *glad* about that. Recently my mom came home and found a hate call on the answering machine. The person was screaming things like, "Why don't you go home to your own country?!" She would have freaked out if she had understood.

♦ *V: Did you learn Vietnamese?*

♦ MN: Yes. I grew up in the white working-class suburb of Plymouth, Minnesota; it was pretty evil. (It's a small town about an hour-and-a-half from St Paul and Minneapolis.) After 12 years we moved to San Diego. When I graduated from high school I moved to the Bay Area to attend U.C. Berkeley. In May '95, I got my undergraduate degree in Women's Studies.

♦ *V: How did your parents support themselves once they got here?*

♦ MN: At first my dad was filling out hundreds of applications for manual labor, like janitorial work. But the sponsor family we lived with had friends who worked in pharmacies, and my dad's a pharmacist. They hired him for a position that usually pays $20 an hour, but only paid him $5 an hour. Eventually, he realized they were messing with him and they started paying him more, but it took a while.

My family was lucky compared to other refugees,

like the second wave of refugee migration commonly referred to as "boat people." They had to deal with really terrifying experiences, being stuck on a 40-foot boat with 100 other people, being attacked by pirates. They had no food or water, and their only hope was to reach international waters and have somebody rescue them. I had a friend who watched Thai pirates cut off her father's ears and then kill him. She was four or five years old when this happened.

♦ V: How many Asian kids lived in this small Minnesota town?

♦ MN: There were maybe four, and my brother and I were two of them. The other two were second or third generation, so they were not as alien to the situation as we were. Sometimes they, too, would join in on picking on us because of our accent. One neighborhood kid was Korean but had been adopted by white people, and he would throw ice balls at my brother. (There *is* such a thing as internalized self-hatred.) It was a weird situation growing up there; people could tell I was a refugee by the way I spoke and looked. I grew up feeling really conscious of being alien, like my limbs or something were placed on my body wrong.

♦ V: Did any other racist incidents happen to you?

♦ MN: When I was ten years old, I was at the Red Owl Supermarket in Minnesota and this middle-aged white woman came up, pointed a finger at me and said [angrily], "You killed my husband!" I had no idea what she was talking about— I was *ten*. It was so weird; I was stunned: "Who is she mistaking me for?" Later I realized that she was referring to the Vietnam war. I felt like I had been mistaken for a monster . . .

In Oklahoma City, where that bombing [allegedly by Timothy McVeigh] took place, there is a large Vietnamese refugee community. Many local white people resent them: "We don't want these people in our neighborhood. They have strange customs; they dress funny." One 26-year-old white woman said, "I don't like them—they can kill you with their feet!" It amazes me that people believe these things. (Though I wish I *could* kill with my feet; maybe someday my parents will pass on this "ancient Oriental knowledge" to me!)

My growing up was a patchwork of weird incidents like that, plus seeing things on TV that I just didn't *get*. On *Magnum, P.I.*, Tom Selleck played a Vietnam vet who got flashbacks all the time. Periodically, a lost Vietnamese girlfriend would show up with the Vietnamese mafia after her—some made-up plot like

slant.

because a girl's gotta do what a girl's gotta do.

number five.

Cover of Slant #5

that. As a kid it was hard for me to register that they were referencing *my* personal history.

In the '80s all these Vietnam war movies came out, like *Rambo*. My parents weren't interested and never took me to see them. It's really hard for me to watch them, even now. I actually sat all the way through *Rambo: First Blood Part Two*. It's the one where Rambo gets to win the war this time. He goes back to rescue M.I.A./P.O.W.'s (that's another topic I could totally go off on, because that whole issue is just a club with which to beat the Vietnamese Socialist Republic with embargoes, etc). The Vietnamese woman who is helping Rambo only lives long enough to die in Rambo's arms after saving him from a bullet. It's awful!

In most of these movies, the Asian woman is "lucky" to live long enough to fuck Rambo or Chuck Norris (or whoever the hell it is) and then die for love of the big strong oiled-up American white man. At the time I laughed because it seemed so transparently stupid, but thinking about it, especially in context of other experiences like the 20-year-commemoration of the refugee camps, I got angry.

♦ V: What was that about?

♦ MN: This was the 20-year-commemoration of the refugee camps at Camp Pendleton. It glossed over all the social and political conditions that forced Vietnamese people like me to become refugees in the first place. Never mind U.S. imperialist intervention—*that* didn't happen! This "commemoration" was really bizarre: there were little kids running around carrying American flags in one hand and mooncake-shaped balloons in the other. There was a huge banner onstage that said, "Thank You, America." Talk about historical and political amnesia?! My parents were really annoyed; we left feeling disgruntled.

♦ V: "Thank you for fucking up our country!" Why did you even go to that?

♦ MN: I was visiting my parents in San Diego, and they asked if I would go with them. And I was really curious to see *how* people were going to commemorate this camp. This was at a place where Marines had been trained before going to Vietnam to burn down villages and whole forests. A Marine came up and handed me this photo of several Vietnamese people lying dead in a street. He said, "Cool, huh?" I said, "Uh, what?" Then he said, "VC, man, VC!" And I went, "Ohmigod." This Marine got a warm sense of national identity from this violent photo, and expected

Anarchy To Me

Anarchy is not what most people think it is. It is NOT burning down buildings you don't like, killing people that you don't especially agree with, and stealing things that don't belong to you, but you just have taken a fancy with.

Anarchy, to me, represents the highest possible moral responsibility you can have toward your fellow human. It is supposed to be a system without a system, where you take care of yourself WITHOUT violating another person's rights. It is where man controls himself with the ultimate maturity, with no need of a law enforcement agency because he knows exactly what's right and he does it. There is no need for a ruler, king or government because humanity will have grown up enough to realize that by hurting another in ANY way is also hurting yourself, and because of that, everyone can live peacefully without conflict, and be happy.

Of course that will never happen the way things are going now. I don't think it's possible considering humanity and its nature. Right now all anarchy is to anyone else is childlike destruction of anything that displeases you, as if a spoiled child didn't agree with the toy he got for Christmas. Grow up people. We are HUMAN. Does that mean anything to you, any of you?

Being human means that you are, or should be, above the animals in behavior. You still have the instincts, urges, animalistic behavior that is part of our nature. But as humans, we have the capacity to go beyond that, perceive right from wrong and make a conscious decision to do the correct thing. It isn't always going to be what you want, but it is always the right thing to do, all things considered.

Many people now, as I see them, are only proving the fact that man still needs to learn more, grow up, think more, and become the human that they are supposed to be.

—George, from *Aim Your Dick #1*

me to identify with him because I was a refugee (i.e., we were on the "same side").

For a long time, whenever I met a Vietnam vet I'd be freaked out and suspicious, because when I was 16, I read about what happened in My Lai [well-publicized massacre of Vietnamese villagers, including babies and old people]. I thought that every Vietnam vet had taken part in something atrocious. I'm still trying to work out all the dimensions involved in these feelings; it's complicated. My best friend, who grew up around all these working-class vets who were totally devastated by the war, is a good counter-balance for me.

♦ **V: What made your parents move to San Diego?**

♦ MN: My dad got a better job; also, my parents hated the snow! And there's an actual Vietnamese community in San Diego (as opposed to Minnesota); my parents had friends there. For the first time, I was able to hang out with other Asian kids. But it was also weird because I was starting to get into punk, which was a departure from what was expected of me from my community. I was an "alterna-teen" by the age of 12.

♦ **V: How were you able to find out about punk?**

♦ MN: In the '80s there was an explosion of punk-ploitation on television. Here I was, Asian with slanted eyes, feeling visually out-of-sync, so seeing punks on TV being visually out-of-sync struck a chord. I felt, "Wow, they're in *control* of how freaky they look. Looking 'other' is something that's always been *imposed* on me—now I can turn that around." And, of course, there was always some editorial about punk being dangerous and offensive to "good" people. I had lots of revenge-driven fantasies of offending "good" people. [laughs] After all, the same people who blew up our mail box in Minnesota went to church on Sundays.

I thought my identification with punk was "intuitive," although looking back, it was really simplistic. But what did I know at eleven or twelve? I just knew I wanted to be this aggressive spectacle, to fit how I was made to feel. Only when we moved to California did I actually see real, live punks!

♦ **V: There weren't any in Minnesota?**

♦ MN: Just heshers (heavy-metal-ers).

♦ **V: Was there more to the tale of your mailbox bombing?**

♦ MN: There isn't a whole lot more to tell; whoever did it was never caught . . . My family's reaction was just, "Oh, somebody blew up our mailbox—surprise, surprise. What did you expect?"

♦ **V: When you were in San Diego, was there any "rebel" peer group you could hang out with?**

♦ MN: I was in middle school doing the alterna-teen thing, listening to lots of Siouxsie Sioux and Depeche Mode. I did have friends who were skaters, but I hung out with these Filipina gang girls. The U.S. Navy traffics a lot between the Philippines and San Diego, so there are lots of Filipino "military brats" in that area.

I went through a long alterna-teen phase. I did the whole skater hair-flop thing with the hair in the face; I wore black all the time. When I was 16, I started getting into punk rock proper, and like many teenagers

Hi. I've gotten a bunch of LETTERS from folks asking how I do the zine by myself. Well, that's an int'resting question 'cause I don't think it's too spectacular, but for some reason, it's a totally absorbing aspect of my life which has taken over my entire apartment (much to the chagrin of my housemates). Then Sarah of mad planet and action girl suggested that I do comics, so I decided to answer both by illustrating the mess I've built up. But believe me, in reality it's worse!

Anatomy of a Zine Editor's Mess...
(or at least my mess!)

this is not what my actual hair looks like normally, but it would if I didn't wash it. I don't think I could get as much height, tho' my hair dreds pretty easily. But this way, it sure adds to the whole mess aesthetic, doncha think?

eyes strained from hours of editing, reading, writing, and laying out stuff!

Roommate's dirty undershirt... thanks davo!!!

Lots and lots of dirty laundry

books!

ORANGE JUICE

more mail

mail

my drink of choice: ORANGE JUICE! However, other options range from JOLT! to hard liquor...

answering mail...

can't find the other sock

stereo, cds', & tapes... and the other sock

pages of text typed up on, yes, an evil computer... HaHa!! sorry, I like computers!

glue stick

SCISSORS

Layout pages for issue whatever

pen

pencil

white-out: essential!!!

RULER

normal eraser

nexto rubber eraser

thing of India ink

pen

envelopes to send out zines

FOLDER FULL OF GRAPHICS, CLIPPINGS, etc.

Drawing from *Aim Your Dick #4*

bought a Dead Kennedys tape. [laughs] Then I stumbled upon a copy of *Maximumrock'n'roll* at some hole-in-the-wall record store and *really* got into punk. I started sending away for zines and records through the mail and writing to lots of people. I don't want to mouth clichés like "Punk rock saved my life"—but it's true! That was really what I needed at the time.

When I first got into punk, I thought it was this open, egalitarian space. The *politics* were a big part of the reason I got interested in punk. It was like, "I may only be 16, but I know about the World Bank and the I.N.S.!"

♦ **V: The D.I.Y. philosophy and the emphasis on radical politics are integral to punk—**

♦ MN: If I hadn't gotten into the punk scene and met people who said, "Well, if you *really* want to understand what's happening here, you should read Noam Chomsky and Ben Bagdikian [author of *The Media Monopoly*]," I probably wouldn't have read those books at that age. Now I have problems with Noam Chomsky because he lets his Western privilege hang out in obvious ways, but at the time his writings were eye-opening.

♦ **V: What year did you get into punk?**

♦ MN: In 1990, when I was 16.

♦ **V: Where did you get the money to buy records and zines?**

♦ MN: I saved money I got from my parents. It wasn't exactly an "allowance," but I got money for birthdays and holidays. I've been saving money religiously ever since I was a child, because I've always had a huge fear of being poor. My parents wouldn't let me work, because they wanted me to concentrate on my schoolwork so I could get into college. They viewed a college education as a way out of refugee/second-class citizen status.

I had lots of revenge-driven fantasies of offending "good" people.

♦ **V: Back in 1991, was Riot Grrrl an inspiration?**

♦ MN: Riot Grrrl is a complicated issue for me. Every conversation I get into about it lands me in these four-day long explanations.

Riot Grrrl is the best thing that ever happened to punk. It's amazing that all these young (mostly white) women have decided to redesign the whole world according to the architecture of their private-made-public traumas and promises of "girl love" wish-fulfillment. Riot Grrrl is amazing in so many ways: as confrontation, as education, as performance, as aesthetic, as support, as theory, as practice, etc.

But it's important to me as a feminist of color to critique Riot Grrrl for the ways in which it has (or hasn't) dealt with differences of race and class. In that aspect,

rather than presenting an *alternative*, Riot Grrrl totally parallels "mainstream" Euro-American feminism. Gender is presumed to be a social category that can be separated from race, class, or even nation. We talk about "women's issues," but *which* women are we talking about? I have a hard time relating to most feminist discourses on body and beauty issues, because they originate from a white middle-class "American" context, and I didn't grow up that way and don't see myself reflected in that.

I don't want to mouth clichés like "Punk rock saved my life"— but it's true! That was really what I needed at the time.

♦ **V: How did you develop a feminist consciousness?**

♦ MN: That's a hard question. When I was growing up, I hated most of the girls I knew—they were all white, and mean as hell in really subtle ways that I couldn't quite grasp.

The boys were *obvious;* they threw balls of snow and ice at us, so retaliation was equally obvious. I could beat up boys (as much as any of us ever really "beat up" other six-year-olds). But it was hard to deal with the social pressures that white girls put on me. Gender is a *social construct,* and the way I grew up (as a non-white, non-European refugee) made me unfamiliar with the "normal" ways that gender was taught.

My parents were busy trying to support my brother and me, sending money to the family members remaining in Vietnam, *and* sorting out their own feelings about being violently uprooted and relocated to an unfriendly, foreign land. Consequently, the gender roles I *did* learn from them were amazingly open-ended. I was encouraged to act out my tomboy impulses, especially by my dad. We'd always be working in the garden growing beans and strawberries, mowing the lawn, climbing trees, and playing in the marshes. My mom was always stressing that we were strong, independent, smart women. So I was raised with the feeling of having survived tremendous difficulties. My parents taught me *subtler* techniques of resistance which involved "distancing strategy": being polite and impersonal toward illicit authority and invasive questioning, so as to not let them into "our world." This kind of refusal to reveal oneself during interrogation is misread by Euro-Americans as acquiescence or passivity.

I really didn't identify with "girl" things. A lot of the subjects white girls talk about in their zines I just don't relate to. Basically, I grew up *counter-appropriating* what I could. For example, I loved Wonder Woman, but told myself she was Asian because she had black

Don't Go There With Me

When Mykel Board writes in his *MRR* column about all the "lithe" Thai boy and girl prostitutes he's bought for a pack of generic cigarettes, he's drawing on a long and still continuing Western legacy of imperialism and slavery, tapping into a colonial imaginary that's always made non-white bodies the objects for the exploitative fantasies/abuses of the empowered white person; a person who may be in the lower strata of social hierarchies "back home" among other white folks (like punk pretends to be) but whose whiteness confers multiple material privileges in relation to Third World people. (. . . a shitty pack of smokes? Let's talk about sex workers' rights to decent fucking wages and alternate, non-exploitative employment opportunities not a part of fucked-up Free Trade Zones, thanks much.) Or when *Second Guess* or *Answer Me!*—with typically myopic and selective attention—wave their collective, good American fists in the air, railing about how Blacklist and/or the Epicenter are actively "censoring" or "suppressing" their constitutional First Amendment rights (the Constitution is a lousy foundation for arguing "freedom;" anyway, it was originally written by and for white, propertied men anxious to protect their privileges), they assume all public space and all possible forums as their "right," that somehow they're entitled to this access and power that many others aren't and whose rights (or lack thereof) they totally fuckin' ignore, ridicule, or dismiss as victim whining. And when Rev. Norb writes a two-page column in *MRR* all about moi, accusing lil' ol' me of oppressing white straight men, he equates my critique of imperial, patriarchal racism with something like state repression or the visceral threat of rape (which he also accusses me of, somehow), as if I had the same access to power and control that in-group members have, to wield these positions of privilege and tap into/be totally supported by dominant hegemonies. Whatever. **—Mimi, from *Slant* #5**

Tôi sẽ giúp bạn an toàn vào trong chỗ phá thai Làm ơn. Đậu xe ở phía sau

This little card was passed out to/by escorts and defenders of an abortion clinic in San Jose, CA, where there's a big Vietnamese population. It reads: "I will help you get inside the clinic. Please park your car in back."—*Slant* #5

---

hair and came from a distant, invisible country. And growing up, one of my favorite songs was "Hit Me With Your Best Shot" which I thought was an original by this leggy Vietnamese-American singer—I didn't know it was by Pat Benatar. That's how removed I was from the dominant cultural loop.

I never read any of those Judy Blume books that girls always read. I didn't care about the "issues" discussed in those books—I didn't want boobs, or expensive clothes, or any of that stuff. My body image was never a big deal to me; I saw all the blond-haired, blue-eyed icons of white feminine perfection in magazines and on TV, but these weren't addressed to *me*. I didn't care about competing for boys because I didn't like white boys either. And it's hardly "girl jealousy" that divided me from those little white girls; it had everything to do with my being Asian, a refugee, etc.

So I'm not sure where my feminism came from. I did have to deal with shit like sexual harassment when I turned fifteen, but it was totally Asian-specific, like this one white boy who approached me and said that he "must have been an Asian man in a former incarnation" because he loved the food, the culture, and "the women." [groans] I think my feminist consciousness was just part-and-parcel of my nascent *political* inquisitiveness at the time.

I used to go to the local library and check out feminist texts. I knew feminism wasn't a "white thing," but they didn't stock Angela Davis or Audre Lorde at the piss-ant trailer that passed for the local library. I didn't find any feminist writing with which I could identify as a woman of color until I went to college. Then all the feelings of being vaguely uncomfortable with white feminisms were fleshed out, and I understood that I wasn't alone in my alienation from the social category that white women had constructed as a political monolith: "all women."

♦ *V: How did your critique of punk develop?*
♦ MN: At first I really bought the "we're all peers here" notion. It took awhile for me to recognize that I felt out-of-sync with the scene. "Little things" began to add up: *Maximumrock'n'roll* in general; cheesy vegan/straight-edge bourgeois moralism tinged with racist and classist overtones; anarchists saddled with boring New Left rhetoric and no sense of *style* (representational aesthetics are important, by the way); white retro punk's comeback neatly coinciding with the rise of the "angry white man" everywhere else in the country—there were so many signs.

Also, there's a definite air of elitism that accompanies the punk rock attitude: of being avant-garde, ruggedly individualistic (which is very much in the tradition of Americanism and Manifest Destiny), and somehow superior to everyone else, including one's family (which is really dangerous for people of color in particular). I had internalized some misrepresentations about "Asian-ness" being not as subversive or radical as punk rock, for instance. Now I resent punks who pretend to understand what it's like to be a racial "other" just because they've got purple hair—they can always shed what makes them "marginal," but I can't.

The really big blow, the thing that just clubbed me over the head, was when this columnist from *Maximumrock'n'roll,* Reverend Norb, wrote that "Asian women's eyes look like vulvii" (and that's why white men love them so much). I was really offended and wrote *Maximum* a letter. I went off on the history of women of color being fetishized for white audiences and how this was really fucked up and racist. I brought up the Hottentot Venus: during the 1800s, this African woman was put on display in museums throughout Europe. Scientists, sociologists and artists obsessed over the proportions of her body. After she died, they cut her up and placed her sexual organs and buttocks on display in the Museum of Man in Paris. (I felt there was a real ideological link here: the fetishization of fragmented, racialized female bodies is so much a part of Euro-American masculine ideologies of conquest.) Meanwhile, Norb's racism was dismissed as just another sexual fetish on a par with "innocent" foot worship or being into corsets or stiletto heels. (It's not!)

♦ **V: Did your article attract any feedback?**

♦ MN: In the issue after my letter got printed, this guy wrote a two-page rant about how evil I was and how I was "oppressing" white men. He wrote something like, "Since you have no sense of humor, you're probably really ugly, too. So you're no longer privileged with my automatically wanting to fuck you because you're Asian." I got so many letters from white men telling me what a bitch I was and to "get off my p.c. high horse" and that "racial and sexual slurs don't hurt anybody." All this forced me to think, "Why am I here in this community that supports and condones people like Reverend Norb? Even if you're not writing this, if you're putting up with it, you're complicit." It really freaked me out and made me feel isolated from this scene in which I'd invested so much of myself. I pretty much dropped out for awhile and stopped going to shows. I still worked at Epicenter but was really unenthusiastic about all of it. I resolved that I didn't want to just "let it go," but realized that further dialogue in that particular forum (*Maximum)* was a waste of time.

A year after that episode with Rev. Norb, I moved to New York. I found out that he had written and recorded a song about me, "Do the Mimi"! The beginning musical bars are "I think I'm turning Japanese" by the

Vapors. Apparently, he had come to Berkeley and someone had pointed me out to him. So, he decided to write this song about how he'd seen me and thought I was "hot" and wanted to rape me. The lyrics basically say + "I wanted to fuck her, but I knew she wouldn't let me, but I wanted to fuck her anyway." It was liberally sprinkled with offensive phrases like "She's my swingin' Saigon siren." I was literally put in the context of U.S. imperialism in Vietnam, where U.S. soldiers "jokingly" lived by the "Mere Gook Rule": Vietnamese were "merely gooks to be fucked, or killed, or both."

Punk rock shelters these kinds of rape/racist fantasies under the umbrella of "creative freedom" or "freedom of speech," but it's always *their* freedom and not ours; *their* power to possess and dehumanize and our lack of power when we confront these not-very-underground ideologies of domination. With a "community" like this, who needs enemies?!

♦ **V: Now you regard your family as your community, more—**

♦ MN: My parents are very supportive of me. My mom cried the first time I shaved my head and dyed my hair red—I think that's a "normal" reaction that lots of parents have, seeing their kids with pink hair and piercings or whatever. Now she knows I do a lot of activist work and simply says, "Just don't go to jail!" She's really supportive of my clinic defense work. I helped organize a women's health conference in April '95 and she showed all her friends the flyers. She's not happy with the way I look, but she tolerates it like a mom. Everything got easier after I moved away—my mom and I get along really fabulously now. For Christmas I dyed my hair black for her and she was so happy! It made me glad that a little thing like that would bring my mom joy: "I can do that—*no problem.* Who wants to be another bleached-blond Asian chick in the East Village anyway?"

But I also count as my "community" all the rad women of color I've met in school. It seemed that half of my class in undergraduate women's studies were other queer Asian women, and we've had many important dialogues. I've also met a lot of women who were once involved in Riot Grrrl and punk and have since moved on to other subcultural spaces (or created their own), and that's been amazing.

♦ **V: What do you think about Asians dying their hair blond or light brown?**

♦ MN: I know that I did it because I really wanted my

hair to be pink, so I bleached my hair. Then I really liked green. This has become very pervasive—it's punk. I don't think people are trying to be "white," because if Asians dye their hair blonde, it's just too obvious that they're not. [laughs] I think it's just an aesthetic—like a punk or a club aesthetic.

♦ *V: For decades, black people were straightening their hair. Then when the Black Panthers started, the movement toward the "natural" hairstyle began: "We're no longer going to try to look like white people; we're going to celebrate our natural hair."*

♦ MN: There's an essay by a black gay scholar, Kobena Mercer, titled "Black Hair/Style Politics." He talks about how that '60s "natural" aesthetic had a very strong political argument behind it: "Black is Beautiful," reversing the values of racist standards toward beauty/ugliness. At the same time, what was defined as "natural" really wasn't—it was just as much a politicized idea about what constitutes "natural" as what doesn't. His whole argument is: all hairstyles are *artifice*; there's no way that they're not.

how tasty was my frenchman

Mercer suggests that we de-psychologize hair-styling and style choices and recognize them as *cultural* practices with complex social and political dimensions that can't easily be chalked up to bad personal politics. And, there is a political value in "counter-appropriation" of the dominant class's style, not to mention the real possibility of pleasure and invention. These are all important issues that we can't dismiss with a mere "he or she's trying to be white."

I got so many letters from white men telling me what a bitch I was and to "get off my p.c. high horse . . ."

♦ *V: What's your critique of academia?*

♦ MN: I think it's a bad idea for progressive or left-leaning people to *not* engage in academia, because so many cultural battles have originated there. Academia is a material site for ideological struggle, and to abandon that space to all the conservative people who are there teaching their agendas, is a bad strategy. There's a lot of work that needs to be done there.

Academia is a big shark pool; it's very "professional" in a way I don't like—I'm just not good at schmoozing! Too often in academia, education is *the process of accumulating knowledge as though it were capital.* Luckily, in the fields I've been in (women's stud-

ies, ethnic studies and cultural studies), the saying by bell hooks seems to take precedence: "Education is the practice of freedom." It's about teaching *critical tools* which enable you to analyze information, theories and representations. There are multiple sites of struggle and we have to deal with all of them. We have to deal with complex issues that aren't easy to just imagine as binary situations (good/bad, etc) because we miss out on much in that reduction, including how we might really effectively deal with them.

♦ *V: Was it difficult to do your first zine?*

♦ MN: The very first *Aim Your Dick* was so easy for me and Marike. She would come and sleep over and we'd have long meetings and energizing cut-and-paste sessions. We'd type furiously and then glue the text down—it was exciting. But for a lot of reasons, it took almost two years to do the new *Slant.* I kept going over it, ripping out articles and putting new ones in. Maybe doing the first zine was easy because I didn't care who my audience was; I didn't think about the "politics of reception." I simply spouted off at the mouth and was just *rabid.*

Now my politics have gotten a lot more complicated. It takes a lot more energy, work and time to explain a topic in depth, rather than just saying, "Capitalism sucks! Fuck it!" Also, I have to switch from the academic language used in my papers to "zine talk," and that's difficult.

My new zine deals with everything that's been bugging me for years: being Vietnamese and into punk rock, being a woman (I'm bisexual), all my ambivalent feelings about Riot Grrrl, me and—

♦ *V: —men; that's a huge problematic area.*

♦ MN: That's a *really* bizarre can of worms. I didn't grow up among many Asians. When I moved to Berkeley there was this group called the "Asian Male Underground" who would graffiti women's bathrooms with slogans like, "Stop dating that hairy white boy!" and "Sisters, stop dating the enemy—date your brothers!" I wrote next to this, "How about if I date another Asian sister—is *that* okay?"

♦ *V: They should have replied, "Fine!"*

♦ MN: That whole thing was so amazing: heterosexist Asian men "taking back their masculinity" from "The Man"! This is still a really hard subject for me to deal with, because I found out that a lot of the white men I dated had weird things for Asian women: "Ohmigod, how could I be that stupid and not notice? Oh no—they're *everywhere;* I can't escape them!" So at first I feel traumatized, then I end up feeling personally disappointed in myself for not being able to have radar to point them all out, when they're not being as obvious as Rev. Norb. My parents are still convinced that some day I'll marry a nice Vietnamese boy, and *that's* really hard to deal with. I don't know quite how to talk about all this yet. It's really hard. V

MIMI'S RECOMMENDATIONS

ON ZINES DONE BY PEOPLE OF COLOR

I've gotten a lot of great contributions for my people-of-color compilation zine, *Race Riot*. I only wish someone had done this for me when I was younger and still struggling with being isolated and besieged. Lauren Martin who does *Forbidden Planet* and *You Might As Well Live* should be given some kind of crown for being fabulous; the same goes for Bianca Ortiz who does *Mamasita*. They've written really good pieces that confront potential white readers while at the same time making a connection with me, a girl of color, because I can relate to the anger and frustration expressed. I love to read zines like theirs; it's what keeps me plugged into punk.

ZINES (ALWAYS SEND 2 STAMPS, PLUS WHATEVER $ IS LISTED BELOW)

Attack Eve, 24816 Barclay Ln., Laguna Niguel CA 92677
Killing the Queen Christina, 421 Central Av., San Francisco CA 94117. 50¢
The Ruby Slippers Milly, POB 16-0963, Miami FL 33116-0963
Karass Jeremy Jusay, POB 140610, Staten Island NY 10314-0610
Samsara Polaris, 8601 SW 142nd Ave., Miami FL 33183
My Letter to the World Tiger Lily, POB 40082, Berkeley CA 94704
Thoughts Adrift James Lin, 4875 N. Magnolia Ave. #308, Chicago IL 60640
Rivals Amy Lam, 1615 E. Denley St., Hacienda Heights CA 91745
And My Foot Goes Forward Kevin Jagernauth, 61A Foxfield Dr., Nepean, Ontario, Canada K2J 1L7. $1
Kreme Koolers Keyan Meymand, 110 Legion Way SE #403, Olympia WA 98501. $1
Forbidden Planet, You Might As Well Live, Boredom Sucks, Princess Charming, Project Listing Lauren Martin, Bard College, Annandale NY 12504. $1
Super Dork Marlene Varela, 150 Balboa Ave., San Jose CA 95116
Scarbaby, Yawp! Johanna Novales, Box 752723, Dallas TX 75275-2723
Pure Tuna Fish Rita Fatila, 16 Fairview Av, St. Thomas, Ontario, Canada N5R 4X4. $1
Sidetracked Mengstin, 7534 Farmington Ave., Portage MI 49002. $1
Smear Leslie, 327 Beechmont Dr., New Rochelle NY 10804. $1
Meniscus Yuan-Kwan Chan, 12793 Misty Creek Ln., Fairfax VA 22033. $1
Strange Fruit Ted Young-Ing. 3435 20th St. #B, San Francisco CA 94110-2517
Asian Takeover, Riot Grrrl Review & Wild Honey Pie Kristy Chan, POB 1791, Fort Myers FL 33902. $3
Cage Dzung Vo, Brown University, POB 4704, Providence RI 02912-4704. $1
Hollyhock Lida, 211 Dewitt Ave., Betteville NJ 07109. $1
Pocho Esteban Zul and Lalo Lopez, POB 40021, Berkeley CA 94704 or POB 63052, E. Los Angeles CA 90063. Pocho24@aol.com. $2
Hijinx Joanie Chen, POB 675, Walnut CA 91788-0675. $1. TigerTrap@aol.com. $1
Planet Drag King Olivia Edith, 3233 Juliet St., Pittsburgh PA 15213. $2.
Crosspatch Rachel, POB 170130, San Francisco CA 94117. $1
Ladies Homewrecking Journal, Mamasita, Mija Bianca Ortiz, 2415 San Pablo CA 94806.
Bamboo Girl Sabrina Sandata, POB 507, NYC NY 10159-0507. $2.

WRITERS

One of my favorite women-of-color feminists is Chandra Talpade Mohanty. My advisor at U.C. Berkeley, Caren Kaplan is developing a theory of transnational feminist practices with her long-time collaborator, Inderpal Grewal; amazing work!

I love the writing of a lot of South Asian feminists: Meena Alexander, Lata Mani, May Joseph, Jasbir Puar, Gayatri Spivak and Mohanty. Rey Chow is a Chinese feminist from Hong Kong elucidating the fetishization of the "third world woman/native" by white "liberals," Marxists and culture-collectors. Trinh T. Minh-ha is a Vietnamese feminist who teaches at Berkeley, and has made one of my favorite films. Gloria Anzuldua, Norma Alarcon, Aiwa Ong, Wahneema Lubiano, Hazel Carby, and Sonia Shah are all doing great, complex work.

There's a fabulous book called *Between Borders* written by Henry Giroux. Another important book is Paulo Freire's *Pedagogy of Oppression*.

For convenience's sake, I won't list all the works by the authors below: *African American* bell hooks, Angela Davis, Ntozake Shange; *Black British* Paul Gilroy; *Chicana* Gloria Anzuldua, Cherrie Moraga, Sandra Cisneros; *Filipina* Jessica Hagedorn, Chea Villanueva (mixed: Filipina/white); *Korean* Teresa Hak Kyung Cha; *South Asian* Chandra Mohanty, Meena Alexander, Inderpal Grewal, Gayatri Spivak, Bharati Mukherjee; *Cuban American* Coco Fusco; *Vietnamese* Trinh T. Minh-ha, Yen Espiritu; *more Asian American authors* Fae Ng, Shawn Wong, Marilyn Chin, Garret Hongo, Lawson Inada, Shirley Ancheta, Walter Lew, David Mura, Nellie Wong.

FILMS / FILMMAKERS / DISTRIBUTION

National Asian American Telecommunications Association Distributes, screens and funds film and video projects by Asian Americans. Runs Asian American Film Festival in San Francisco.
Women Make Movies Distributes and screens women's film and video works. Feminist, queer, labor, international and more. Definitely worth checking out.
Pocho A series of videos by the Pocho boys. One in collaboration with Coco Fusco, a Cuban American feminist cultural critic.
Frameline Gay/lesbian/bi/queer/etc, film and video distribution.
Marlon Riggs *Black Is, Black Ain't, Ethnic Notions, Tongues Untied.*
Julie Dash *Illusions, Daughters of the Dust.*
Renee Tajima *Who Killed Vincent Chin? Yellow Tale Blues, Declarations: All Men Are Created Equal? Jennifer's in Jail,* more.
Lourdes Portillo *The Trial of Christopher Columbus, Mirrors of the Heart, Vida, Las Madres de la Plaza de Mayo,* more. Also Isaac Julien, Richard Fung, Christine Choy, Valerie Soe, Shu Lea Cheang, Helen Lee, Lizzie Borden, Pratiba Parmar, Trinh T. Minh-ha.

ANTHOLOGIES

Piece of My Heart: A Lesbian of Color Anthology, Our Feet Walk the Sky: Women of the South Asian Diaspora, The Very Inside: An Anthology of Writing by Asian and Pacific Islander Lesbian and Bisexual Women, Home Girls: A Black Feminist Anthology, Making Face, Making Soul, This Bridge Called My Back, Making Waves, Miscegenation Blues, Premonitions: A Kaya Anthology of Asian North American Poetry

ASIAN AMERICAN WRITER'S WORKSHOP has a bookstore and a catalog: 37 St. Marks Pl. NY NY 10013. Tel: 212.228.6718. FAX: 212.228.7718. E-mail: aaww@panix.com

THEATER [V. Vale's additional recommendations]

CULTURE CLASH. Herbert Siguenza, Ric Salinas and Richard Montoya. Amazing Chicano "living theater" satirizes and entertains while educating with music, dance, skits, impersonations, historical recreations, ethnic history, and jazzy routines.
MIGHTY MOUNTAIN WARRIORS. Asian theater group from San Francisco.

From Aim Your Dick #4

My Political Statement. (who says all us feminists don't know how to laugh...?☺)

65

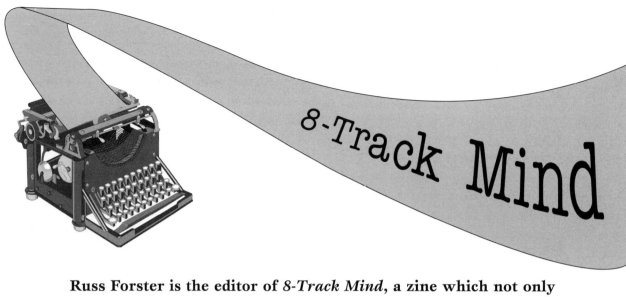

8-Track Mind

Russ Forster is the editor of *8-Track Mind*, a zine which not only investigates 8-track tapes but also non-digital recording/playback systems. Transcending purely technical concerns, *8-Track Mind* details and fleshes out the "analog lifestyle" in pages full of enthusiasm and eccentricity. Recently, Russ produced a 16mm documentary film, *So Wrong They're Right*, featuring 8-track enthusiasts across America (VHS and Beta available for $25 ppd, PAL foreign version $35; see address below). His 8-track instructional video is scheduled for release December 1997; write for details. Today, 8-tracks provide the cheapest music available—they can still be found in thrift stores for 50 cents. Everything, from Pharaoh Saunders and Ornette Coleman to Iggy Pop's *Metallic K.O.*, Leo Diamond and Martin Denny, is accessible—even Lou Reed's *Metal Machine Music*. (Send $2 cash for a sample copy [or $8 for a 4-issue subscription] to Russ Forster, POB 14402, Chicago IL 60614-0402.

♦ *VALE: Did you start collecting 8-tracks in the '70s?*

♦ RUSS FORSTER: No. Even though I'm 33 years old, I never had any 8-track equipment back then; I just had vinyl. A few friends owned cars with 8-track players—not me. But in 1987, a neighbor moved to Los Angeles and left behind her 8-track player and a bunch of tapes. I guess she felt she didn't need them anymore.

I'd been going to thrift stores for years, mainly to buy clothing. All of a sudden I had a free 8-track player, and I started noticing all these tapes and equipment in thrift stores. Previously, they had just been *invisible.* I've always been a music fan, and suddenly having such cheap access was a huge revelation. Finally, I could afford to take chances, and discovered all this music I'd missed the first time around: country, soul, easy listening, etc. I had grown up as a typical adolescent hard rock fan—that was *all* my friends and I listened to (you were chastised if you listened to anything else). Now this whole new world was open to me at 25 cents a shot—sometimes less.

♦ *V: Where did you grow up?*

♦ RF: I was born in Chicago but spent most of my life in Elmhurst, Illinois—Carl Sandburg lived there for awhile, but there's little else to recommend. It's close to Oakbrook, home of McDonald's World Headquarters—I always force visitors to go to the Ray Kroc Museum. There's an amazing photograph of Walt Disney and Ray Kroc in the same Red Cross Army Unit in World War I. At any rate, that's the most exciting thing there.

When I got into 8-tracks, I was living in Chicago. Gradually I found other people who were also into 8-tracks, and we started hanging out. We would host bowling nights where we'd bring our 8-tracks to a bowling alley that had previously been populated just by gangs. Actually, *they* wouldn't bowl, so basically we had the whole bowling alley area to ourselves. We'd dress up, we'd dance—a local TV station even did a feature on us.

Russ Forster: 8-tracks inspired not just a zine, but also a state of mind. Photo: V. Vale; Illustration: Eric Rodenbeck

8-TRACK MIND

Journal of the Analog Movement

20th ANNIVERSARY ISSUE

INSIDE: MEET YOUR 8-TRACK MATE
A BRIEF HISTORY OF 8-TRACK TECH
CONFESSIONS OF AN 8-TRACK JUNKIE
PLUS: CLASSIFIEDS, FIND OF THE MONTH

Cover of the 20th anniversary issue of *8-Track Mind*

I started traveling, and discovered other little groups of people who were also obsessed by 8-tracks like me and my friends. There seemed to be a spontaneous generation of similar ideas cropping up everywhere I went. I got the idea to start a magazine because it was a way to meet and stay in touch with people.

♦ *V: You started collecting 8-tracks in the late '80s—*

♦ RF: Those were the glory days, when tapes were plentiful and you could still find amazing things in thrift stores. It was so exciting and so much fun to discover something you didn't even know existed, like the SEX PISTOLS on *8-track!* Today, pickings are a lot slimmer.

♦ *V: How many tapes do you have in your collection?*

♦ RF: The largest number I've had was about a thousand. But I give away almost as many as I get, so my collection has slimmed down to around 600. If I don't listen to one, I try to give it to someone who *will* appreciate and listen to it. There's an ethic among 8-track fanatics: we gotta find a use for 'em. The worse thing you can do is throw them away—that's the ultimate slap in the face.

I think 8-tracks have an interesting shape; some people don't play 'em but just display them proudly on their walls. I know a few artists who use them in their artwork—any tapes neither I nor anyone else wants get funneled to them. There are interesting artistic aspects that haven't been fully explored. I met an artist who created an 8-track sculpture which integrated both their sound and visuals. Warhol painted a Campbell's soup can, but now people are taking the actual objects and making art out of them instead of just making reproductions. The objects *themselves* become the art.

♦ *V: Well, didn't they come in a rainbow of colors?*

♦ RF: Sure! [laughs] Some people know which colors are associated with which labels. There are even special colors for quadraphonic tapes! A friend in San Francisco has all this great quadraphonic equipment he got from thrift stores and garage sales. On one player, the dial looks like a radar display. When music plays, you see a visual representation with four different points marking the four different channels. It's a lot of fun watching the little squiggles move between the four different points.

♦ *V: Like "follow the bouncing ball" in old sing-along musicals. Quadraphonic sound is another forgotten technology—*

♦ RF: Some people who aren't exactly into 8-track *are* into *quadraphonic 8-track*. The vinyl quadraphonic technology was not precisely distinct; it required encoders, decoders, and all this other processing. Vinyl didn't truly have the separation, but reel-to-reel and 8-track had four distinct channels that could be separated fully. Sound fanatics who want true four-channel sound get into quadraphonic 8-tracks, and those tapes are the hardest to find by far.

Listening to a quadraphonic tape is pretty amazing. A lot of tapes were specifically remastered for quadraphonic sound, with music and sounds that circle the room. A particularly good example is Pink Floyd's *Dark Side of the Moon*—you actually hear the sound of people running as the footsteps travel from speaker to speaker all around you. It's an amazing full-room experience that's not duplicated by the recent surround sound or Dolby technology. Those are not true quadraphonic sound; usually the bass is in the middle (on the theory that bass isn't directional) and other sounds are positioned on the sides. Surround sound *is* interesting and it does sound like movies in theaters, but it's not quadraphonic sound which travels to different areas and circles the four corners of the room!

♦ *V: Does quadraphonic sound require you to face a certain direction?*

> **There's an ethic among 8-track fanatics: we gotta find a use for 'em. The worst thing you can do is throw them away.**

♦ RF: An audiophile would probably set up a room with a chair positioned so the listener could best hear all four channels. However, most people into quadraphonic aren't quite that anal-retentive. They'll just do some drugs, sit you down on a bean-bag chair in the middle of a room and put on the Moody Blues or whoever they feel like hearing at the time. The sound may not be perfect, and it may not be coming at you evenly from all directions, but it's still pretty amazing.

♦ **V: It was fortunate you got a player along with the 8-track tapes—**

♦ RF: If I hadn't gotten a player I might never have gotten started. Also, that neighbor left behind a broad spectrum of really great tapes—everything from Charlie Rich to the B-52s. Isaac Hayes' *Hot Buttered Soul* became one of my favorite albums. If I'd only inherited hard rock tapes, I might not have gotten as excited about the possibilities of 8-tracks. But she left behind mostly music that was new to me, or music that I wouldn't have expected to find on 8-track, like DEVO.

Actually, I can't believe some of the music that came out on 8-track, like the Vibrators' first album, *Pure Mania*. What decisions led to *that?* Punk records weren't big sellers, so for the most part punk was never released on 8-track, but the few exceptions leave you scratching your head. Such discoveries are exciting. If I found the Vibrators on vinyl it would be *nice,* but it wouldn't exactly be a revelation. With 8-track it's: "Ohmigod—*this* came out on 8-track?!" [laughs]

One of the biggest surprises (one that people talk about a lot) is the fact that Lou Reed's *Metal Machine Music* came out on *quadraphonic* 8-track! This is a highly coveted item, probably because it's so extremely unlikely: "Why did this come out at all? Why is it quadraphonic? Was there really four-channel separation in the original master recordings?" I don't know the answer to any of those questions—I'm still waiting to find a copy! If I do, then I'll have to find a quadraphonic *player,* which I still haven't gotten. Actually, I found one, but it doesn't work, so one of these days I'll have to find someone to fix it. I'm not exactly an electronics expert, but I've gotten pretty good at repairing 8-track tapes.

♦ **V: Why?**

♦ RF: When you get into 8-track, one of your first realizations is: sooner or later every tape you find is going to fall apart! I'm working on an 8-track instructional video which will show how to avoid most true (or terminal) disasters. The most common problem with 8-tracks is: the factory splices break. If you know what you're doing, you can fix all your tapes *before* this happens—I call this procedure "pre-emptive splicing."

Basically, an 8-track tape contains eight distinct tracks of information on a reel of quarter-inch tape which is on an infinite loop—the head is spliced to the tail and theoretically it could keep playing forever. This splice uses a length of metallic tape. Are you familiar with those radio station cartridges (known to the trade as "carts") that were used in the '70s up to the '80s? They look like 8-tracks, are usually made of clear plastic, and hold between 30 seconds to three minutes of information. Like the 8-track, this cart is set up as an infinite loop with metallic tape as the splice. After playback, the tape is automatically stopped at the splice and cued up, instantly ready to play again. Commercials, PSAs (Public Service Announcements) and sometimes songs would be put on separate carts. So if you wanted to play a commercial, all you had to do was grab the commercial cart, shove it in the player and it would start playing without delay.

> **If I found the Vibrators on vinyl it would be *nice*, but it wouldn't exactly be a revelation. With 8-track it's: "Ohmigod—*this* came out on 8-track?**

There *are* 8-track players that give you the choice of stopping when the metallic splice is reached. However, most 8-track players change programs and continue playing when that point is reached. There are four stereo programs on an 8-track tape, and for each program two tracks create the stereo sound. The playback mechanism contains two heads—it's actually playing two different tracks at the same time. You're familiar with the concept of "tape bleed"? If the head is just 1/100th of an inch out of alignment, you'll hear music from tracks you're not supposed to be hearing. Fortunately, on most players the heads can be adjusted to produce perfect sound.

♦ **V: Can anybody do that, or do you have to take it to a repair place?**

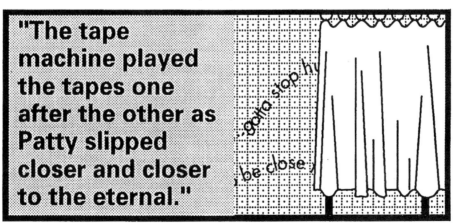

"The tape machine played the tapes one after the other as Patty slipped closer and closer to the eternal."

Patty was the leukemia victim who convinced the Carpenters to visit her at her hospital death bed. From *8-Track Mind #78.*

♦ RF: Good luck finding one! The key to 8-track enjoyment is *self-sufficiency:* teaching yourself maintenance procedures. That's why I'm making the 8-track instructional video: I want to help people *do it themselves.* These days, you're not going to find many technicians who are knowledgeable about 8-track, and if you do find one, they'll charge you an arm and a leg! It's much better to try and do as much yourself as is humanly possible. Another thing—you'll want to collect as many players as possible, because if one breaks and you aren't able to figure out how to fix it, you can just grab another one. I usually have at least half a dozen on hand!

♦ *V: How much do you pay for these players?*

♦ RF: Whenever I see one in good shape for under $10, I buy it. I'll check it out and make sure it works. I pretty much pick them up any time I can.

♦ *V: What are "fade outs"?*

♦ RF: Before 8-track, the previous infinite loop tape technology was 4-track, which basically mimicked an LP record. One program of a 4-track tape would contain one side of an album, and the other program would contain side two. Usually the tapes followed the LP format, with the timing worked out so there wouldn't have to be any fading in or out.

With 8-tracks, that analogous relationship between a tape "program" and an LP "side" changed, because now you had twice as many programs as sides. In other words, now only half of an LP side fits on a program. If songs were short, it wouldn't matter, but in the '70s, songs got longer and longer, which meant that something like "Stairway to Heaven" would get cut in the middle! On an 8-track, there was no way to be able to play that in its entirety straight through—the song would fade out, there'd be a *click,* and the song would fade back in. Needless to say, this drove Led Zeppelin fanatics crazy—but personally, I like it! [laughs]

"Stairway to Heaven" is just too long to listen to in one sitting, but I can take it if it's cut in half. Also, now I think of it as two separate songs! I've met a few people who have grown up hearing "Stairway to Heaven" cut in half, and they think that's the way it should sound. When they hear it played in its entirety, it sounds *weird* . . .

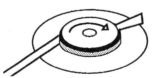

The key to 8-track enjoyment is *self-sufficiency* . . . That's why I'm making the 8-track instructional video: I want to help people *do it themselves.*

At any rate, the "fade in/fade out" made it easy for the record companies. They would record all 8 tracks simultaneously, and this gave them some "sloppage" area: a song would fade out, pause, and then fade back in on the next program. Also, the timing didn't have to be perfect; it didn't matter if there was extra tape next to the splice. The technical aspects of 8-track were part of its downfall, but part of its beauty, too!

♦ *V: How long could an 8-track play before the next program change?*

♦ RF: Generally, the entire 8-track would be about 40 minutes long—the length of an average vinyl LP. This had to be split up into four programs (in this case) each being about 10 minutes long. So there would be 10 minutes' worth of 1/4-inch tape traveling at 3-3/4 inches per second. The linear feet of tape didn't amount to much—one of the reasons 8-track was considered an improvement over 4-track: the same amount of information could be recorded on half the amount of tape. This appealed to the manufacturers, because 1/4-inch tape was relatively expensive.

♦ *V: Did the earlier 4-track format require a huge reel-to-reel machine?*

♦ RF: No. It was a cartridge system that came out a couple of years before the 8-track. It was similar to the

---

STEPS TO FOLLOW FOR 8-TRACK LOOP-I-CIDE

1. Take apart the cartridge.
2. Remove the recording tape.
3. Cut a length of recording tape proportional to the amount of time needed for the loop (3-1/4 inches per second.)

4. Wrap the recording tape around the hub, leaving a couple of inches sticking out from the center.
5. Bring tape to the front of the cartridge and align. The tape must be a bit loose. If it is too tight the tape will jam at the splice.
6. Overlap the recording tape, adjusting its length to the desired tension. Cut the tape diagonally with scissors.
7. Splice the tape together with adhesive tape (I use regular Scotch magic tape). Make sure you apply the tape to the back of the recording tape.
8. Trim excess adhesive tape.
9. Lay the tape back into its correct path.

radio station carts in that thc mcchanism lackcd a pinch roller (the little rubber wheel under the tape), whereas 8-track has a pinch roller. The 4-track cartridge had a hole. After inserting the cartridge into the machine, you'd slide a lever and a pinch roller would swing up and drive the tape across the head.

You can recognize a 4-track tape immediately; its shape is slightly different from an 8-track. This format was fairly short-lived: from approximately 1963–1969. 8-track was introduced in 1966, causing an immediate decline in 4-track sales. The whole story behind this involves a lot of politics.

♦ **V: Who invented the 8-track?**

♦ RF: William Lear, famous for the Lear jet. He had all the right contacts: friends in high places, whom he'd supply with planes. Whereas Earl Muntz, the developer of the 4-track, was just a Southern California audio enthusiast. He didn't have the contacts or the money to develop 4-tracks to the technological level that 8-tracks attained. His 4-track players didn't work all that well, and if you dropped a cartridge, it was a goner! They would open up, tape would be all over the place, and you would have to scoop up the mess and put it in the garbage. Whereas with 8-tracks, they can withstand being dropped or thrown against a wall (almost)—they're sturdy and are built to take a lot of abuse.

The 8-track is widely considered the earliest recorded-sound format for the automobile, though 4-track was actually the first—it just didn't have widespread success. But a lot of famous movie stars had 4-tracks in their cars—it worked a lot better than a record player! [laughs]

♦ **V: Did they have those?**

♦ RF: Yes, record players that played 7" records were built for cars. They incorporated some kind of gyroscopic mechanism to counter the bumps in the road, but they didn't work too well. Four-track provided the first reliable playback system; you could play a whole album's worth of music pretty easily in your car. Then the 8-track improved on that and just took off.

♦ **V: So 8-track was a technological improvement?**

♦ RF: I think so. I visited Sam Auld, one of the co-inventors of the 8-track, who lives near Reno, Nevada. He was an inside witness to all the innovations, and he told me his reasons why the 8-track was superior. The quality of the cartridge was better. The players were much more shock resistant and, in general, a great deal of effort went into reducing "wow and flutter" to a minimum. If you were in a car equipped with a 4-track player and you hit a bump, you'd hear the tape "squiggle" (a drastic change in the music), whereas 8-tracks were designed to overcome that. Eight-track players in cars are remarkably unaffected by bumps. You'd have to hit a pretty large hump to really affect the music.

With 8-tracks, a program could only contain half of an album side—which meant that something like "Stairway to Heaven" would get cut in the middle!

♦ **V: Was Sam Auld nostalgic about the early days of sound technology?**

♦ RF: He was overjoyed that there were still people like me who were interested in the technology he was instrumental in creating. He didn't believe people like us existed until we came and interviewed him, and he was excited that someone would even ask him all these questions.

The 8-track was just one of many projects Sam worked on with William Lear, whom he described in glowing terms. Before Lear produced the jets bearing his name, he helped launch the Motorola corporation. Later, he wanted a music system for his Lear jets, so he went to Southern California and bought a quantity of 4-track players, going so far as to distribute them

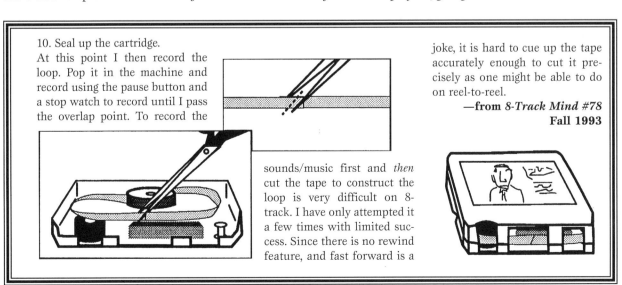

10. Seal up the cartridge.
At this point I then record the loop. Pop it in the machine and record using the pause button and a stop watch to record until I pass the overlap point. To record the

sounds/music first and *then* cut the tape to construct the loop is very difficult on 8-track. I have only attempted it a few times with limited success. Since there is no rewind feature, and fast forward is a

joke, it is hard to cue up the tape accurately enough to cut it precisely as one might be able to do on reel-to-reel.

—from 8-Track Mind #78
Fall 1993

THESE BOOTS WERE MADE FOR WALKING

MODEL RQ-830S

JUST SLIGHTLY AHEAD OF OUR MIND

INSIDE YOUR *EIGHT-TRACK MIND:* READERS REVEAL THEIR LOOPY STORIES

in the Midwest. Soon, however, he discovered there were serious problems with the technology. So he got his top engineers together and said, "We're going to create a better system and we're going to do it within the next six months." And they did! They worked day and night, and within six months developed a pretty amazing system. Then Lear used his contacts with RCA, the big auto manufacturers, and everybody else he knew and began promoting his system. He knew a lot of famous movie stars, wealthy business people, etc; they began spreading the word and it quickly took off. By 1966, 8-tracks were selling far more units than Lear ever imagined—millions of people were listening to them.

Lear was the kind of inventor who would encounter a problem, sit down and figure out a way to solve it, market it and make a lot of money: "Wouldn't it be great if I had a business airplane that was small enough to take me wherever I wanted?" Lo and behold, the Lear jet appeared. Lear's wife is writing a biography about him that promises to be amazing. Almost all of his inventions were successful; somehow he had his finger on the pulse of what Americans wanted.

My 8-track instructional video will trace the history of how the 8-track was developed. Before the '50s, the existing tape recorders used metallic tape. Plastic tape didn't hit the commercial mainstream until the late '40s, after we stole it from the Germans during World War II. Before that, everybody used metallic tape or the earlier wire recorders.

♦ *V: How does a wire recorder work? All I can imagine is a wire going around a spool—*
♦ RF: I've never seen one in operation but I've heard they've had a resurgence. Recently, Les Paul made a live recording on a wire recorder in Thomas Edison's laboratory in New Jersey, then played it back to people who were gathered there. By all reports, it was an amazing recording. If you were a music purist, you probably wouldn't be into wire recordings because they sound "tinny" and a little flat. But to some ears that's an interesting sound that cannot be obtained with any other technology.

For similar reasons, ribbon microphones have had a

resurgence—the kind that Frank Sinatra would croon into. I think David Letterman also has one on his desk. That microphone produces a sound you can't get any other way. To many ears it's not a good, full sound because it's tinny and trebly, but some people want that. When we were making my 8-track documentary, we used $3 microphones to get an 8-track sound for the background music. 8-tracks didn't have a wide dynamic range; the high end and the low end were lost—

♦ *V: 8-tracks have less fidelity than cassettes?*
♦ RF: 8-tracks were *better* than cassettes until the late '70s, then Phillips put a ton of money and research into improving cassettes. But if similar research had gone into 8-tracks, I think they would have ended up being superior. One *inherent* superiority is that the tape travels at twice the speed. During the first few years of 8-track, a lot of marketing was aimed at audiophiles, but they persisted in sticking to their reel-to-reel decks, which go even faster. So when manufacturers figured out that there wasn't a high-end buying audience out there, they started cutting corners, based on the belief that most 8-track buyers didn't care about "high fidelity." By the late '70s, manufacturers wanted to get rid of the 8-track format. The people who were listening to 8-tracks were listening to Led Zeppelin and Rush in their cars and cranking it up so loud you couldn't tell what you were hearing, anyway! [laughs]

It was the compact size of cassettes that ultimately won the war against 8-tracks: "Americans like smaller."

Sam Auld believes that it was the compact size of cassettes that ultimately won the war against 8-tracks: "Americans like smaller." Look at the Walkman—so small you can carry it in your pocket. Small TVs—people love 'em. In Chicago I've seen people take them into restaurants and watch 'em while they eat, and they always draw a crowd. People might not be buying

8-TRACK AS CAPITALIST TOOL?

8-TRACK ANTIDISESTABLISHMENTARIANISM

A LOOK BACK, A LEAP FORWARD

Covers of *8-Track Mind #79, #73, Winter 1991 issue, #81, #76, and #78.*

them *en masse* yet, but everybody's excited about a small TV. *I* don't get that excited because I can't see anything on a screen that small, but there is something "American" about wanting smaller, better, faster . . . as well as larger, better, faster.

♦ **V: Didn't a lot of '70s cars come equipped with 8-track players, complete with a custom cartridge made exclusively for the "Cadillac of the Year"? The music was usually easy-listening compilations.**

♦ RF: Yeah—those are actually highly-coveted tapes. The guitarist from White Zombie is a huge collector of 8-track automobile samplers. I've been trying to get him to write a story about this, but since he's in a successful rock band he doesn't have a lot of spare time. I have gotten some pretty amazing submissions, completely unsolicited. And, with some exceptions, I'll print whatever comes into my mail box, generally verbatim or with slight editing.

♦ **V: How did 8-Track Mind begin?**

♦ RF: A small community of 8-track collectors developed in Chicago. In 1989, I was touring with a band and in Cambridge, Massachusetts, we met some people who were rushing off to their local thrift store to buy 8-tracks. I said, "I was just there and bought all of the good stuff!" They were really upset—well, *pseudo*-upset. There's always a camaraderie among "trackers," as I call them. [laughs] But on this tour it blew my mind to meet all these people in a completely different area—I didn't know about them and they didn't know about me—and we were all collecting 8-tracks and using the same jargon . . .

♦ **V: What jargon?**

♦ RF: Some of it involves the different components: pressure pads, pinch rollers, splices, breaks, etc. I've also created jargon like: *trackers, tracking, 8-track mind, the 8-track lifestyle.* When two people who are into 8-track get together and start talking *seriously,* usually everyone else in the room will start rolling their eyes! That's how I know we're talking a different language—in about ten minutes, other people get lost. [laughs]

Anyway, after I met those people in Cambridge I came back to Chicago and got together with other 8-

track fans. We discussed the idea of doing a publication to reach "all these underground networks of 8-track enthusiasts around the country." There seemed to be some interest, but nothing got going until we met this guy named Gordon Van Gelder. He claimed to have had a magazine called *8-Track Mind* in the late '60s to the mid '80s. I say "claimed" because I don't necessarily believe a lot of what he said—I've never seen any of these early magazines, never heard anybody talk about them, and the Library of Congress doesn't seem to know about them. He also said other things of dubious veracity; I'm not sure how we ran into him. At any rate, he had this idea and was really gung-ho about it: "Yeah, you could do it! Take my idea and we can run with it together." Gordon wrote the "Letter from the Editor" for the first four or five issues of *8-Track Mind,* and then he dropped out.

♦ **V: Where did everybody meet?**

♦ RF: We had meetings in my old apartment in Wicker Park, a "hip" Chicago neighborhood, and first worked on a manifesto, beginning with our "Eight Noble Truths" and "Statement of Purpose." Initially we were just brainstorming, trying to envision a philosophical bent for our publication.

We decided to broaden our editorial scope to include the "analog lifestyle," because a lot of us were also vinyl enthusiasts who were highly critical of digital media. What we liked about vinyl was very similar to what we liked about the 8-track (and to a certain extent, cassettes). They are analog formats. With analog sound you have magnetic waves on magnetic tape representing sound waves, whereas with digital you have 0s and 1s representing waves, and there's something incongruous about that. We felt there was a philosophical problem with digital sound.

Basically, *8-Track Mind* is about 8-tracks, 8-track collecting and the 8-track lifestyle. A small group of us wrote, did layout, and a friend copied 100 issues for free. Gordon Van Gelder claimed that the last issue he put out was #68, so we started ours at #69 in 1990. We gave them out to friends and sent one to *Factsheet Five.* Then we made 100 more, managed to get rid of those and started thinking we were a "real" magazine because we'd distributed 200 copies! [laughs]

At that point we were amazed we'd gotten rid of 200; I thought that at most we'd reach maybe 50 people, but now we print 500 copies of every issue and it's become a quarterly. I get way more contributions than I could possibly print. I figured that at some point interest would start dropping off and people would get jaded and think that it wasn't "hip" anymore and that would be the end of it. But circulation keeps growing. Some of the initial writers have dropped out, but they've been replaced by a new generation of enthusiasts. Actually, it seems like every four issues we have a new group of writers who are really excited—the faces might change, but the enthusiasm doesn't. *8-Track Mind* has gone on for six years now, and it doesn't seem to be slowing down.

♦ *V: You've certainly made your contribution to the recycling movement, because a lot of people were just throwing 8-tracks in the garbage—*

♦ RF: Actually, recycling is important to me, and I try to emphasize this idea in my film, at least as an underlying concern. We flippantly refer to the "8-track lifestyle," but what it's really about is figuring out creative ways to use what you have, instead of using a lot of resources to create new things that are inferior, or that are not really needed. There's absolutely no reason to buy new appliances when there are great 40-year-old appliances that will probably outlive you and me, because they were built with care and with the conscious intent to last a long time. And despite their bad rap, 8-tracks were built with longevity in mind—Sam Auld said they were tested to endure a *thousand* hours of play! That's a lot of play for one tape. I doubt if I'm getting 1000 hours out of my cassettes!

Statement of Purpose

We of the *8-Track Mind* are dedicated to our one pursuit: to keep analog alive (in whatever form) for the coming day of its ultimate victory. We will supersede all formats yet to emerge. We and our followers adhere to the following doctrine:

**THE 8 NOBLE TRUTHS OF THE
8-TRACK MIND**

0) Understanding one's fate leads to greater acceptance.
1) State of the art is in the eye of the beholder.
2) Society's drive is on *attaining* rather than *experiencing.*
3) In less than optimum circumstances, creativity becomes all the more important.
4) Progress is too often promises, promises to get you to buy, buy.
5) "New" and "improved" don't necessarily mean the same thing.
6) "Naive" is not a dirty word.
7) In seeking perfection has the obvious been overlooked?
8) Innovation alone will not replace beauty.

I have found that once you get an 8-track to work, it pretty much works and *works.* The sound quality doesn't deteriorate. Any deficiencies in the sound are in the original recording and there isn't much you can do about that. There was a lot of very complex engineering involved to make them run smoothly and consistently. That's why I collect and swear by 8-tracks—if they were falling apart, I wouldn't have a collection of 600 of 'em. They've lasted longer than a lot of my albums. They're also a much safer secondhand buy because you can't really scratch an 8-track. You can immerse it in mud [laughs] and get dirt inside, but it's amazing how robust the tapes are.

Now there are companies like Sony that manufacture the players, the music, the music videos . . . they rake in money like crazy whenever a new format appears.

I do happen to like the sound of scratchy records, so I won't ever give up vinyl. And contrary to some people's opinions, I'm willing to lower myself to buy CDs. I don't really like the sound, but there's a lot of music I won't be able to hear any other way, like new music or hard-to-find reissues of rarities. The one advantage of CDs is their longer playback time. But you could do that with 8-tracks, too—it's just that not many record companies took advantage of that capability. There *are* a few 100-minute 8-tracks.

♦ *V: Wow—that's like the length of an opera. Is there much opera on 8-track?*

♦ RF: No. Some classical music was released in the early years when record companies were appealing to audiophiles, but again, it seemed that 8-track audiences were younger and just wanted to hear the latest hard rock or Top 40. Supposedly, the manufacturers conducted extensive demographic research, ending up heavily marketing to adolescent males about to get cars!

♦ *V: Somehow it doesn't seem like there's a heavy "collectibles" market in 8-tracks—*

♦ RF: Iggy and the Stooges' *Funhouse* is sought by collectors, because the 8-track has a different cover! The cover photo was originally on the inside LP jacket—one of the few instances where the 8-track cover differed dramatically from the original. This isn't all that interesting to me, because I don't buy 8-tracks for the artwork. It is small and poorly reproduced—you're not going to get much out of it. However, RCA's earliest 8-tracks were packaged in dust-protective plastic boxes accompanied by miniature booklets. I have a *Sound of Music* package and the booklet must be 40 or 50 pages. It includes extensive liner notes and tells how the film was made.

In my film, one person speculates that if 8-track packaging had been more informative, a different audience might have developed. But somewhere down the line manufacturers decided that 8-tracks were just going to be thrown around in the car: "There's no *need* to include any interesting information or graphics!" But in the early days when the emphasis was on excellence, 8-tracks were probably as good as vinyl. Then the manufacturers consciously decided to lower the quality.

♦ **V: Did they start using cheaper grades of tape?**

♦ RF: Yes. They also began duplicating at speeds higher than recommended for optimal sound quality. In every imaginable way they began skimping on quality, and then they turned around and said, "Oh, 8-tracks are laughable and they sound terrible. Why don't you buy our new cassettes?" This was a scam to make you re-buy all your music and buy a new player as well—does that sound familiar? Now there are companies like Sony that manufacture the players, the music, the music videos, the movies whose soundtracks are also marketed . . . they rake in money like crazy whenever a new format appears.

♦ **V: At least the Sony mini-disc hasn't taken off. Their ad campaigns never mention their deficient 8-bit sound quality—**

♦ RF: [laughs] No—perhaps people *are* getting a bit more discerning. A few people realize they were sold an untrue bill of goods with CDs.

♦ **V: When they first came out, there was a TV commercial claiming they were indestructible. It showed them being put into a washing machine—**

♦ RF: [laughs] Yeah, a skipping CD is one the most annoying things I've ever heard, and there's *nothing* you can do about it. If a record skips you can often clean it and get it to play through the skip. Even with an 8-track, there's a few things you can do. If the tape has gotten "waffled," you can actually iron the tape with an iron set on low heat, but you have to use a towel or some kind of padding so the tape doesn't melt. Mind you, I haven't actually *done* this myself, but I know people who have! This procedure has been written up in the pages of *8-Track Mind,* so it must be true!

John Lear is one of the foremost UFO experts in the country, and this further incites the belief that William Lear was at one time abducted by aliens who gave him his technological revelations.

♦ **V: Were 8-track recorders ever manufactured?**

♦ RF: Very much so—even quad-recorders! In my film, I interviewed John Peterson from Seattle who sent me

a tape of John Lear (William Lear's son) talking about research into UFOs. John Lear is one of the foremost UFO experts in the country, and this further incites the belief that William Lear was at one time abducted by aliens who gave him his technological revelations. [laughs] I like this notion a lot, even though I don't necessarily subscribe to it. At any rate, when I first heard John Lear it was in an interview that John Peterson had recorded onto 8-track off the radio.

Occasionally you find 8-tracks in thrift stores that were recorded off the radio in, say, 1971. You get a little slice of history: the commercials, the current Top 40, the PSAs which can be really interesting—they tell you what people were worried about at the time. These are not too common, but from a historical viewpoint they're pretty exciting finds.

With a quadraphonic 8-track recorder you could use two stereo microphones (one for the front and one for the back) and record your own band in simulated quadraphonic! I still haven't come across any

The *8-Track Mind* Defined
A Glossary of Terms

4-Track: The first pre-recorded tape format available for stars' cars. Spaciously accommodated two stereo signals ("programs") on an infinite loop of 1/4" magnetic tape. Tape design is similar to 8-track but they are not as sturdy and lack an internal "pinch roller."

8-Track: William Lear's improvement on the 4-track concept. Four stereo signals ("programs") make for 8 "tracks" of information packed across a loop of 1/4" magnetic tape. Sturdy casings ("carts"), resistance to extremes in temperature, long play life, and internal rubber wheels called "pinch rollers" were some of the improvements Lear initiated.

8-Track Lifestyle: Cheeky term describing a state of mind marked by resistance to modern marketing techniques, and creativity revolving around finding new uses for items which most people in a disposable First World culture would discard. Cleverness vs. consumerism, with a spirit of whimsy thrown in.

Analog: Recording formats which utilize systems of sound information storage which physically mimic the structure of sound waves. Electromagnetic "waves" on analog-recorded magnetic tapes and wave-like "grooves" on long-playing records are the most prominent examples of analog recording systems.

Cart: Short for "cartridge," most commonly used to describe 4-track-like infinite loop stereo cartridges once used by radio stations to store up to three minutes of much-reused information. Also used as a "jargony" term for 8-track (or 4-track) cartridges.

Click: The sound of an 8-track player changing "programs."

Collectible: An item which is acquired for market value and/or nostalgia rather than its originally intended use.

Fade-out: 8-track technique used to consolidate "program" lengths at the expense of song integrity. A song would be cut into parts, with an artificial reduction in volume at the conclusion of the first part, followed by a "program" change (with its accompanying "click"), and an artificial increase in volume leading to the onset of the second part. The reductions and increases in volume ("fade-outs" and "fade-ins") were used to make the transition less jarring than a simple severing of the two song parts would provide.

LP: Long-playing record album, which consists of a 12" diameter vinyl disc with spiraling grooves cut into the top and bottom containing sound information.

Pre-Emptive Splicing: Term created by Russ Forster to describe the replacement of an 8-track tape "splice" before it is allowed to break on its own volition.

Pinch Roller: 1" to 2" diameter rotating rubber or plastic wheel which moves under and guides the magnetic tape loop in an 8-track player.

Program: Stereo or "quadraphonic" sound signal formed by two or four "tracks" of information respectively on an 8-track tape. There are four programs of sound on a stereo 8-track tape and two programs on a "quadrophonic" tape. Most stereo 8-track tapes have programs of ten minutes in duration; "quad" tape programs are around 20 minutes long.

Quadrophonic: Also referred to as "quad." An electronic sound system which delivers four distinct (different) signals to four separate sound reproduction "speakers." Only truly distinct in the 8-track and reel-to-reel formats.

Reel-to-Reel: Also referred to as "open reel." Ultra high-fidelity sound recording format utilizing 1/4" magnetic tape coiled onto plastic or metal "reels" (similar to film reels). Not user-friendly, but a favorite of audiophiles.

Splice: Joining point of two "ends" of material such as film or magnetic tape. In an infinite loop magnetic tape cartridge such as 4-track or 8-track, the "beginning" and "end" of a single strand of tape are joined together at the splice.

Splicing Tape: In 8-track, also referred to as "sensing foil" (at least by Radio Shack stores, the last place known to sell a metallic splicing tape appropriate for 8-track tapes). Sticky adhesive tape used to connect "ends" of a splice together.

Tape Bleed: Unintentional mixing of "tracks" in magnetic tape sound recording formats generally caused by a misaligned playback head.

Track: A single, distinct signal of recorded sound information on a magnetic tape sound recording format.

Tracker: Jargon term created by *8-Track Mind Magazine* which refers to an 8-track tape and technology enthusiast.

Tracking: Verb form of "tracker."

Waffling: A "scrunching up" of magnetic recording tape which often occurs after a catastrophic tape splice break in 8-track tapes.

Wire Recorder: Sound recording system utilizing metallic recording tape, developed before plastic-based magnetic tape technology was acquired from Germany by the U.S. in World War II.

Wow (and Flutter): Distortion in sound reproduction caused by unwanted vibrations of "analog" sound reproduction devices.

—**Russ Forster**

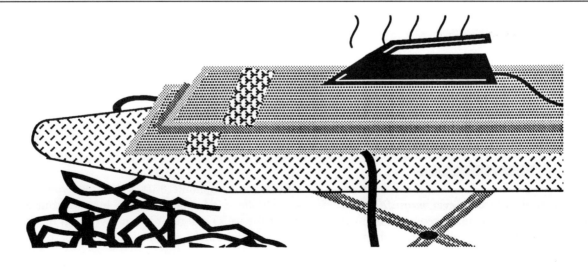

Illustration from 8-Track Mind #75

home-made tapes, but they would be exciting to find. Imagine discovering Grand Funk Railroad basement tapes recorded in quadraphonic sound in Flint, Michigan (quadraphonic came out after the time they were in their basement. I actually own a reel-to-reel tape of one of their practice sessions, but I've never played it because I don't have a player). Who knows what else might be out there—Boston's early demos on quadraphonic? [laughs] There's always exciting finds and surprises in the world of 8-track.

♦ **V: *You were the original editor and publisher of* 8-Track Mind?**

♦ RF: Let me try to clarify that. *8-Track Mind* began in 1990. In 1991 I moved to the outskirts of Detroit after my friend Doug von Hoppe had moved to New Orleans to work in film there. People were starting to go off in different directions; our 8-track collective was breaking up. Since I was the main person who was keeping the magazine going, I brought it to Detroit with me and became the full-fledged editor and publisher. Then Gordon Van Gelder wrote me a couple of very nasty letters (in '91) and disappeared off the face of the earth. I took over the writing of the "Letter From The Editor" and from then on was in charge. I also changed the structure of the magazine to become what it is today: basically, a forum for people who are interested in 8-tracks.

In Detroit, most people I met thought *8-Track Mind* was a big joke; I got no support. I couldn't find a single store to take it. Slowly it started doing better on the East and West coasts, and then it got national distribution through Tower Records, etc.

I had set aside some money, planning to attend film school. Then it dawned on me: "Why not just make a film?!"

♦ **V: *How do you distribute in Detroit now?***

♦ RF: Basically, I go around town and give away my magazine—I don't try to sell it; that's too much effort. Since my film came out, there are about four or five people locally who anxiously await each issue. It's been tough trying to develop any kind of "collective feeling" in this city. Detroit is quiet; it's good if you seek seclusion to do work by yourself, but if you're looking for social stimulation I wouldn't recommend it.

♦ **V: *What's your educational background?***

♦ RF: I have two bachelor's degrees under my belt.

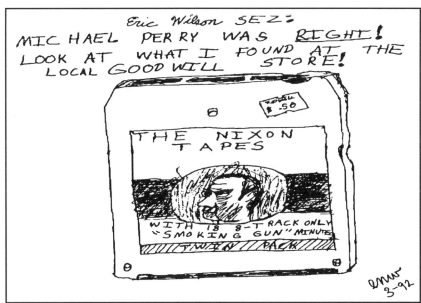

Eric Wilson SEZ: MICHAEL PERRY WAS RIGHT! LOOK AT WHAT I FOUND AT THE LOCAL GOOD WILL STORE!

THE NIXON TAPES WITH 18 8-TRACK ONLY "SMOKING GUN" MINUTES TWIN PACK

from *8-Track Mind #79*

One is in Economics from the University of Chicago—coincidentally, the place where the first self-sustained chain nuclear reaction took place. (It took place under the football field.) I can't recommend the Economics program, at least on the undergraduate level—it was appalling that I graduated without having taken a single course in Marxian or Malthusian economics. The curriculum was straight Milton Friedman—he had taught there. Reagan had just taken office and everyone in the Economics department was overjoyed—now the Friedman camp had a friend in Washington. I was constantly writing about what crap it was, so needless to say I didn't get good grades. But I did graduate with a degree.

I got another B.A. in Urban Studies at Elmhurst College where my mother taught. Through that program I was able to visit the Soviet Union in 1987, when it was still the Soviet Union. That was a great experience. We'd go to different regions and talk to urban planners, transportation officials and developers. I started to see how things get done—how decisions get made, how bureaucracies work. I got ideas on how to set up my *own* little bureaucracy—I definitely rely on other people to help get out *8-Track Mind*. Now the magazine breaks even, which is nice. I don't intend it to be a career, though.

♦ **V: *How did you fund a feature-length 16mm film? The film stock alone costs thousands—***

♦ RF: The film cost about $25,000. I just set aside and planned for the money to pay for the film stock. To a certain extent I could be considered a "trust fund baby"; I've got stocks and bonds that earn interest and I don't have to do anything. I did work at Kinko's for awhile. Detroit is an extremely cheap place to live—in the city of Detroit proper, you can buy a house for $30-$50,000. The homes are beautiful, but the neighborhoods are less than stellar. You wouldn't want to own a lot of expensive items because your house will be regularly broken into. I know a few people who live there and their solution is to simply own nothing of value. Everything they own is bought in thrift stores, and most people wouldn't bother stealing *any* of it! If you can live that kind of lifestyle, then Detroit's your place to be!

♦ *V: Describe your filmmaking process—*

♦ RF: The cinematographer that I worked with, Dan Sutherland, bought a camera specifically for this project. He'd been wanting to do a film and this was just the impetus he needed. We piled into a van with as much equipment as we could scrounge and went around the country (10,000 miles) interviewing people. We drove to Seattle, San Diego, Dallas, Cambridge—all over the place.

♦ *V: Did you stay with people at their homes?*

♦ RF: Yes. People were amazingly forthcoming with hospitality and willingness to let us stick a microphone in their face. We were on such a tight schedule that usually this would happen within 15 minutes of arriving at their home! Outside Chicago, we did all the travel and filming within a month's time, averaging over 300 miles a day. We had very little money, so luckily people contributed food and shelter. Only once did we have to rent a motel room; that was in North Carolina and it cost a whole $25. [laughs]

Here's how the funding really happened: awhile ago I had set aside some money, planning to attend film school. Then it dawned on me: "Why not just make a film?!" Through the magazine I had met some really interesting people, and I love documentaries about weird, eccentric people. So I thought, "This is right up my alley; I should *do* it." I had made a few short films before, and I knew people like Dan with film expertise. As soon as I got the concept, everything seemed to fall into place.

So many people gave me puzzled looks when I mentioned my film project that I felt, "Yeah, this *is* so wrong that it's right. It seems completely right to *me* . . ."

I sent a questionnaire to people and friends whom I thought would be interesting to interview (mostly *8-Track Mind* readers) and was amazed that so many people were totally into it and had great ideas and suggestions. The film worked really well. It was definitely a collaborative effort and I think that's what made it a really good experience for people. I wasn't like some investigative reporter trying to catch them with their pants down; I asked them ahead of time what they wanted to talk about. This saved a lot of money, too.

♦ *V: Did you cut your own negative?*

Russ Forster's documentary film, *So Wrong They're Right*

♦ RF: Yes, but I wouldn't recommend it—it was a nightmare! Now at least I know the basic techniques that will help me as an editor later on.

The film was finished in January, 1995. I submitted it to every possible festival: Sundance, Telluride, etc, and amassed a pile of rejection slips an inch high—I guess Sundance is not the place for me! But at the Chicago Underground Film Festival my film won "Best Feature-length Documentary." It's also showing at the New York Underground Film Festival and some smaller festivals. I've talked to people who've attended the Sundance and Toronto and even the Seattle festivals and they complain how uninspired and uninteresting the work is . . . like those festivals have become just a clearing house for people wanting to make fast money.

♦ *V: What inspired the title of your documentary, So Wrong They're Right?*

♦ RF: Someone in the film who expresses ambivalence toward 8-track nevertheless concludes, "I love 8-tracks because they're so wrong that they're right." To me, that statement comments on the people in the film, the technology of the 8-track, and even the idea of making a film about 8-tracks. So many people gave me puzzled looks when I mentioned my film project that I felt, "Yeah, this *is* so wrong that it's right. It seems completely right to *me,* yet to most of the world it's the craziest idea they ever heard." [laughs] Yet the film will

About the Film

So Wrong They're Right is a 92-minute documentary encapsulating a 10,000 mile journey around the U.S. in search of a group of 8-track (those clunky plastic pre-recorded cartridges from the '70s) fanatics, or "trackers" as they have been dubbed. *So Wrong They're Right* follows the travels of *8-Track Mind* editor Russ Forster and fellow enthusiast Dan Sutherland in search of other 8-track minds. The result is over 20 interviews which delve into reminiscences, rants, political diatribes, fantasies, fix-it tips, sales pitches, and everything else defining the skeptical yet inquisitive mind of the '90s 8-track enthusiast. It's not a film about nostalgia; rather, it serves as a statement of outrage from a population of consumers who are tired of being told what to consume.

Producer, Director, Sound Recordist, Editor:
    Russ Forster
Cinematography, Lighting: Dan Sutherland
Soundmix: Jerrell Frederick
Soundtrack Music:
    Lary 7, Wally Pleasant, Bob Jordan, Mr Bucks,
    Duane Thamm Jr, Scot Konzelmann

be considered Oral History in years to come; I documented a subculture that would have remained subterranean if I hadn't dug it up. A lot of people have noted that you don't have to be interested in 8-track to enjoy the film. All you need is to be interested in people—especially weird, eccentric people.

It turned out that doing a zine literally opened up a whole new universe of possibilities.

♦ *V: What about your 8-track instructional video?*
♦ RF: Again, I think it will help those who are starving for more information about the care and maintenance of 8-tracks. Maybe someday I'll self-publish a book about all the ins and outs of 8-tracks. I would like it to be meaty and full of information—the kind of book that sends readers scurrying to find *other* books.

♦ *V: What splicing tape do you recommend?*
♦ RF: Radio Shack still sells metallic splicing tape. I think they sell it mainly because early cassette phone-answering machines use for an outgoing message a cassette tape with an infinite loop that uses metallic splicing tape. It operates much like the radio station cart; it plays the message, advances to the splicing tape and stops, all cued up for the next time a phone call comes in. Radio Shack still sells the splicing tape for that purpose, but you can also use it for 8-tracks. It's called "Sensing Foil" and costs about $3.99 a roll, but actually it's splicing tape: metallic on one side and

sticky on the other. It's good quality. My splices have lasted eight years; I've never had a single splice break.

♦ *V: You use this to prevent future tape breakages—*
♦ RF: Yes; whenever I bring home a new tape the first thing I do is give it a pre-emptive splice. I have a special 8-track machine that will advance to the splice and then *stop;* I don't even have to wait for the splice to break on me because the machine stops the tape before it breaks. Then I'll take the cartridge out of the machine, pull a little bit of the tape out and replace the splice.

♦ *V: You could offer a service to people who don't want to do it themselves—*
♦ RF: [laughs] When they invent the 48-hour day I'll consider that. Right now I have enough on my hands just promoting the film and producing the magazine. I did as much as I did on the film because I couldn't afford to have anyone else do it. I directed, did the sound recording and mixing, edited, and like I said, had a crash course in negative cutting which was horrible—I wouldn't recommend that to anyone. But now I have a 92-minute, feature-length documentary about 8-track fanatics around the country which contains 30 different interviews. It's a lot more interesting than most people expect and it's not really about nostalgia—even though most people automatically assume it's a nostalgia film. Some people in the film aren't *old* enough to be nostalgic—one interviewee was seventeen. To her, 8-track is a "new thing" that was handed down from her uncles, parents and grandparents, and she became enthusiastic about it.

The film is actually about *people*—specifically the subculture of "trackers." I think it parallels documentaries like *Vernon, Florida* and *Wild Wheels*—it's really about obsessive and eccentric personalities. I hope to be able to make more films—I do consider myself a filmmaker on some kind of level. I want to continue doing the magazine as well—8-tracks are still a big part of my life, and I've met so many friends all over the country because of them. It turned out that doing a zine literally opened up a whole new universe of possibilities. V

The Panasonic RQ-235 "Dynamite." Photo: Erin Fahey

Otto von Stroheim publishes *Tiki News*, dedicated to the preservation, celebration and revival of "Tiki Culture," which includes surviving Tiki bars and restaurants, apartment buildings, statues, masks, lamps and torches, hibachis, lights, cups, graphic designs (on menus, etc), shirts with tiki designs on them, necklaces, giant tiki forks and spoons, tiki torch fuel, a 20 ingredient Mai Tai from a former Kelbo's employee—the list goes on and on. For the latest issue send $3 (or $12 for a 6-issue subscription) to *Tiki News*, 2215-R Market St. #177, San Francisco CA 94114. E-mail: Ottotemp@aol.com (Make checks payable to "Schwarz Grafiken".)

♦ *VALE: Why did you start publishing* Tiki News?
♦ OTTO VON STROHEIM: It was a cause, a compulsion. I have a lot of friends with tiki mug collections in Los Angeles and San Francisco, and over the years I saw their collections grow from five mugs to ten to 15, and now several of them have full-blown tiki bars at their houses. After putting a lot of time into researching tiki culture, I thought: "Why don't I try to package all this knowledge I've gained into something I can share with other people? That way I can create more of a community." A lot of people were asking me fairly obvious questions, and I thought I could put out a newsletter and answer a lot of these questions upfront; then people could gain more of an appreciation.

One of my major goals was to save places like Kelbo's which was taken over by a strip joint in 1994, even though people like Joey Sehee [lounge entertainer and bandleader] were trying to save it. In the greater Los Angeles area it seems like there used to be thousands of tiki bars, one on each corner, where mostly local white home-owners would come in after work. Now only a dozen (or less) remain, and I wanted to save those. Also, I wanted to build an appreciation for tiki culture. A lot of the

articles I publish are "travelogues," because people should be encouraged to track down and visit the remaining tiki environments. Once you start visiting the bars and seeing the old menus and photographs of all the old places, you realize, "This used to be a *whole other world.*"

♦ *V: The tiki bar, with its decor of bamboo, tiki statues, masks and lamps, offered a welcome respite from the confines of the rational, logical mindset, which modernistic interior design reinforces. When did tiki bars start?*
♦ OVS: The tiki bar scene started with Don the Beachcomber's in 1934. I just got a plate from Trader Vic's that boasted "From 1934," but in 1934 Trader Vic's was still a hotdog stand. It didn't really open as a Polynesian restaurant until 1948. There were bamboo, exotic, Hawaiian-style nightclubs all over L.A. in the '20s and '30s, but only Don the Beachcomber's was truly *tiki,* having switched from a more nautical-style decor to a trader-style place featuring hand-carved Polynesian artwork.

When you go to a place like the Tonga Hut in North Hollywood, you'll notice details like the hand-made lighting fixtures, a kidney-shaped dropped ceiling—the place is artistic and it was all built by the owners.

TIKI TIKI

Otto von Stroheim: A case of life imitating art. Photo: V. Vale; Illustration: Eric Rodenbeck

Kelbo's was also built by the owners—self-made. *It's total folk art to the max*—yet nobody cares about it. It hasn't been documented in any art or architectural

Cover of Tiki News #2

publications that I know of. There were all levels of craftsmanship involved, from John Doe at the corner bar doing carvings for his own bar, to some exceptionally skilled carvers and designers. Basically, this was an incredible art movement that was nationwide, coast-to-coast and all-encompassing (places like Kansas, New Mexico and Texas had tiki bars, as well as Canada, Mexico and Europe due to Thor

---

Once you start visiting the bars and seeing the old menus and photographs of all the old places, you realize, "This used to be a *whole other world.*"

Heyerdahl, as well as the Bahamas). They were so prevalent, and then they were all wiped out. It's amazing that nobody documented anything—this blue collar cultural phenomenon just came and went.

♦ *V: Perhaps a lot of people awoke* en masse *from their utopian escape dream and thought it was foolish or kitsch, and immediately felt ashamed and wanted to dissociate themselves from something they now perceived as "corny"—*

♦ OVS: That might be quite accurate. When I talk to a lot of 65-year-old people about this, their attitude is: "Why do you care about *that?* Why would you even want to know?"

♦ *V: They don't even know when they had it good—*

♦ OVS: Right, and of course their kids didn't want to carry on that tradition. However, in the late '60s–early '70s the surfers were wearing tiki necklaces and wearing Hawaiian shirts—there was still a strain of tiki in

the surf culture, but that was the end of it. After the mid-'70s tiki was gone. People today ask me, "What's left?" I say, "Well, I've got seven issues of my fanzine—check 'em out!" Some people think that all the tiki bars have disappeared, but every week somebody tells me about another tiki bar they've discovered. A friend of mine, Max Buda, has a collection of *three thousand* matchbooks (another fun thing to collect) from different establishments, all with tiki designs on them, and these imply the existence of thousands more.

♦ *V: Tiki culture also had its music, which Martin Denny personified—*

♦ OVS: You could *live* off just Martin Denny music, as far as tiki music goes. Denny, Arthur Lyman, Les Baxter and others have been extensively re-issued recently.

♦ *V: The tiki carvings are a primitive art form; amateurs could carve their own. There ought to be a neo-renaissance of tiki-carving!*

♦ OVS: That's happening. Paul Musso in San Francisco carves tikis for his friends, and Bosko in San Diego also carves tikis. Crazy Al is making tiki incense burners. There is a Tiki carver shop called Mai Tiki in Florida that's been around for years. Since you make them yourself, you automatically have your own style. Whereas if you're entering the field of modern furniture design, you really have to work hard to make a name for yourself and create something that's your own. But if you're carving tikis, immediately whatever you make will probably be recognizable as yours.

Cartoonists and fine artists are now doing art with tiki themes. Fantagraphics just published Mary Fleener's book of tiki cartoon art, and she hand-cast some tiki necklaces to help promote it, too. I'm trying to encourage the graphic arts production as well. Charles Schneider is a fairly well-known artist who was into tiki art back when Amok opened their first

---

Basically, this was an incredible art movement that was nationwide, coast-to-coast and all-encompassing.

---

store in the '80s; he painted their wall mural. Then he got out of it. I contacted him and told him I'd like to publish any tiki material he might have, and he was inspired to start making tiki drawings again. *That's* my payment for doing *Tiki News*—to think I might have inspired someone. I'm an artist myself

How to Create Your Very Own

TIKI BAR

Bachelor pads of the '50s and early '60s relied on cocktails as lubricant for smooth nights at home. Along with soft Latin or Polynesian rhythms, nothing created a more sophisticated atmosphere for establishing that exotic mood than a well-stocked, warmly lit tiki bar.

Recreating that refined atmosphere is still possible in the '90s.

Vintage postcards from the magnificent but long-vanished Polynesian restaurants of greater Los Angeles provide inspiration. Locations such as the Luau of Beverly Hills, Don the Beachcomber of Hollywood, The Islander on Restaurant Row and Beverly Hills' Trader Vic's depict the essential ingredients.

Tiki bars are layered spaces. Create depth by layering exotic textures, objects and colored light. For texture: bamboo, thatch, tapa cloth, fish-netting and reed fencing. For objects: tiki statuary, tiki mugs, ceramic or wooden bowls, coconuts, silk ferns, starfish and anything nautical (port holes, life preservers, rope). For color and light: low wattage (7, 15, 25 watt) colored bulbs suspended inside pufferfish, bamboo fixtures, conch shells, multi-colored glass and plastic fishing floats. Deftly hidden old-fashioned Christmas lights work, too.

Pick a dark spot in your living room conducive to conversation, preferably a corner or wall with shelf space (for mugs, booze and glassware). Attach reed fencing to the wall with split bamboo as a border. (To split bamboo, hold the pole vertically and with a sharp knife push down from the top with the grain.) Create a ïhutî by placing thatch atop a row of two-foot bamboo poles projecting downward from the wall. Staple tapa cloth accents to adjoining doors or walls. Unless you already have a wet bar, free-standing bamboo bars work fine as the centerpiece. A trio of sturdy, swiveling rattan bar stools are a must. Get an old *Mr. Boston Bartender's Guide* from a used bookstore for tips on stocking a full bar. Hang light fixtures from underneath the thatch hut or from the ceiling. Fish netting stapled loosely to the ceiling masks unsightly cords. Strategically distribute nautical and natural sea objects, tikis, mugs, silk ferns and other bric-a-brac on walls, shelves, etc. Weave Christmas lights amongst the objects for subtle drama. Direct lighting of any kind is too harsh—you want your bar to GLOW. Try old-fashioned Christmas lights.

Now, under the soothing spell of Arthur Lyman, Martin Denny and Les Baxter, sip a Navy Grog as guests mingle beneath the layers of light and texture of your tiki bar mood exotica.

—Pete Moruzzi, from *Tiki News #3*

Pete Moruzzi basking in the glow of his tiki bar. Photo: Pete Moruzzi

and I put little drawings in *Tiki News,* but I don't credit myself; the art looks more anonymous, like clip art. It's like the matchbooks and menus we find now, which don't have an artist credit or copyright.

Cover of the 1995 Exoticon Covention program.

I helped Jeff Berry put out the *Grog Log,* which is a bar guide illustrated with collages from found menu art. My friend Bosko created original art for the cover. There were some gaps ("Hey, I need another tiki in that corner!") so I did some drawings to fill in the gaps and flesh out this stolen found graphic art. The Viper Room ripped off a tiki drawing that David Purcell had made for *Tiki News* and used it on a promotional flyer—I wish they'd credited us, but I guess they just thought it was clip art. Oh well—I'm sure that back in the old days Trader Vic was irked on a daily basis by how many people were ripping off his concept. There was Trader Nick's (Pismo Beach), Trader Dick's (in Reno), Trad'r Sam's (San Francisco), Trader Rick's, Trader Frank's, Trader *whoever*—they all ripped off Trader Vic's.

Tiki Bob's in San Francisco was started by a former bartender at Trader Vic's who realized, "These guys have a line out the door, and they're turning away people who aren't wearing a sport coat and tie. I'm going to start a tiki bar right up the street and open it to people who don't have a sport coat." For years he made a living off all these Trader Vic's *rejects!*

♦ **V: And now there's an "Exoticon." Who started that?**

♦ OVS: Me and my friends, Steve and Strike. Steve is my age and comes from the same background: used to be a punk rocker, and now works in a record store because he loves music and wants to get free records. He's Bohemian to some extent. He and Strike got together and thought, "There are all these bands doing exotica and lounge-style music that don't get to play anywhere, and there are vendors like Haywire who sell tiki mugs but don't know how to find their audience. We should have a

Tiki Manifesto

TIKIS ARE BEING DESTROYED AND LEFT TO ROT AT AN ALARMING RATE. THE LOSS OF A TIKI IS A LOSS TO OUR SOCIETY. THE PAST TWO DECADES HAVE SEEN THE DEMISE OF WHAT WE CALL "POLYNESIAN POP."

IT IS OUR MISSION TO PRESERVE ANY AND ALL REMAINING ELEMENTS FROM THE POLYNESIAN POP ERA OF THE MID-1950S TO MID-1970S.

WE ALSO RECOGNIZE PRE-TIKI EXOTIC ELEMENTS AS PRECURSORS TO THE TIKI ERA AND POST POLYNESIAN POP ERA ARTIFACTS AS EXTENSIONS OF THE TRADITION.

REDISCOVERY AND PRESERVATION OF THESE ELEMENTS AND ARTIFACTS ARE ESSENTIAL AND WILL BE EXECUTED AT ALL TIMES TO THE BEST OF OUR ABILITY.

WE WILL NOT REMOVE OR OTHERWISE HINDER ANY ELEMENTS IN THEIR ORIGINAL SETTING UNLESS THOSE ELEMENTS ARE IN IMMINENT DANGER.

NOR DO WE ENCOURAGE THE AGREEABLE SALE AND/OR FRIENDLY REMOVAL OF THESE ELEMENTS FROM THEIR ORIGINAL SETTINGS. LIKE NATURE WE BELIEVE THESE ELEMENTS TO BE FOR PUBLIC ENJOYMENT.

REMOVAL AND PRESERVATION OF ELEMENTS FACING IMMINENT DANGER IS NOT ONLY CONDONED, IT IS ENCOURAGED.

TO REMOVE TIKIS AND OTHER ELEMENTS NOT FACING DANGER IS TO TRAMPLE UPON ALL EXISTING MORAL AND ETHICAL CODES. BESIDES THAT, IT'S BAD LUCK!

WE INTEND TO CREATE A FORUM FOR SHARING CURRENT AND PAST INFORMATION REGARDING ANY SORT OF TIKI CULTURE. ALL INFORMATION WILL BE DISPERSED IN AN EFFORT TO PROMOTE GROWTH OF CURRENT TIKI CULTURE.

convention." And it was packed; people came from San Francisco, Berkeley, Arizona and all over. Combustible Edison and the Phantom Surfers told all their friends about it, and they also played. The place held 1500 but 2000 people showed up. I think most people were happy to be exposed to what they saw.

♦ **V: *How was this event funded?***

I'm sure that back in the old days Trader Vic was irked on a daily basis by how many people were ripping off his concept. There was Trader Nick's, Trader Dick's, Trader Sam's . . . Trader *whoever* . . .

♦ OVS: Even though we had no money, we managed to get a lot of people to advance us what we needed. For example, we rented a bunch of tikis, a waterfall and some palm trees from Oceanic Arts in Whittier, who did a lot of the original carvings for Don the Beachcomber and other restaurants in the '50s, as well as later work for Disneyland. At first the owners, Leroy and Bob, were going to trade us just a few tiki rentals for an ad space in our program, but they ended up giving us a huge amount—whatever we wanted, basically—in exchange for their $150 ad. The Cacophony Society came in and built a tiki bar and sold tiki drinks—that added a lot to the atmosphere. Things like that happened all down the line. We were trying to sell vendor tables for $100, and nobody had bought any. But at the last minute a lot of people came in and bought 'em, and all the vendors did really well so they were thanking us: "Sign us up for next year!" (If they had lost money, they would have wanted to kill us.) The event took place at the Park Plaza Hotel where a lot of movies are shot, like the opening scene of *Wild at Heart* where Nicolas Cage bangs a guy's head on this huge flight of stairs.

♦ **V: *Some people in Berlin were inspired by our* Incredibly Strange Music *book to put on an exotica-type event. Everyone dressed up luau-style, and they sent me photographs. It was wonderful in spirit but they probably didn't have a lot to work with (can you get bamboo in Berlin?!). But they had a few Martin Denny albums, and were also trying to make music like that themselves.***

♦ OVS: That's where it gets really interesting, when mutations occur and spread. What they did was better than making a Pearl Jam cover band. Isn't that *payment* in itself—didn't that make you feel good when you saw it? That's why we do things like publish *Tiki News*. Feedback and meeting interesting, fun people is the *real* payment . . . **V**

OTTO'S RECOMMENDATIONS
Publications
Grog Log
Jeff Berry's Polynesian bar guide, $12 from Schwarz Grafiken, 2215-R Market St. #177, San Francisco CA 94114. (Make checks payable to "Schwarz Grafiken.")
Kiss My Pineapple #1 & #2
$2 each (cash) from Beth Allen, 1538B Fulton St, San Francisco CA 94117. Beth is now in a band, The Loudmouths, and sadly has (at least for now) ceased to create her zine.

Note: *Tiki News #7* is an attempt at a comprehensive guide to "tiki culture" music currently available.

Mail Order:
Tiki incense holders $16.50 from Allan Evans, POB 553, Sunset Beach CA 90742 (213) 264-7275.

Tiki buttons, cuff links, bottle openers, necklaces, etc from Tiki King. Catalog $1 to POB 345, Felton CA 95018.

Custom Tiki mugs and hand-carved palm tikis. Send $1 for information from Bosko Hrnjak, POB 300024, Escondido CA 92027.

Matchbook from the Islander restaurant

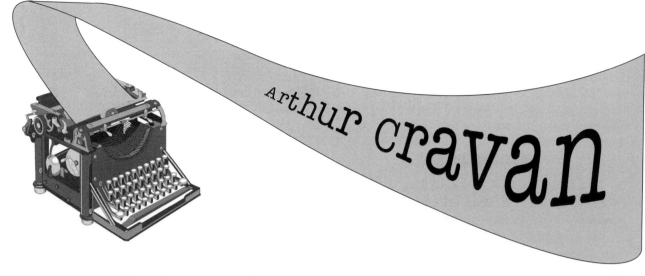

Arthur Cravan

Dean lives in Prague, The Czech Republic where he does an e-zine dedicated to Arthur Cravan [pronounced cra-*van*], a contemporary of Duchamp who anticipated many late 20th century cultural trends and attitudes. Born in the Bay Area, Dean was a member of obscure San Francisco punk bands such as Oedipus; he has several "weird 45s out on weird labels—didn't everyone?" Presently he earns a living via computer skills. His Arthur Cravan e-zine address is: kravan@login.cz.

♦ *VALE: How did you end up in Prague?*
♦ DEAN: I went there in '92 and discovered an old friend was living there, Bob Bell, who used to be in a band during the '70s San Francisco punk scene. Prague is a good place for expatriates to live; people mind their own business. I've seen a lot of persons with facial tattoos there; recently I saw someone who had his face and neck tattooed in *paisley.*

I think we're oozing into a New Dark Age, and I want to be low profile during this period.

Personally, my world view has been that of a Perpetual Tourist ("PT"), and I've managed to live in several countries for extended periods of time. I think we're oozing into a New Dark Age, and I want to be low profile during this period. I like the idea of the nomad, and transportation is getting cheaper all the time. "PT" (it has different meanings: perpetual tourist, poetic terrorist, thoroughly prepared) is a philosophy written by an English ex-barrister who makes his money publishing books about how to be a tax exile. (W.G. Hill, Scope Intl Ltd, 62 Murray Rd, Waterlooville, Hant, P08 9JL, U.K.) Wherever you are, tourists are always given more slack than locals or green-card holders, so it's best to be a "tourist."

I periodically visit San Francisco to buy software—it's half the price. Otherwise, Prague is really cheap as far as food goes, and rent's not too bad. Now you can actually get vegetables—there's a place called Fruits of France that flies vegetables in every Thursday. The national dish is pork, sauerkraut and dumplings—goulash is big, too.

Prague is interesting—it's getting better all the time. There's very low unemployment so all the natives seem to be happy. All the buildings and cobblestones are getting redone, and there are a lot of American expatriate writers thinking they're Hemingway or Fitzgerald in Paris during the '20s. I went to a "sports bar" where there must have been *two thousand* American twenty-somethings hanging out. I have no idea what these people do for a living; it wasn't vacation time . . . That's a great Duchamp poster there, showing him with a punk haircut—
♦ *V: I think Duchamp anticipated most of the trends of the 20th century. He had an early shaved-design haircut that predated punk or rapper hairstyles; he dressed in drag and used an alternate gender name, "Rrose Selavy"; he denounced the art scene to play chess, yet he was still producing art anyway. His final creation was a deliberately cheesy "pornographic" installation that forces the viewer to be a voyeur looking straight at a nude woman with her legs spread . . .*

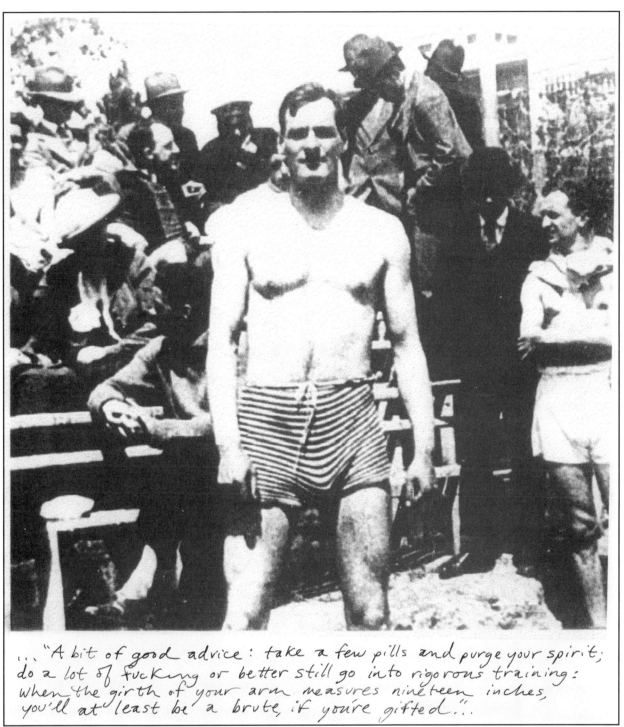

... "A bit of good advice: take a few pills and purge your spirit; do a lot of fucking or better still go into rigorous training: when the girth of your arm measures nineteen inches, you'll at least be a brute, if you're gifted."...

Arthur Cravan: the poet pugilist. Photo supplied by Dean.

♦ D: Do you know who Arthur Cravan was? He was a boxer-poet-wild man-provocateur who's been my hero for 30 years, and he seems to be getting more popular. Just like Duchamp, Cravan anticipated a lot of things—in fact Duchamp appreciated Cravan and got him a ticket from Barcelona to New York and procured him that famous lecture at the New York Independents Exhibition in 1917. Cravan was supposed to expound on modern art movements to society ladies, and he came in reeling-drunk and started tearing his clothes off and was taken away by a couple of policemen. Duchamp said, "Wonderful lecture!" and persuaded Walter Arensberg to get him out of jail.

♦ V: So why did you do an e-zine?

♦ D: It's really cheap to do, and your distribution is already in place—you've got massive distribution. Also, e-zines don't consume trees, and they're instantly editable, changeable and update-able, whereas if you publish a paper zine, it's fixed—if you've made a typo, you have to live with it. And with an e-zine, you can even change your views.

The only thing I don't like about e-zines in general is that they're short on graphics and long on textual content. But being in Prague, the Internet helps keep me in touch—I was surfing the net and came across the Caffe Trieste [San Francisco bohemian landmark] sign and thought, "Ah, nice!" (Someone who hangs out there has a home page featuring their sign as a logo.) So I feel I can be "in touch" with San Francisco—or anywhere—while I'm away.

Censorship is rearing its ugly head on the Internet, but a lot of people are fighting against it. It's hard to do because there are so many ways to get through to people—it's not centralized or local in nature. I find wonderful things just by browsing; you can find people interested in specific subjects no matter how bizarre they are. Overseas, it's a much better source of information than reading the *International Herald-Tribune,* for example. You can get less-mainstream information and points of view and culture; you can tune in on what's up with the 20-somethings; what's current.

♦ **V: How much do you pay your Net server in Prague?**

♦ D: A lot compared to America. Here they're *giving* it away because it's very competitive; over there it's not. It costs about $200 a month for on-line time; they charge by the minute. I always check *Hotwired;* they update their site all the time.

♦ **V: Tell us more about Arthur Cravan—**

♦ D: His real name was Fabian Avenarius Lloyd and he invented the name Arthur Cravan; there are no other Cravans anywhere. I regard him as one of the most unsung heroes of 20th century art; the situationist Guy DeBord described him as "the only person he ever respected." Cravan was a very early zine creator;

Photo of Cravan from the collection of Dean.

Cravan wrote great poetry, was Oscar Wilde's nephew . . . and was intelligent enough to go into the ring dead drunk so he didn't get hurt very badly!

---

his self-publication was called *Maintenant.* It was printed on butcher paper, and he stood outside art galleries selling it. It was filled with reviews that completely blasted all the artists of the day—so much so that once a group of a dozen painters waited for him and ambushed him in the street.

Cravan's whole life was one performance art piece. To quote *Four Dada Suicides:* "His parents were English, his language was French, his passport was Swiss. His last-known driver's license was issued in Berlin, his last-known address was in Mexico City. As a teenager he was expelled from boarding school and rode boxcars from New York to California, working as a butcher, orange-picker and lumberjack along the way. In his 20s he studied the classics, boxed in Athens and Barcelona, and lectured on modern art in Paris and New York . . . He made a lasting impression on his contemporaries, who never tired of describing his personality, appearance or behavior."

It's hard to find information in English on Cravan, although he's described quite well in Robert Motherwell's *The Dada Painters and Poets.* The best description, by the art critic Roger Conover, is in *Four Dada Suicides.* Cravan was a nomad with different passports who traveled a lot. He was called "the brutal critic"; he criticized the way artists looked and their athletic abilities and pretty much didn't touch on their paintings because they didn't seem worthwhile to him! His criticisms consisted of such phrases as: "He couldn't throw a stone more than twenty feet," "ran with great difficulty," "looked like an inflamed armpit," "a flabby cheese." He was really wonderful in how he insulted people.

Cravan's insults to Apollinaire and his cohorts landed him in jail for character defamation. Upon release, Cravan announced that anyone who would like to see him silenced for good need only reserve a seat at the nightclub Noctambules, where he would end his career as a critic by committing public suicide, following a speech during which he would wear only his jockstrap and put his balls on the table for the benefit of the ladies. The club was packed with eager voyeurs on the night of the event—and after berating the assembly for wanting to make a spectacle of death, Cravan gave them a boring lecture about Victor Hugo.

Cravan wrote great poetry, was Oscar Wilde's nephew, and fought with Jack Johnson (the ex-heavyweight champion of the world) and was intelligent enough to go into the ring dead drunk so he didn't get hurt very badly! To quote *New York Dada 1915-23:* "Far more significant than the footnote he left in pugilistic histories was the undying legacy of his outrageous behavior, which played a unique role within the development of an artistic and literary avant-garde. Arthur Cravan was, as Gabrielle Buffet-Picabia later asserted, "a man who personified, within himself and without premeditation, all the elements of surprise to be wished for by a demonstration that was not yet called 'Dada.'"

The situationist Guy Debord described [Cravan] as "the only person he ever respected."

Supposedly he drowned in Mexico in 1918 while out on a boat, but after he disappeared, there were all these Cravan sightings. If in fact he did make it out of there, he sold a lot of counterfeit Oscar Wilde works to major collectors—so he was a forger as well as many other things. He's a very 20th century guy at the *beginning* of the century, not at the end. I think he's like William Burroughs or John Cage or Marcel Duchamp in terms of his originality. He influenced all the early Dadaists and Surrealists, who greatly admired his life and considered it as art. *That's* why I do an e-zine on him! **V**

ARTHUR CRAVAN BIBLIOGRAPHY
compiled by Elizabeth Burnham

Ashbery, John, *Double Dream of Spring*: "Some Words" from the French of A.C.

Begot, Jean Pierre, Editor. *Arthur Cravan: Oeuvres.* Paris, Lebovici/Champ Libre 1987.

Conover, Roger L. Introduction to *Mina Loy: The Last Lunar Baedeker.* Highlands, NC, The Jargon Society, 1982.

Cravan, Arthur,. *Maintenant.* Jean Michel Place, editor. 12 rue Pierre et Marie Curie, 75005 Paris, France.

_____. *Double Dream of Spring* [no publishing info]

Debord, Guy. *Panegyric.* London, Verso, 1991 (page 13).

Green, Malcolm, editor. *The Dada Almanac.* London, Atlas 1993 (page 169).

Hale, Terry, editor. *Four Dada Suicides.* London, Atlas Press, 1995.

Knabb, Ken, editor. *The Situationist International Anthology.* Berkeley, Bureau of Public Secrets, 1989 (page 107)

Marcus, Greil. *Lipstick Traces.* Cambridge, Harvard University Press, 1989 (pp. 193, 198, 334)

Motherwell, Robert, editor. *The Dada Painters and Poets.* 2nd edition, Boston, Hall, 1981.

Naumann, Francis M. *New York Dada 1915-1923.* New York, Harry N. Abrams, 1994.

Sainz de Zasca & Escobar, "Arthur Cravan," *Poesia #38,* Madrid, Ministerio de Cultura, 1992.

Vaneigem, Raoul. *The Revolution of Everyday Life.* Seattle, Left Bank Books, 1983 (4.4, 12.1).

PLAZA DE TOROS MONUMENTAL
DOMINGO 23 ABRIL DE 1916
A las 3 de la tarde
GRAN FIESTA DE BOXEO
en la cual tendrán lugar
6 interesantes combates entre notables luchadores, 6
JACK JOHNSON = ARTHUR CRAVAN

Finalizará el espectáculo con el sensacional encuentro entre el campeón del mundo

Jack Johnson
Negro de 110 kilos
y el campeon europeo
Arthur Cravan
Blanco de 105 kilos
En este match se disputará una bolsa de **50.000** ptas. para el vencedor.

Véanse programas

PRECIOS (incluidos los impuestos)

SOMBRA Y SOL Y SOMBRA: Palco sin entradas, 20 pesetas.—Silla de ring 1.ª fila con entrada, 36 ptas.—Silla de ring 2.ª fila con entrada, 28 ptas.—Silla de ring 3.ª y 4.ª filas con entrada, 15 ptas.—Sillas de ring 5.ª, 6.ª, 7.ª y 8.ª filas con entrada, 12 ptas.—Barrera con entrada, 10 ptas.—Contrabarrera con entrada, 6'50 ptas.—Sillón delantera de Palco, con entrada, 8 ptas.—Sillón tendido de Presidencia con entrada, 8 pts.—ENTRADA GENERAL, 3'50 pts.—Entrada de carnets (impuestos) 0'60 ptas. SOL: Silla de ring 1.ª fila, con entrada 18 ptas.—Silla de ring 2.ª fila con entrada 12 ptas.—Sillas de ring 3.ª y 4.ª fila con entrada 8 ptas.—Silla de ring restantes con entrada 6 ptas.—ENTRADA· GENERAL 2 ptas.

Sobs. de Lopez Robert y C.ª, impresores, Asalto, 63

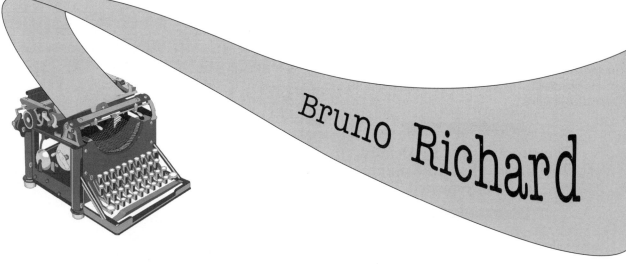

Bruno Richard

One of the most prolific and persistent self-publishers is Bruno Richard. With collaborator Pascal Doury, he publishes under the name "Elles Sont de Sortie." Since 1976, Bruno has created an estimated 100,000 graphics, many of which appear in the over 50 books he has published. Most of these books were given away or traded with other self-publishers all over the world. (Send something in trade to Bruno Richard, 15 Passage de la Trinite, Paris 75002 France.)

♦ *VALE: What's your background?*
♦ BRUNO RICHARD: I was born August 30, 1956 in Mauritius. One of my earliest memories was seeing a volcano erupt, and afterwards collecting volcanic stone. At the age of ten, my family moved to France. I attended a very good state school for students who lack both parents. This was near Paris in Meudon, Sevres, where Celine lived—his wife still lives there. I was raised Catholic and one year I was head of my class, so the teacher gave me a big plastic Jesus as a prize.

At school I became friends with Pascal Doury; however, he was thrown out of school for stealing apples from a neighboring orchard. I lost contact with him for four years. Then we ran into each other and discovered that we both were still drawing, just as we did when we were children. We decided to do something together. We both had a lot of drawings at home; we wanted them to be seen, yet there was no way to make money with them, and no one was willing to print them. So we decided to print some books ourselves. We had little money and it seemed that the only way we could afford to print was to do linoleum printing. That was a very annoying process, because it took so long to dry—
♦ *V: To produce artwork, you had to carve the linoleum with tools—*
♦ BR: Yes, and then you put on the ink and print each page with a roller, by hand. You could only print one color at a time. When 50 copies were finished we put the sheets into an envelope—it was like a portfolio.

♦ *V: Describe the content—*
♦ BR: It was a little booklet, 6″x9″—actually we don't like our first three books because they're a little bit "young." I included some letters from girlfriends because everybody has these kinds of text but nobody talks about them. I decided I wanted to expose all the hidden parts of daily life.

Later on I did a book of portraits which were just large drawings of cocks and cunts, trying to establish a new archetype of beauty based not on the face but on the sex.

We brought our first publication around to various stores, but this turned out to be exhausting and we only got rid of about 20 copies. Soon after, Pascal went into the army because this is mandatory in France. (I got out by crying inconsolably for three days and being insane.) They assigned him to work on an army magazine, and he began stealing materials (like film and metal plates) to produce our own publications. This was 1977, and in France there were no easily available xerox machines or computer printers. We printed our second collaboration and split the cost—$150 each for 150

Bruno Richard in his Paris apartment

copies. We started calling ourselves *Elles Sont de Sortie.*

♦ **V: *What does that mean?***

♦ BR: We found this phrase in a newspaper, only it was actually written *Ils Sont de Sortie.* As a joke we chose to use the feminine "elles," and once somebody included us in their listing of feminist magazines. The translation reads: "The girls are going out."

♦ **V: *How was the distribution?***

♦ BR: Most stores wouldn't take them, and the few that did only took them on consignment terms, so that if they sold a few months later, we could collect the money due us. But we never went back to the stores! [laughs] Actually, we went to a *few,* but only one or two copies had sold, so it didn't seem worth it to go back to the rest of the stores to collect the money due us.

♦ **V: *At first you only distributed locally?***

♦ BR: Yes. The French underground weekly newspaper *Charly* ran a column by Willem, a supporter of underground comics, so we sent him some of our work. He wrote about us in one of his columns, and people began to write us and look for our books in stores.

♦ **V: *What was in the next two issues?***

♦ BR: Pascal made many drawings which critiqued the army. One illustration portrayed his commanding officer as a butcher chopping up sausages. I made drawings of life in the barracks—the army really is a theater for homosexuality, with all these men flexing muscles, sweating together, living through the same problems and fighting.

Our fourth project was on the theme of "Health and Sickness." We included a lot of medical-style drawings but didn't follow the theme exactly—I included pho-tobooth photos of my sex, for example. (Later on I did a book of portraits which were just large drawings of cocks and cunts, trying to establish a new archetype of beauty based not on the face but on the sex.) We also included insulting letters which Pascal and I had written to each other: "You fuckin' bastard, you believe in art, you are nothing, you just make bullshit"—that kind of thing. Futuropolis distributed this issue.

It's more interesting to do something when you're alive than just living!

Number five was on the theme of "Adventure, Holidays and Pleasure." Inside Pascal told a story of fucking a neighbor girl. After awhile he fell in love with her, but she didn't want him anymore. Actually, Pascal was really shy; this had been his first girlfriend. Living next door, he could overhear her fucking other guys and this made him crazy—one day he broke everything in his room to avoid hearing the noise. Another time he slid a big drawing under her door to make them stop.

We also included many drawings about holidays and people lying on the beach. I included a transcript of me phoning this girl to ask her out, and it was full of banalities: "Hello, how are you?" Fine." "What are you doing tonight? Perhaps we could go out for coffee?"

We also did a Wallpaper issue (#6) and later one called *Pornographie Catholique* (#10) in which Pascal

and I talked about our personal finances: how much we spend on rent, how much salary we earn, what we do with our money—all this is taboo and nobody talks about it. At the time I was working for an ad agency, and some people were shocked because I was so young yet earned so much money.

I kill people in my drawings, but they are just images—lines on paper.

♦ **V: Did you make any money off your publishing?**

♦ BR: A little bit, but it was never enough. Over the past 20 years we managed to produce 45 books. Recently somebody asked me if I'd like to do a book with them for no money, just a copy of the book, and I agreed. That's often the way it works. All the books are different—we change the size, the type, the topic, every time. It's all done just to do something before dying. It's more interesting to do something when you're alive than just living!

♦ **V: Well, one of your rewards is meeting people all over the world—**

♦ BR: Everybody I ever liked, I would send them a free copy of my book. I would write, "I like what you do very much. This is what I do. Is there something you could send me in exchange so I could see more of your work, because it is not readily available to me?" When I travel I look at magazines and find things that interest me; then I try and meet the people who produced them.

♦ **V: Don't you often stay with people you've met through the mail?**

♦ BR: Yes. The first time I went to Los Angeles (in 1978) I saw a small advertisement in *Slash* magazine for a Gary Panter exhibit. I went to the opening and brought my work and said, "I would like to meet Gary," and met him. He asked me where I was staying and I said, "I don't know yet." He told me that I could stay with a friend of his.

♦ **V: After you visited L.A. you came up to San Francisco in 1978. How did you contact me?**

♦ BR: Caro [graphic and video artist and co-director of *Delicatessen*] had visited San Francisco the year before, discovered *Search & Destroy* and worked on it. He gave me your address. Caro was very involved in the punk music scene. Now, some people think we are "kings of the underground" because we have done a lot. That's because most people quit very quickly: they put out one or two or three issues and give up. They don't make any money and then they get bored and become interested in doing something else.

♦ **V: How do you produce art while working a full-time job?**

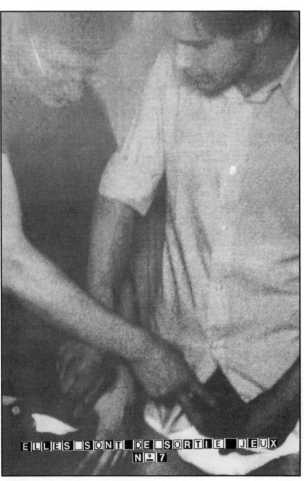

ELLES SONT DE SORTIE JEUX N°7

♦ BR: I draw three to five hours every morning before I go to work (4:30–9:00 AM), and sometimes I draw at bedtime if I'm alone. That's all I can do. For me, work is a kind of "regularization"—if I didn't work and stayed alone in my room drawing all day like a monk, I would suicide myself. That's why I need a regular job, and that's why I hate weekends! Besides, my job pays for all my publishing.

♦ **V: Describe the range of topics that you've included—**

> ## By adding all the scratches, I make the *form* dirty as well as the content.

♦ BR: I like to destroy pictures. Often I'll find a photograph and then redo it in a drawing my way—only then am I completely satisfied. When something touches me, like a photo of a girl—even if she's not nude, I'll make her nude. When I find a picture that touches me very much, I'll do it in my way, like "Guernica" was for Picasso.

Sometimes I have a concept. I did a book entitled *Sexy Politzei;* "sexy" plus "politzei" (a German word for police). For that book I chose pictures of policemen that I'd collected, but not photos of them beating people—that's too easy. I preferred to find very ordinary snapshots of policemen and to show a different viewpoint of them. I redid those pictures and added sex and violence to them to reflect the world as I see it. My drawings depict the awfulness and comedy in this world, like George Grosz who did biting drawings of the bourgeois, the military, prostitutes, etc. And because people's perceptions are broken or fragmented, I do pictures that reflect different states of mind . . . that reflect what this world makes you feel. (That's *part* of what I do, at least.)

People tell me that my pictures are very dirty or violent, but the world is like that—my pictures don't *begin* to reflect what is really there. With my kind of pictures, you learn how to "read" violent imagery and then maybe you don't buy the violence on TV with its happy car or plane crashes and mass murderers. Then, people tell me that I am doing "dirty" things: "You shit on a plate, you piss in a glass! That's very dirty! You put fish on your sex, you put meat on your sex!" [referring to SX-70 polaroids Bruno published]—that's nothing compared to what happens in Rwanda in Africa where many people get killed. I kill people in my drawings, but they are just images—lines on paper.

I also show the bad side, the dark side of "true love"

because I don't think true love exists! For example, when people look at pin-up girls, they're imagining the vulva and having sex with the girl—that's already what they have in their mind. When I redo these photos in my way, I just add more tits, draw a larger vulva, add scratches. And even though it's what a lot of people have on their mind, it's unacceptable. By adding all the scratches, I make the *form* dirty as well as the content.

Self-publishing is good, but sometimes it feels like there's too much to read—so much, that nobody knows what's going on anymore.

I also like to show intimacy, because people rarely show that. When you love somebody you know how they do things: when you are intimate with someone there is no taboo about watching that loved one shit or put on lipstick. In life, many things are taboo, talking about how you shit, how much money you earn, etc. Showing your girlfriend at home shitting or pissing reflects a certain kind of truth. People ask, "Why are

you interested in this?" I think everybody is interested—the difference is that I show it.

♦ *V: For the past 20 years, you never cared that your books lost money?*
♦ BR: No. I have a regular job to make money, so I don't have to compromise. If somebody asks me to do a book, but says, "I don't want that on the cover," I just say, "Forget it—I'll do it myself." If they let me do what I want, that would be okay.

The best compensation is making contact with people. You need people to see your work; you do things to be shown. Although . . . I was reading yesterday about a girl who was knitting a large fantastic hanging. Somebody from the Museum of Fabric wanted to display it, and she said, "First let me finish it." When he came back she showed him a big pile of wool—her idea of finishing the work was to unravel it! To her, the act of destruction had completed the artwork.

However, most people do what they do for money. Some people, like Matt Groening, started out just drawing for themselves, but now he's making a lot of money with the Simpsons. Mariscal from Spain is the same; he was doing underground comics and now he has his own Disney-like company producing toys, furniture, fabric, etc. All cartoonists want to have their own Disney company! Once Gary Panter said some-

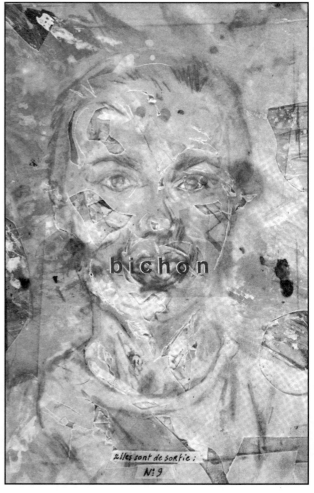

thing very funny; he said, "I want to be the Walt Disney of Death." Even he wanted to make money with that concept! [laughs]

♦ **V: When you take the rides at Disneyland, a lot of the fun derives from the fear of death.**

♦ BR: Now, everything is all mixed up and nobody knows why they do things anymore, except out of self-interest or self-promotion and to make money, of course. Nobody knows how to judge what is good and what is not good. It was easier in the past, like back in the hippie days where the music and graphics supported each other and "made sense." Even in punk, there was a certain aesthetic—punk music made you destroy pictures, for example. In graphics there was a lot of shouting and protesting through visual deconstruction . . . taking images and phrases from official media and making them say something completely different, like in a collage. Now, it's very difficult to know what will "work" anymore. Self-publishing is good, but sometimes it feels like there's too much to read—so much, that nobody knows what's going on anymore. ▪V▪

SOME OF BRUNO'S SELF-PUBLISHED BOOKS:

Elles Sont de Sortie, numéro 45 "Dead end Loves" September 1996

E.S.D.S., numéro 43 "Tortures Nazies Maladis" July 1995

E.S.D.S., numéro 41 "Polaroï pornographiques recadrés mâle et femelle" June 1995

E.S.D.S., numéro 40 "Dirty Love Autopsy" 1994

E.S.D.S., numéro 36 "Photomatons pornographique" and "Mort pornographique" April 1992

E.S.D.S., numéro 22 "Négres vulves Noires bites" October 1988

E.S.D.S., numéro 19 "Kolor Love, rose mâle, bleu femelle" November 1986

E.S.D.S., numéro 16-18 "Femmes déguisées en femmes Hommes déguisés en hommes" 1984

E.S.D.S., numéro 14 "Afrikan Baohaos numéro 1" January 1983

"Graphic production. 73-83. 1000 dessins sauvages" April 1983

E.S.D.S., "Nathalie 1" 1982

E.S.D.S., numéro 11 "Sexy Politzeï" September 1982

E.S.D.S., numéro 10 "Pornographie Catholique" 1982

E.S.D.S., numéro 9 "Bichon" 1980

"Néon de Suro fullet monografic de divulgacio" by Bruno Richard 1980

E.S.D.S., numéro 8 "Portraits. Suicides Graphikik (sic) Bichon Dora Maar récupération Spécial veufs" December 1979

E.S.D.S., numéro 7 "Jeux" 1979

E.S.D.S., "French Magazine of Love" August 1979

E.S.D.S., numéro 5 "Aventures Vacances Loisirs" 1978

E.S.D.S., numéro 4 "Santé et Maladie" 1977

E.S.D.S., "Spasmes" 1977

E.S.D.S., numéro 1 1977

International Mail Art

After 15 years in Dallas, John Held, Jr. recently moved to San Francisco. He publishes a zine about mail art, *Bibliozine* (currently up to 52 issues), and in 1991 published a hardback reference book, *Mail Art: An Annotated Bibliography,* which lists relevant books, magazine and newspaper articles, and catalog essays. An enthusiastic mail art correspondent and world traveler, John may be contacted at PO Box 410837, San Francisco CA 94141.

◆ *VALE: What is mail art?*

◆ JOHN HELD, JR: There are probably as many definitions of mail art as there are people who are doing it. When you give a definition of mail art, it tells more about you than it does the medium. In *my* definition, it's a process rather than a product; mail art is the process of interaction with an international network of artists. The focus is on the transfer of aesthetic information. Mail art isn't merely postal based: there's mail art on the Internet and there's fax mail art. Mail art can adapt itself to all these different communication technologies because it's not really about the mail; it's about information transfer.

> **When you give a definition of mail art, it tells more about *you* than it does the medium.**

There are a lot of genres within mail art: zines, artists' publications, artists' postage stamps, rubber stamp use, tourism (which is mail artists meeting each other in an expanded performance setting), performance art, sound art (a lot of cassettes are exchanged in mail art)—the list goes on and on. All these kinds of *marginal art forms* are harbored within the mail art medium.

I've always had trouble with this question: "Should

I capitalize the term 'Mail Art'?" Sometimes I want to capitalize it because I think it should be recognized as an art movement like Dada, Fluxus, or Nouveau Realism—all of which have been influences on mail art and are "capitalized" art movements. But lately I've been thinking that it's not really a movement. Dada, for instance, lasted approximately seven years; Nouveau Realism five years; and Fluxus began around 1960 and some people say it died with George Maciunas in 1978 or so. But mail art has been going on since Ray Johnson developed and globally expanded the art form in the late '40s. That's 50 years ago!

Ray Johnson is the figure most commonly identified with founding the mail art movement. He was a student at Black Mountain College in the late '40s. His classmates included John Cage, Robert Rauschenberg and Merce Cunningham. Josef Albers was one of his teachers. Johnson was very much in the center of this new milieu that was forming around Cage, who was also very important to Fluxus. The Fluxus art movement had its beginnings in a class that Cage taught at the New School for Social Research in New York in 1957. George Brecht, Dick Higgins, and Allan Kaprow were among the people in that class. Then George Maciunas came in later and developed Fluxus. Johnson was also involved with Fluxus, but he was too much of an iconoclast to join a movement.

There's a story that Johnson told a younger artist shortly before he died. He said that he started mail art when he was living with John Cage in the early '50s.

32 USA

John Held, Jr. Photo: V. Vale; Illustration: Yimi Tong

sQUiRts

A children's journal of flows

- Public Masturbation
- Rioting as Potlatch
- Exposing the Waco Whack-off
- Anal-sewing with Mother Theresa

Cage had gotten a letter from Robert Rauschenberg with just a piece of gold foil in it. I've also heard that Johnson took the idea of mail art from A.M. Fine, a poet in New York City circles, who was doing poetry postcards. Johnson himself said that he was doing mail art much earlier in the '40s with another artist friend named Arthur Segunda. With Johnson now deceased, it's pretty hard to pin down exactly how mail art started—at least in his eyes. He was the type of artist who was always perpetuating a kind of mythology; he would never give a straight answer.

> **[Ray Johnson] relished being "the most famous unknown artist in America."**

There's lots of precedents for mail art. In the 1800s, the American painter Frederic Remington was decorating his mail; Van Gogh did this as well. In 1915, Marcel Duchamp glued together four postcards and sent the resulting "object" to his patron, Walter Arensberg. The writing in the postcard bore no resemblance to "normal" communication: none of the verbs matched the nouns. When Duchamp was in Argentina, he sent a book to his sister, Suzanne, and told her to hang it on a clothesline.

♦ *V: You visited Ray Johnson in 1980. What was his Long Island house like?*

♦ JH: It was a little pink suburban house with no furniture. There were cardboard boxes everywhere.

♦ *V: [laughs] I take it he was a bachelor—*

♦ JH: Yeah, he was a bachelor and he was gay. A lot of people in that circle were. It's no secret that Cage, Rauschenberg, Ray Johnson, et al were gay. In their cultural milieu, they had that sexual orientation bonding them, as well as their artistic outlook.

Ray Johnson did very sophisticated art work in addition to mail art. The more sophisticated pieces are being stressed lately because there are people trying to market him now. He would never participate in promoting himself while he was alive, and thwarted a lot of efforts to make himself known. He relished being "the most famous unknown artist in America." [laughs]

♦ *V: Didn't Ray Johnson jump off a bridge a couple of years ago?*

♦ JH: January 13, 1995. It was never confirmed that he purposely jumped off the bridge, because no one witnessed the event. Most people think it was a suicide.

♦ *V: How did he support himself?*

♦ JH: It's funny, he used to always cry "Poverty!" Yet when he died there was $400,000 in his bank account. That's kind of a mystery. Somebody said that his parents died and left him a house in Detroit. Perhaps Rauschenberg gave him a picture and he sold it. A lot of influential people were his friends. I've never heard any real explanation.

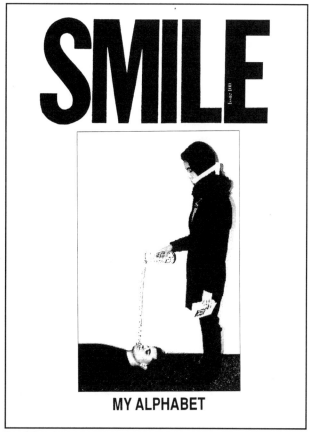

MY ALPHABET

A *Smile* is a *Smile* is a *Smile* is a *Smile*. Covers of *Smile*: (from left to right) issue #9, #7, #6 and #100, each produced by a different person.

Anyway, mail art has been going on for about 50 years. I think it's more like painting or sculpture or printmaking—all these activities that are not capitalized. It's an art medium.

♦ **V: A medium of expression as opposed to a theoretical movement—**

♦ JH: Exactly. There's no theory concerned with mail art at all; it's an open system that anybody (ranging from professional artists to senior citizens) can feed into, and doesn't exclude people. It's like sculpture, where you can use wood, ceramics, various metals, etc in any style.

♦ **V: Who's involved in mail art?**

♦ JH: Most people are from very small towns in places like Japan or Poland, who are reaching out to other people. Their correspondents become their closest friends. Mail art is a very life-impacting art form: the avant-garde's dream of blending art and life. The act of letter writing is very much an activity in daily life, and some people say that mail art isn't art at all. It definitely is a cultural activity. It's a non-commodity art because it isn't sold; it's a gift among friends. Sometimes it's stretching it to call it "art"; mail art, like the Fluxus movement, really tries to break down those boundaries between art and non-art, as well as art and life. It's a boundary breaker, just as the mail goes across countries.

♦ **V: Internet activity on the computer is protected under international law. Many people, who would otherwise have been censored by their governments,** *have a forum for their ideas and an international audience to expose them to. Does mail art ever become political?*

♦ JH: Correspondents avoid certain divisive political and religious issues—but sometimes they find *you.* Clemente Padin, an active networker from Montevideo , Uruguay, was arrested in the mid-'70s for satirizing the military. He was imprisoned, tortured and released only after a world-wide mail art letter-writing campaign to secure his freedom. Genesis P-Orridge was brought to trial for sending supposedly obscene postcards through the mail.

Mail art is a very life impacting art form: the avant-garde's dream of blending art and life.

Sometimes you get giddy with the freedom of expression. What is trying to be conveyed is a kind of universal brotherhood with a shared interest in art; a utopian community-making. Mail art is very much its own community. It has developed its own myths; it has its own patron saints like Duchamp and Johnson; there's a lot of shared imagery that goes back and forth. Mail art is very anti-copyright, so people pick up an image and then modify it and send it around. It's also anti-entropic: you put something in motion and it continues to grow and transform in ways that the originator would never be able to imagine. That's one of the beauties of mail art: things get so mixed up and there's a loss of ego for the betterment of the mail art community.

One of the important modes of expression in mail art is rubber stamps; *everybody* seems to have a rubber stamp. In Eastern Europe, it was very difficult to obtain rubber stamps; bureaucrats there keep them locked up in special rubber stamp vaults. So, mail art artists started carving erasers to make their own rubber stamps.

♦ **V: *The rubber stamp is a cheap way to mass-produce an image or idea . . .***

♦ JH: It's perfect. And it's also a way for someone to develop an identity within the mail art network. People might not know you as a person, but they recognize your rubber stamp. Ray Johnson's trademark, for example, was a bunny head.

Rubber stamp history in art goes back to Kurt Schwitters, who was using them in his collages around 1919. There was a big show of rubber stamp art at the French National Postal Museum in 1995. It included contributions from Russian Constructivists, Leger, Warhol, Arman, the Nouveau Realists, Fluxus, etc. There's a trail of rubber stamp usage that runs through modern art, but it really burst forth with mail art.

A lot of mail art deals with communication theory, and one part of it says: to get your message across, you have to have a very short, succinct message used repeatedly so that it becomes recognizable. You're dealing with a lot of different cultures within mail art; it's not primarily a literary medium because you're crossing a lot of language boundaries. You need that short burst of visual statement to be effective, and in that regard the rubber stamp is very effective.

♦ **V: *There have been a small number of rubber stamp art shows—***

♦ JH: And a lot of people don't want mail art "historified," as they consider it a very fluid, noncommercial medium. They're afraid that if mail art is historified, the next step is commodification—

♦ **V: *People will be marketing all these rare Ray Johnson letters—***

♦ JH: —which is already happening. There are a lot of purists in mail art who think that the only mail art show should be: no fees, everything mailed in gets shown without "critical" judgment, etc. Which is exactly what Ray Johnson did when he organized the first mail art show at the Whitney Museum in 1970. Most curators judge the artwork submitted and decide what to show, whereas in mail art there is no judgment passed. Nothing is sold, so you don't have that star system in place. However, a lot of current "art stars" have done mail art in the past: Gilbert and George, Christo . . .

♦ **V: *Can you sum up the influence of mail art?***

♦ JH: Mail art had an impact on punk graphics and punk zines; people like Genesis P-Orridge and Monte Cazazza were big mail art participants in the early '70s before punk. Another impact was on the rubber stamp art movement, which is still proliferating. And then there's the Internet.

♦ **V: *There is a lot of publishing going on in mail art. What are some of the different approaches?***

♦ JH: I have over 555 mail art periodicals and zines from 27 different countries in my archive. I'll try to summarize some of the different types:

1) *Found Art* uses everyday materials, such as pages from telephone books. Since a lot of the content is cross-cultural, images appear more frequently than text. There's a mix of the cultural, political and social.

2) *Hybrid* (Canadian) Colin Hinz was into science fiction, so his publication is a blend of mail art and science fiction. It was mimeographed, like old science-fiction fanzines.

3) *Assembling* The late Guillermo Deisler was a Chilean communist allied with the Pinochet government in Chile. When Pinochet was assassinated, Deisler had to leave for Bulgaria and then East Germany. He was very influential in spreading mail art throughout Eastern Europe. His assembling magazine, *UNI/vers,* contains visual poetry by other artists; he assembled it all and sent copies to all the contributors.

4) *Multiple Origins. Smile* is an example of a zine

Cover of Held's book on mail art.

of multiple origins; people all over the world published *Smile* zines which had nothing to do with each other except they all share the same title. I have a whole collection of these *Smiles* from different countries.

Stewart Home published a British *Smile;* he also tried to apply the same idea (of multiple origins) to the punk band format. He started a band called White Colors and tried to get other people to start bands with the same title, but it didn't work as well. Home borrowed this idea from Neoism, a "movement" where anybody could publish or create under the name Monty Cantsin. This idea is anti-entropic in that you publish a magazine and it doesn't just sit on the shelf, it inspires other people to publish their own magazines using the same title. It also mystifies a lot of people: "What's going on here: all these *Smile* magazines from all over the place?"

A more complex example of an assembling publication was done by P. Petasz from Poland; I have an example dating from around 1980. He set up a "Common Press" with himself as central coordinator, and assigned numbers to different people who each became the editor.

There were certain rules: you can't charge money, you have to print a certain amount of copies, etc. Every publication was different, but they all bore the rubric, "Common Press." There's about 60 of them. But it was always Petasz you wrote to and said, "I want to publish a Common Press," and he would say, "Okay, you're Number 42." This is one of the most sought-after "collectibles" in mail art; there are people trying to collect all of them.

Zines are all about community building and finding other kindred spirits.

♦ *V: It seems that mail art and zines have a lot in common—*
♦ JH: A key idea here is that zines aren't just an American phenomenon. There's a lot of cross-cultural, international interaction in the zine world—to me, that's the most interesting aspect. Zines are a way of communicating messages that aren't being broadcast by the mass media. So, it's interesting to get zines in the mail to see what other people are thinking, but it's especially interesting to see what people are thinking in other countries—culturally, politically and economically.

Zines are all about community building and finding other kindred spirits. One nice thing is: with zines and mail art you don't have to be the best-looking person in the world, or dress right. Any "status" has to do with your ideas. And when you finally meet somebody after 10 years of writing to them, you have this tremendous history together, so you naturally embrace! Well, it doesn't always work out, of course, but when it does it's so rewarding. So many times I've just paid for a train or plane ticket, and crashed at correspondents' homes. They're all artists, so they know all the most interesting places to visit, off the beaten track.

Mail art especially means so much to people in places like the former Soviet Union, e.g., Estonia or Yugoslavia. In fact, I went to Yugoslavia in '94 right after the embargo ended. Somebody there did an interview with me and said, "It seems in your travels you always go to the outer corners." I replied, "I go to the outer corners to discover the inner self." If you can reach people who are separated from you geographically, linguistically and culturally, and establish some sort of bond between yourself and them, think what you could do with another American!

♦ *V: It's really an integration of art and life, without the mediation of museum-business culture—*
♦ JH: Right. The "Art World" is so uninteresting; all you do in it is promote yourself. Whereas mail artists promote mail art and the network. So many people are willing to share; it becomes easy to publish a zine like *Smile* where the effort is cooperative and interactive. You're doing it for the community and not just for yourself. ◼

JOHN HELD GLOSSARY

Albers, Josef (1888–1976): As a painter, Albers was described as the "nearest person in contemporary art to a technician." He joined the Bauhaus in 1920 and left for America soon after Hitler closed down the school in 1933. He is best known for his famous and endless series "Homage to the Square."

Black Mountain College, North Carolina: Much of the work reflected interest in Zen, chance operations in art and a move towards integration of the arts.

Fluxus: Began as a loosely organized cooperative of artists held together by their common opposition to the traditionally established art world. Concerned with the fusion of art and life, Fluxus sought wider accessibility and social responsibility for art. As a result, the work is often elusive, transitory and conceptual. An international art movement that began in the early '60s, it included such artists as Yoko Ono, Nam June Paik and Dick Higgins.

Maciunas, George (1931–1978): A leader, organizer and theorist who was a central figure in the Fluxus movement. He has been credited for coining the term in 1961.

Candi Strecker

A pioneer of the current zine scene, Candi Strecker has been publishing zines since 1979. Her postmodern pop sociology humor publication, *Sidney Suppey's Quarterly and Confused Pet Monthly*, is still being produced, and the two classic issues of *It's A Wonderful Lifestyle*, her '70s zine, are still available. Send a SASE for a catalog or $2 for the latest issue of the *SSQ&CPM* to Candi Strecker, PO Box 515, Brisbane CA 94005-0515. The holder of an advanced degree in library science, Candi lives with her husband Matthew Householder (whose hobby is restoring and dealing in early portable radios and other electronic arcana) and her 4-year-old daughter Nicola (named after Mr. Tesla, of course).

♦ *VALE: Why did you begin publishing a zine?*

♦ CANDI STRECKER: I was 23 years old, out of school and working my first job. All my library school friends had moved to different towns. I was feeling lonely and out of touch and I wanted to *stay* in touch, so I got the idea to publish something and send it to all my friends. I happened to be working in an office that had xerox machines and typewriters—that was as advanced as the technology was back then! I was working in the editorial offices of *Mathematical Reviews*, a major publication surveying the math field, and they were switching over to a primitive version of computerized typesetting at the time. They used a special IBM typewriter that was a piece of "interim" technology—it produced typesetting-quality output.

♦ *V: I think it's called a "proportional spacing" typewriter—*

♦ CS: That sounds right. Anyway, I would sneak in after-hours and use that to typeset maybe one little paragraph—I was so shy and nervous in those days. I was fascinated by the idea that if you had access to the right equipment, you could create a publication that was indistinguishable from something officially published by "The System." This felt like an immense power, even better than being able to print your own money—it was as if you could print counterfeit *ideas!*

At the same time I started playing around with cutting and pasting—that was another powerful kind of magic! You could take a grocery store ad and totally alter its original meaning—then if you xeroxed it, the paste-up lines were invisible and it looked completely original. So rubber cement, xerox machines and typewriters all came together in March '79, and I did my first zine. I made just eight copies and sent them to people I knew. After that, for the next eight months I was actually publishing monthly!

♦ *V: What was the content?*

♦ CS: I was trying to do humor writing—the kind of thing that people still put in their first issues: funny newspaper headlines, weird little articles clipped from the mainstream press about gruesome car accidents, stupid criminals who leave their credit cards behind, etc. I also liked clippings that highlighted the enormous *banality* of everyday life. I included small record reviews because I was interested in punk rock—it was a big deal to me, although I wasn't as involved as someone who would start a band or devote their whole life to going to clubs. My zine was fairly brief in that first year—six or eight pages.

♦ *V: What was it called?*

♦ CS: *Sidney Suppey's Quarterly and Confused Pet Monthly*, which I'm *still* publishing, though approximately *yearly* instead of monthly. That's just a name that came into my head totally out of the blue! The first half was based on a custom from the last century, which you can still see in older magazines like *Harpers* or *Forbes*, where the founders of a magazine got to name it after themselves. I had an image of this Victorian patroness of the arts named Miss Sidney Suppey. It was fun to imagine her hair up in a bun, like Miss Manners, funding this little arts magazine. This was a notion that had nothing to do with what was in the pages. Anyway, that accounts for half of the name. The other half was an idea for a psychology magazine for pet owners called *The Confused Pet Monthly*. Then I had an idea that struck me as just hilarious: what if these two magazines had *merged* at some time in the past, resulting in a ridiculously unwieldy name? Actually, I thought both of these up years before I ever did a zine; I was reading science-fiction zines and said to myself, "If I ever do a zine, I'll remember these names." And so I did. But I wish I'd thought of a simple one-word title instead, because now I'm stuck giving this explanation 20 years later! [laughs]

♦ *V: At first, you weren't charging money for your zines?*
♦ CS: Absolutely not! It took *years* before I started charging people. At first all the copies went to friends, and later many copies were "trades." One of the nice things about doing zines is, once you get into the network, you have something to trade with other people who do zines. I still had a retro '60s notion that it was a bad thing to charge money—this was just something nice that I was doing for free. But once I got it into my head to charge money, I was a much happier person about doing the work! [laughs]

When I was first doing a zine in 1979 . . . it was it was almost impossible to explain that I wanted things copied on *both* sides of the page!

♦ *V: The word "zine" was not always in people's vocabularies. One of the first xerox punk zines I remember seeing was* Sniffin' Glue *from England, which started in 1976. Xerox technology hadn't been available for very long—it wasn't around in the '60s, as far as I know—*
♦ CS: There must have been some point when xerox machines became really *available* to people. Office copy machines were often strictly regulated, so that you had to be sneaky and bold to make even a *single* non-work-related copy for yourself. When I was first doing a zine in 1979, there was a copy shop on the first floor of the building where I worked, and it was almost impossible to explain that I wanted things copied on *both* sides of the page! They seemed to think that

Candi Strecker with portable radio collection. Photo: Olivier Robert

Cartoon by Candi from *SSQ&CPM Vol. 5 #3*

was their use of mimeograph machines. There's a cult of mimeography even *now*; some people who do science-fiction zines make a big deal about doing it on mimeo (not xerox or desktop publishing)—even going so far as to get this certain kind of paper that isn't manufactured anymore, called *Twiltone*. It was like blotter paper but thinner, and had a real "spongy" or pulpy quality to it. It gets nice mimeo results. But because of their mimeo tradition they ignored xerox for years—though it seemed to me an obviously superior printing technology.

In the mid-'70s when I was peripherally involved with science-fiction fandom, I occasionally saw some of these fanzines but never much liked what I saw. Most of them seemed very dorky and middle-aged to me. Because of the long history of sci-fi fandom, they were filled with a lot of in-jokes and internal references, and as a young Turk—a young *punk*—I felt, "To hell with *that!*" However, I did like the idea that you could publish something yourself and circulate it—that had appeal.

I've always been a hugely voracious reader—the kind of person who checks out the maximum number of books from the library every week. In the late '60s, when I was in junior high, I had two gal friends who were into *Star Trek*. We would write our own little six-page scripts about Spock kissing someone (or whatever) and show them to each other, and in a way this was similar to doing a zine. Anyway, that probably led me to explore the shelves labeled "science fiction."

In high school, my best friend and I read a lot of science fiction. Neither of us had a lot of money, so we would buy different books and then trade them—that way we got double the reading for our dollar. Also, we were both heavily into Marvel comic books and that was another fun obsession. The fact that I was into "guy" things like reading science fiction or comic books didn't faze me—I was such a weirdo in high school and so totally on the margins of society that I couldn't do anything to make it *worse!*

xeroxing was only for archiving purposes, like making copies of tax forms or magazine articles. They hadn't yet grasped the concept that it was a *printing press* that people could use to produce their own publications . . .

Recently I had the idea of publishing a "greatest hits" compilation of my earliest zines, which have been out of print for years. I went through all my back issues, taking notes, and spotted the very first time that I used the term "zine"—in 1979, the year I started publishing. If I used it then, I must have thought that readers would understand what I was talking about. So I actually have some lexicographical evidence!

♦ V: *Before you did your publication, were you reading other zines?*

♦ CS: That depends on what you mean. In science-fiction fandom, the fans have a long tradition of self-publishing going back to the '30s and even beyond. One strange feature of science-fiction zine publishing then

♦ **V:** *But you had at least one girl friend who shared your interests and supported them—*

♦ CS: Yeah, but I think I would've done this anyway, because I was that kind of person. Anyway, I had a lot of science fiction reading under my belt by the time I went to college and met my husband, who showed up at school with a bookcase of 300 science-fiction paperbacks. I hadn't been into accumulating books quite *that* heavily, and I was really impressed that he had all these books and had read them—including *Moderan* (by David R. Bunch) which he had read in high school.

I was such a weirdo in high school and so totally on the margins of society that I couldn't do anything to make it *worse!*

♦ **V:** *When did you get married?*

♦ CS: My husband and I have been married 20 years—we're the oldest couple of our generation! [laughs] We met the third day of our freshman year at Kent State. I was a teenage bride when I was 19—isn't that weird?

♦ **V:** *You went to Kent State with DEVO—*

♦ CS: Actually, they were out of school already, but they were still hanging around. I first saw them perform in 1977 when they were just local dorks, and this was very inspirational to me. They would play some bar and get a million beer bottles thrown at them!

♦ **V:** *Wasn't Kent State a "progressive" college?*

♦ CS: It has that reputation because of the shootings, but it was not cutting-edge. It was more of a "cow-town school"—like going to Chico State in California. Most of the students were from a blue-collar background, and a large number were commuting from home, so it felt like a community college. There were some great teachers and hip people there, but it was predominantly an educational school to churn out school teachers for the next generation.

♦ **V:** *How did you find out about Marvel Comics?*

♦ CS: In the late 1960s when comics were being publicized in other media for the first time. Rock stars would say, "This song was influenced by *Spiderman*," or, "I like to get high and read the *Fantastic Four* or *Dr. Strange*." A kind of cross-fertilization was happening; for example, in one issue of *Dr. Strange*, the writer Tom Wolfe makes a walk-on appearance! A lot of fresh talent was coming into the comics field, with writers like Roy Thomas behind artists like Barry Smith, Neal Adams and Frank Frazetta, who were creating jaw-dropping drawings. That time was a high-water mark for comics—the early good years of the *X-Men*, for example.

When I was in the eighth grade, I learned a useful trick: if I read in the media that "college kids are into such and such," it turned out to be exactly right for my reading level. I remember reading that "college kids are into Vonnegut," so *I* got into Vonnegut. I read that "college kids are into Marvel Comics," so I checked that out.

♦ **V:** *Were there many women writing science fiction?*

♦ CS: There were a few, like JOANNA RUSS or URSULA K. LEGUIN, but women were not the mainstream. Nevertheless, the late '60s and early '70s were excellent years to be reading science fiction. There was a "New Wave" movement of experimental and groundbreaking writing, and J.G. Ballard was part of that. I read everybody who was in the *Dangerous Visions* anthologies: Roger Zelazny, Samuel R. Delany, Thomas Disch, Gene Wolfe, Philip K. Dick, John Brunner (my copy of *Stand On Zanzibar* was all marked up with my comments). That's *still* a great book, and personally it had a lot of impact on me. Most of Brunner's books have a conventional narrative line, but that one was more in the style of Tom Wolfe's "New Journalism," told in fragments with a real kaleidoscopic effect, and was a lot of fun to read.

Stand On Zanzibar includes a character named Chad C. Mulligan who's a renegade pop-sociologist. Within the novel's universe, he's the author of the famous book *You're An Ignorant Idiot*, and he functions as sort of a truth-teller character. Every few chapters he is brought in to say something clever that explains this future world. I remember thinking, "That's what *I* would love to be: the person who looks around and makes sense of everything in such a brilliant way that it permanently affects the way people see the world they live in."

♦ **V:** *In your zine, you kind of do that—*

♦ CS: As much as possible he's been a role model for me. He made a *living* at it, though!

♦ **V:** *You were somewhat involved in science-fiction zines, and then you got into the punk rock scene— why didn't more people do that?*

♦ CS: Science-fiction zines were very introverted; the people never seemed to look beyond the sci-fi circle. So

In the late 1960s a kind of cross-fertilization was happening; for example, in one issue of *Dr. Strange*, the writer Tom Wolfe makes a walk-on appearance!

in 1977 when punk was starting, I thought, "How can you be talking about *The Future* (allegedly) and not see this Big Thing that's happening?" There's a weird unacknowledged conservatism in science fiction.

♦ **V:** *Perhaps it's because a lot of sci-fi fans were nerdy white males without women in their lives—*

♦ CS: That's the stereotype, but science-fiction fandom has really changed since the early '70s *because* women have joined in. It used to be a totally male

province, like model trains. My generation changed the face of that forever. Now at science-fiction conventions, the attendees are divided about 50/50. The genre itself has grown so big that it has internal gender divisions—there's "hard" technology sci-fi with a mostly male audience, and a huge growth in fantasy fiction which attracts more women.

We saw ourselves as a new generation: we could read *and* we could dance and wear black leather jackets.

Another thing that has changed the face of sci-fi fandom is computers. Science-fiction fans used to be such nerds, totally on the fringes of society and working weird little odd jobs. Very few of them had what you would call *careers*; their skills and personalities put them on the fringes of the working world. Now their computer skills are in great demand and they have disposable income to spend at conventions. Nobody ever talks about this, but it's a major change. Today this outcast social group has an enormous economic foundation.

♦ *V: And more women are involved—*

♦ CS: There are definitely more female writers. The genre is open to female writers. More fans take feminist issues seriously and discuss them. But in a funny way, science-fiction fandom (at least at conventions) is more of a social/party scene than a venue for serious literary criticism. Just as at punk rock shows, while people talked about the music and the revolution they hoped it was going to lead to, they were also hoping to get laid that night! [laughs]

♦ *V: Back in '79 when you did your first zine, you weren't doing it to be part of a scene—*

♦ CS: Absolutely not. The only zine network I knew about was the science-fiction fanzines, and I didn't want to be part of that. Eventually, however, I discovered a few cool people within science-fiction fandom, and we called each other "the punk rock fans." We saw ourselves as a new generation: we could read *and* we could dance and wear black leather jackets. These people were the first audience for my zine, outside of my personal friends and co-workers. I started out making eight copies but was quickly up to 20, mailing them cross-country and so forth.

At that time, my favorite technological discovery was press-on letters—I just worshipped them because they made your publication look so *real*. If I could manage to get $2.50 together, I'd rush out and buy a sheet of Letraset and use *everything* on the sheet, including the borders and punctuation marks—that's how poor I was. I got quite clever about using every bit.

♦ *V: Your first issue has an article about different kinds of paper clips. How did you research that information?*

♦ CS: Actually, I just made it up! [laughs] It was a *humor* article. That issue was done on three different manual typewriters. I included the "solution" to a puzzle from the previous issue, which of course didn't exist, and a recipe for angel-food pie.

♦ *V: You also "borrowed" an editorial from a March '79 issue of* Fast Service, *the magazine for fast-food restaurant managers—*

♦ CS: Working in libraries, I'd discovered all these weird trade magazines for every possible industry. One of my favorites was *Modern Plastics*—I always thought that would be the greatest name for a band. Actually, there *was* a Japanese band called the Plastics.

♦ *V: Your second issue has a critique of television. What are your thoughts on television?*

♦ CS: I watch huge amounts of it! [laughs] What better window is there onto the world we live in?

♦ *V: But TV keeps you from doing real work—*

♦ CS: I was in a bookstore yesterday reading a book in which the author claimed a lot of kids in high TV-viewing households also do a lot of reading on their own—they just tune the TV out. Maybe that's the best thing you can do: learn early to ignore it. My family had the TV on day and night when I was growing up, yet I did nothing but read. This may defy all common sense . . .

♦ *V: In your second issue, you also used quotes from a 1950s* Reader's Digest.

It was hard for me to tell anyone I was doing a zine. Especially because no one would have known what I meant.

♦ CS: Old magazines supply great materials such as the weird graphics in the ads. My zine hobby has given me an excuse to collect boxes and boxes of them, from the '30s through the '70s. Anything interesting that I discovered I would write about, like *The Dreams of Donald Roller Wilson*, a book about a modern surrealist-like painter who lives in Arkansas—check him out! In my first few issues I was very "serious" about being humorous; I thought it was my job to enlighten the world through satire. After a few issues I began "loosening up" and enjoying the freedom to put in anything I wanted to.

♦ *V: You mixed in recipes, collages and headlines. What feedback were you getting?*

♦ CS: I was plowing ahead without it. I think most of the people who received those early issues didn't quite know what to make of them! But from the science-fiction/punk circles I gained my own personal gadfly and

THRIFT SHOP CONFIDENTIAL
— PART II —
STILL MORE FUTURE COLLECTIBLES

"HAVE YOU EVER NOTICED THAT 90% OF ALL THRIFT SHOPS HAVE AT LEAST ONE BREAST PUMP?"
—REID OF DICKTOOL, IN CORRESPONDENCE

CHINESE CHECKERBOARDS! MASS-PRODUCED, COLORFULLY PRINTED ONES LOOK GREAT HUNG ON THE WALL.

CHINK[] CHE

SHRINER GLASSES
USUALLY HAVE SOMETHING TO DO WITH CAMPAIGNING FOR LODGE OFFICES.
ELECT EUGENE "BUD" OSTERWALD 19 71 GRAND VIZIER AL-KAZAM TEMPLE
ACTUALLY, ANYTHING WITH A SHRINER OR FEZ MOTIF IS PRETTY GROOVY.

CANDI STRECKER · 1991

SOCK MONKEY DOLLS
HAVING ONE SITTING ON YOUR COUCH IS JUST REGRESSIVE NOSTALGIA. BUT 15 OR 20 IS A SERIOUS DESIGN STATEMENT.

CLIP-ON BED LAMPS
THESE ELECTRIC READING LAMPS THAT ATTACH TO THE HEADBOARD OF A BED ALWAYS REMIND ME OF SCREWBALL COMEDY FILMS.

PAIRS OF HANDCRAFTED "GAY 90'S" PLATES, DECORATED WITH FELT & GINGHAM & SEQUINS. WEIRDLY APPEALING.
George   Doris

"LIVE SLOW, DIE OLD, AND LEAVE A GREAT ESTATE SALE." —CS

Cartoon by Candi from *SSQ&CPM Vol. 5 #5*

supporter, Luke McGuff, who was always telling me, "Publish more! Do this, and do that!" I didn't think that *all* of his suggestions were good, but he was always on my back about how I should keep going. He began publishing a zine, *Mollocca*, shortly after I did, and he still puts out publications. [Luke's address: POB 31848, Seattle WA 98103-1848. Currently, he produces the zines *Project Z* and *Minifictions*.]

♦ V: *You ripped off graphics from slick magazines—*

♦ CS: And subverted the texts as well. I got to be pretty good at parodying fashion magazine writing—I think I had that down cold.

♦ V: *One of your fashion parodies reads: "Here she is showing off her latest pick-up, while modeling a typically tasteful outfit which she calls, 'perfect for the everyday things that I love to do—going to rummage sales and seedy drive-ins, sneering at members of the upper middle class, or just turning over the compost heap.' Her beauty secrets: natural mango, tongue-strengthener, rubber spiders . . ." You were going to garage sales, partly out of poverty—*

♦ CS: But also because it was the thing I loved to do! Ann Arbor was a really expensive place to live, and we were so poor. A large proportion of students at the University of Michigan came from New York. They were rich, elite, "wallowing-in-money" kids. You could practically live off their garbage. Whereas Kent, Ohio, had been very cheap; everybody was blue-collar and living on peanut butter. At the time, poverty was considered very hip, so even rich kids would pretend to be poor. When I moved to Ann Arbor I had a sudden shock: suddenly it was the preppie, pre-Yuppie years!

So, in irritation, I wrote a rant in Vol. 1 No. 8: "1. Move away from Ann Arbor and make a lot of money. 2. Come back with the money and buy a lot of nice things. 3. Take them all back home with you."

♦ V: *Look, this early issue is mimeographed—*

♦ CS: It's *ditto*: the purple-printing stuff teachers use to print up worksheets in elementary school. Cheaper and lower-tech, with even fewer images and "repeats" than from mimeo. Someone gave me a ditto machine, and for awhile I was including some dittoed pages in my zine. But I loved the xerox machine because it could reproduce my collages; a ditto machine did text only.

♦ V: *This article, written when a lot of people were reading Robert Anton Wilson's* **Illuminatus Trilogy,** *is still relevant: "The Three Fallacies of Conspiracy Theory: 1. That your life will suddenly become more interesting. 2. That you will be selected to be let in on the Big Secret. 3. That everything you have ever heard, read, or seen will suddenly fall into a Meaningful Pattern." Are people still obsessed by conspiracy theories?*

♦ CS: Yes, but now they're right-wingers instead of left-wingers. Hasn't all the Republican fervor of the past few years been fueled by conspiracy theory? You know, those way-out people who are moving to Idaho with guns and enough supplies to stock a bomb shelter.

♦ V: *The zine* **Paranoia** *focuses on conspiracy theories, as does* **Flatland** *. . . You did a review of Samuel Delany's* **Dhalgren**—

♦ CS: That's in an article I wrote called "Punk Rock as Foreshadowed in Science Fiction," and *Dhalgren* seemed very punkish to me. I was too young to write

THE ENDS OF AN ERA

No one knows what possessed my otherwise un-flashy father when he bought a 1956 Ford Crown Victoria in two-tone pink-and-white. Maybe it was those perky kitty-ear tail-lights....

YOW! Promise me anything, but give me a NASH METROPOLITAN

One swell car, the '49 Ford -- so poised, so baby-simple (is that a pacifier in its mouth?)

The 1951 STUDEBAKER perversely exaggerates the Ford's rocket-nose. This car looks as if it just put a whoopie-cushion under your seat.

In 1954 these THINGS on a Cadillac were called "Dagmar" bumpers (we'd call them "Dolly Partons" today....)

Hey Four Eyes! The Rambler was much maligned in the Corvette era, but it looks quite lively compared to today's bland Detroit product. (1959)

Kustomizing by Kandi Strecker, 1982

ARE WE NOT VALIANTS? Two 1960 versions of my second-favorite car. Check the varied window-shapes on the wagon!

(These tail-lights have been revived on the 1982 Toyota Tercel)

A BAD IDEA REPEATED:

'58 Lincoln
'62 Chrysler

I just can't decide whether the "gull-wing" rear of the '59 Chevy is inspired or insane.

the article well, but I had a *concept*. I also wrote, "Why We Need a Nerd Liberation Movement."

♦ *V: Tell us more about your inspirations—*

♦ CS: Underground newspapers, the kind you could pick up for free on college campuses in the early '70s. If you didn't like the message from the mainstream, you could print your *own*. They were there saying any damn thing they wanted to, and that was inspiring.

When I was going to school in Ann Arbor, there were all these zany flyers thumbtacked onto telephone poles signed by "The Last International." They were simultaneously funny, subversive and political, and would make you stop and question concepts you had held without thinking. They turned out to have all been made by a person named Bob Black who was living in Ann Arbor going to law school. His idea was simple: xerox a message on sheets of paper and go around in the dark of night posting it everywhere. No one needed to know who you were, and I liked that. Back in those days I was very shy and secretive, and it was hard for me to tell anyone I was doing a zine. Especially because no one would have known what I meant.

Candi with husband Mattthew and daughter Nicola at a flea market.

Another big influence on me was an anthology of pieces from *high school* underground newspapers, entitled *Where Will You Be In 1984?* The idea that even high-schoolers were self-publishing was encouraging. Another influence was *underground* comics—a particular favorite being *American Splendor* which was self-published by Harvey Pekar. Back then, there was an attitude in the media that if you weren't from New York or California, you weren't shit. *American Splendor* originated from *Cleveland*, and was a big encouragement.

But basically, the biggest inspiration was the early punk rock concept of *Do It Yourself*. D.I.Y. was a big topic then, so much so that it became an abbreviation. I think that's why there were so many regional music scenes in the early punk years, like in Akron or Athens. People started doing things themselves right where they were, instead of moving to New York or L.A. and hoping somebody would "discover" them.

Back then there was no pressure to be like (or unlike) a certain zine. Today, if you want to do a zine you can write to 20 people listed in *Factsheet Five* and see what zines are like before you even begin to do yours. It makes it easier, gives you a template to fol-

low, but it kind of spoils things, too.

♦ *V: There's such a variety of zines being done now.*

♦ CS: There's much more specialization—it's almost like a marketplace specialization. If somebody came to me for advice, I would say, "Find a topic that nobody else has." But that's a shame because *I* had no topic when I started my zine—that was the beauty of it.

♦ *V: Anything you wanted to discuss, you could—you weren't constrained a priori—*

♦ CS: Right. I often wrote about bands I liked, but I didn't feel I had to produce a punk zine in any way. During one month I was reading a lot of books so I wrote about books that month, the next month maybe not at all. After a certain point I got a little more involved with the zine network that existed, though it was still very much a word-of-mouth thing. *Factsheet Five* began in the early '80s. The editor, Mike Gunderloy, came out of the science-fiction fanzine world, too. He was also into leftward politics, and some of his motivations came from that. But in the early days a good proportion of the zines he reviewed were science-fiction fanzines.

When *Factsheet Five* started out, it wasn't the definitive guide it is today. Now it can make you or break you, depending on whether or not you're included or how favorably you're reviewed. Some people blast *F5* as though it represents the most heinous aspect of "The Establishment"! But back in those days, *Factsheet Five* wasn't this central place where all zines would filter through; it was just one of *many* places where people could learn about zines. Almost everybody who did a zine would list other favorite zines, so instead of one central directory, there were many. If I read five different zines, each might mention five other zines, and if you sent for all of them you'd get a picture of a much bigger world. Depending on which doorway you came through, you could get a radically different picture and perspective.

♦ *V: What are some zines that no longer exist?*

♦ CS: I have copies of a publication from 1970—not exactly a zine—called *Slattery's Review*. I was 14 years old and living at home where my parents watched a certain genre of TV shows that don't exist anymore. The shows featured a host who'd interview all kinds of weird people. The guests were not stars from the entertainment media, but people from UFO societies,

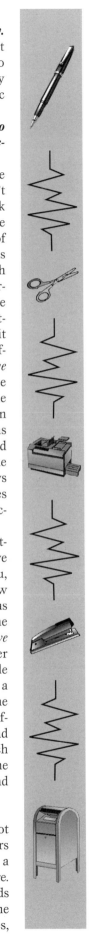

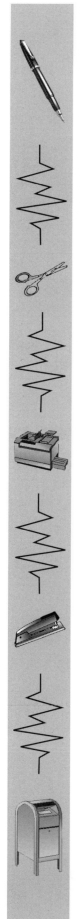

Jeanne Dixon-type psychics, neo-nazis and early gay liberation groups like the Mattachine Society. These pioneering gays would wear masks on TV because they didn't want their identities to be known: "We prefer just to be left alone." But no other TV show at the time would have allowed them on *at all!* Most of these guests were peripheral rather than extreme kooks—fringe people. One talk show host I remember was Alan Douglas, a very dignified and charming guy with a devilish silver beard. I always liked his show best. Some other hosts in this genre were Joe Pyne and Alan Burke.

There was a circuit of these talk shows and the same guests would circulate among them. One memorable guest was a nutty raconteur named Desmond Slattery. He would always say, "Send a dollar for my newsletter, and I'll send you a copy," so 14-year-old me sent off a dollar.

FACTSHEET FIVE

Factsheet Five remains the zine of crosscurrents and cross-pollination despite its new look, and is brought to you by Mike Gunderloy, sometimes to be found at Superlative Manor (aka BBBTLE), 41 Lawrence St., Medford, MA, 02155; phone (617) 391-3496. This is Pretzel Press publication #368, and is intended for direct mailing to lots of folks. Frequency: irregular. Press run: 150 copies. Begun 15 September, 1982. 4th issue. All rights reserved.

If there is an "X" or other rude mark after your name on the envelope, you're not going to get the next issue unless you indicate some sort of interest.

The Second FF Contest is still open. To recap, what book is dedicated: "To Bob Geiser, for reasons that need not be explained here—and to Bob Dylan, for Mister Tambourine Man"? Prizes include a lifetime subscription to this rag, and other valuable considerations to be announced at a future date.

Current plans for the Factsheet are to continue production on a roughly bi-monthly basis at least through the early part of 1983. I'll continue to use offset unless I end up really broke. Contributions to defray costs will be greedily accepted. I'm also looking for people to write music and movie reviews, or whatever, to be published here. I'd also like to know about any off-the-wall publications that I should try to review here. In an issue or two, I'll probably be asking for, or demanding, stamps to cover postage costs for those still interested in my immoral words. Be warned.

I'm also considering making *FACTSHEET* #6—which ought to be out in January or so—a roundup issue of sorts, containing addresses for all those people I've discussed in previous issues. If you're listed, I think you'll end up being known by about 200 extremely crazy people.

****

"Looking forward to tapping into the network of tasteful freaks you correspond with"—Cardinal Feng

—*Factsheet Five* (1982) exerpt from Candi's collection

♦ *V: It cost just six cents to send a big envelope through the mail—*

♦ CS: Right; if only that were still possible. He always had a pet cause to promote, like a bird sanctuary in South America, or the device sold through his newsletter that was like a mouse-trap for cats. It featured a bird figurine. Supposedly your cat would jump at it and then it would snap back with a loud noise, and because of this bad experience, the cat would never again attack a bird. This was his device to "Save the Songbirds!" He also sold little bags of herbs like Valerian root. On TV he'd ramble on about the same topics he'd rail about in his publications. He also had a couple of chums who would occasionally appear with him on shows and get mentioned in the pages of his newsletter. One article outlined his "Six Month Plan to End the Vietnam War."

In those days most hosts on these shows were liberals instead of conservatives; a total flip-flop from today's talk show world. The idea seemed to be that the mainstream world was conservative, therefore liberal hosts airing liberal ideas would be irritating enough to be entertaining. The fact that today's talk show hosts are all conservative implies that we're actually a *liberal* culture—we just don't realize it. That's the only hope I cling to! [laughs]

Speaking of unsung heroes of the world of self-publishing, there's Cheryl Cline, whom I discovered around 1980. She was living in the Bay Area long before I moved here; she was born and raised in Concord and still lives there. When I first saw her zine, I thought, "This person's trying to achieve what *I'm* trying to achieve; she has the same vision." There were parallels: we were women of the same age, we both came out of science-fiction fandom, we both liked punk rock, etc. One of her early zines was titled *My Secret Life in the Mail*, which reflected her interest in rubber stamps and mail art. That was another big inspiration: *mail art* and the collage work and rubber stamps that were usually part of it.

♦ *V: You're mentioned in her zine, as well as two other early San Francisco zine-makers: Tina Said who published* Bridal Shower *('80s zine) and G. Sutton Breiding, who did* Punk Surrealist Cafe.

♦ CS: Cheryl was also involved with another early zine context involving an organization-structure called the APA, which stands for Amateur Press Association. They existed to publish a newsletter which circulated only to contributing members of the group. If you wanted to be a member, you had to contribute a certain minimum amount of writing. Let's say there were 50 members in the APA. You'd send 50 copies of your APA-zine to the person called the Central Mailer, who would collate everyone's contributions and then send each member a bulky compilation.

There are quite a few active APAs in science fiction—some general, some specialized—there are probably half a dozen *Star Trek* APAs alone. There's a

Women's APA (AWA) which started in the '70s, and Cheryl was involved with that. An unfortunate tendency in APAs is that a lot of bickering or "flaming" goes on, very similar to what's happening now in Internet groups where people will say something obnoxious just to get a rise out of others. They get a reaction, it goes back and forth, and it all goes on far too long. I've never been involved in the APA movement myself. I also like the idea of limiting my readership to a certain arbitrary group.

Back to Cheryl: she's a very intelligent writer about rock and pop music and its larger place in society. She was a Women's Studies major at U.C. Berkeley and has compiled a bibliography of diaries and journals written by women in America, which is published by Scarecrow Press (the library publisher). Her zines are great; she's able to critique the arts and society while still speaking plain English, without lapsing into academic jargon. Her writing is a delight to read—very opinionated and funny. One of her zines, *Lumpen*, was devoted to intellectually justifying heavy metal music. It wasn't exactly a *defense*, but it took this subject (which, until then, I had dismissed) and put it in a certain sociological/historical perspective so that it all made sense. She made me ashamed of having dismissed that music so facilely.

One of Cheryl's favorite topics has been the way women are marginalized in rock music. Any band liked by young girls is immediately trivialized by critics: "Oh, they must be a teeny-bopper band." Her David Lee Roth issue dealt with that.

Lumpen was devoted to intellectually justifying heavy metal music.

Cheryl is currently publishing a semi-pro magazine called *Twangin'*, which is about country music that's *not* in the Top Ten. Right now the world of country music is very glossy and slick and poppy and its stars sell in the millions, but performers that don't fit the glossy Nashville image can't get airplay. So she writes about the *interesting* music that's being produced on the margins of commercial country music. Some of her articles deal with people who started out in punk rock and moved into country later. [Cheryl Cline, *Twangin'*, 2230 Huron Dr, Concord CA 94519]

♦ **V: She listens to a lot of records to find the interesting ones—**

♦ CS: Right. The last time I saw Cheryl she told me that certain back issues of her zines are now highly "collectible" because she published a few pieces by William Gibson before he became famous. Here's another "cyberpunk" piece she wrote, "Dining With John Shirley."

Back cover of *Lumpen*

My personal nomination for the best zine issue ever published, with the perfect marriage of form, content, wackiness and everything else, is Cheryl's issue titled *The Wretch Takes to Wrestling* (a pun on Virginia Woolf's phrase "The wretch takes to writing"). This was in 1980, before wrestling became popular with hipsters and was shown on MTV—back when it was still this contemptible fringe, blue-collar entertainment. She produced this beautiful issue on Twiltone paper, and used two-color mimeo ink to mimic the blood of the wrestlers on the cover. It contains pull quotes like, *"We love to make our opponents suffer!"* and is just delightful.

♦ **V: You contributed to it as well, back in 1980, with an essay on the car ads shown between the wrestling matches: "Ben's commercials are to a true connoisseur of the tube like Grandma Moses' paintings are to an art collector. TV commercials in their purest form, untainted by sophistication and prepared within a very limited budget." The idea of early TV commercials considered as naive art . . .**

♦ CS: The world should know about the massive output of Cheryl Cline; somebody should reprint it all. She did a lot of other zines, including *Shake!* and *Mama Oom Mow Mow* and *In a Blue Moon*. And she's the only person I know who has her own xerox machine, which I envy. Every zinester should have one!

♦ **V: [looking at Cheryl's zine] "My Secret Life in the Mail is available for trade and correspondence. Send no money."**

♦ CS: Those were the politics back then. In those days, almost everybody (including myself) would say in their editorials, "This is *your* magazine too—send me your contributions! It's not an ego thing on my part." Now it's "Send me some money and shut up!" [laughs]

♦ **V: Here's Cheryl's review of the Bikini Girl zine: "I like Bikini Girl, the boots, the boys, the sad Sues and the glad Sues, TV Guide cut-ups, the Chinese fortunes, the psychedelic glasses, the little red records, the interviews, the reasons given for not attending school dances, the un-prose, and the pink, pink paper. What more can I say? A peachy-keen zine." Hey—the word "zine" is being used in 1981.**

Cover of *The Wretch Takes to Wrestling #5*

And here's a big list of mail art people to write to; one says: "Send me hate mail, prayers, anatomical illustrations, or surprise me." Every issue features hand-done rubber stamps in six or eight colors— what a labor of love just to produce this . . . So in the early '80s you built up a zine network—

♦ CS: Like I said, a new wave of punk rock blood came into science-fiction fandom. Luke McGuff was one of my first big contacts, and he put me in contact with a lot of other zine publishers who had one foot in punk rock and another in science fiction but were not limited by either one. Cheryl Cline was a major figure, and so was Rich Coad, a San Franciscan who did a zine called *Space Junk*. The title was taken from a DEVO song; also, that was a popular phrase at the time when *Skylab* was crashing down to earth. Luke McGuff prodded me to send my zine to people like them. The letters were flying thick and fast coast to coast, and shortly thereafter my husband and I made our first trip to San Francisco. We met all these people I'd been corresponding with, and hit it off quite well with them. Within a couple of years my husband persuaded Atari to pay him to move to the West Coast. In late '83 we wound up in San Francisco. *That's* how we made our escape from the Midwest.

Now, almost 15 years later, I'm still in contact with most of the people I met in the early '80s, even though we're all middle-aged now. [laughs] I just kept publishing zines. Now I have over 500 names in my database, and it's still growing! I never intend to stop publishing, although the biggest threat to my zine endeavors is, ironically, commercial success. I've started get-

ting paid quite well for writing articles for a local weekly. And once you start getting *paid* for writing— well, they say money changes everything, right?!

♦ *V: But in your articles for other publications, you don't have the freedom to include irrelevant recipes and miscellaneous articles. You also don't do the layout and graphics and include your own cartoons, so that part of your talent is not being expressed—*

♦ CS: That's a very good point. I really enjoy screwing around with the graphics and throwing in random quotes and articles clipped from somewhere, which has been part of what I've done from day one. I like merging text and visuals together and if I only did writing I wouldn't have that outlet.

I wonder what the history of zines will read like 40 or 50 years from now. There are probably grad students writing about it right now. Just don't let 'em weasel free copies out of you, is all I can say! If you're on the *alt.zines* bulletin board on the Internet, there are all these wheedlings: "I'm writing a term paper about zines, and I'd like to see some copies. Will everybody please send me a copy of their zine? Thanks!" "Yeah—*right!*" It's the old "I'm writing a paper" trick. However, that's part of the game in zines: being poor and being cheap: "Oh, please, send me this."

♦ *V: That's why trading started.*

♦ CS: But at least trade means you're actually *giving* something in exchange. But there can be a lot of inequity in that. I send somebody my beautifully produced 18-pager, and receive four little pages of scribbles and think, "Gee, I'm not real happy with that." But that is something we all have to live with.

♦ *V: Zines didn't really take off until the '90s—*

♦ CS: Right; now *Factsheet Five* actually has to admit that they can't review every single zine. The early *F5* was padded with record reviews, book reviews, and articles that had nothing to do with zines.

The biggest threat to my zine endeavors is, ironically, commercial success.

As far as my zine-making goes, I guess the real mystery is, "Why didn't I quit?" I guess I had no reason to do anything else. [laughs] I had found my own personal art form. It's a hobby that draws on different parts of my personality. There's my lack of discipline—with zines, I can work by my own schedule. I can put things off for months until I feel more inspired, or take as long as I want to track down the perfect piece of clip art. My anal-retentive librarianness makes me keep folders of clippings that *might* be of interest someday. All these talents came together—a little bit of graphics here, some writing there—zines were the medium for *me*!

♦ **V:** *You published a zine just about the '70s—*

♦ **CS:** I became obsessed with the '70s when the very first inklings of '70s nostalgia started to surface in the late '80s: "Ha ha, remember the Partridge Family?" I became troubled by the way the '70s were being trivialized for amusement, and thought: "But there was so much *more* going on." During the '70s I had paid a lot of attention to each weird little pop phenomenon, trying to make sense of the world around me. Fads like streaking or CB radio made me think, "What does this signify? What does this tell us about who we are and where we're going?"

Bikini Girl deals with cultural images of "girlness" that in reality have little to do with us. These images repel us, but they also fascinate us in a snake-like way.

When you only talk about the Brady Bunch and skip the Kent State shootings, you create a one-sided picture of an era. It's not that one is silly and the other is serious, but that both were happening simultaneously. So I started delving into my personal memories in a weird kind of interior time travel. I didn't want to just say that something happened, I wanted to say what it *meant* to people at the time. Take the gas shortages of the mid-'70s. The shallow way of remembering that was: "Remember when we had to wait in line to get gas?" But if you were *living* that reality, you were wondering if this was going to be a permanent condition. Maybe in the near future there would be no cars, and what would that mean? Was this the end of the world as you knew it? Should you move within walking distance of your job? Should you move to the country and grow your own food? It was very serious, despite the joking, and felt like an end-of-the-worldness.

♦ **V:** *Several people shot other people while waiting in line—*

♦ **CS:** Right. Also, in the early days of the gas shortage around 1973, truckers were going on strike in a very revolutionary manner. You tend to think of these rednecks as very conservative and rightwing, yet suddenly they were more radical than the college kids! It felt like all the tables were being turned, and you weren't quite sure where you stood anymore. Things happening had a lot of strange resonances that people don't always remember, and *that's* what I wanted to get down on paper. I felt that by doing this, I would make everybody confront these issues—they couldn't be swept under the rug in joking nostalgia any longer.

The more I reminisced and researched the '70s, the more info I had, until I had much more stuff than I could shoehorn into a typical *Sidney Suppey's Quarterly*. Finally a friend made the obvious suggestion that moved me into action: "Just do a *different* zine!" So that's what I did. So far I've done two 36-page issues of *It's A Wonderful Lifestyle*, my zine about the '70s, and I'm not sure if a third will be enough—it might take a fourth. I wish somebody would give me a book contract on this. Anyway, that's how I came to be a dual-zine publisher. I wanted to keep my unfocused and more personal-oriented zine, and I wanted to pursue a specific interest in a lot of depth, too, so now I have a zine for each.

♦ **V:** *I like the idea of doing a lot of different zines—*

♦ **CS:** Recently, the biggest impact on my zine production has been being a mother. It's made me a lot more serious about myself. I always had a spotty work history; I didn't have a career in the '80s or '90s. And I didn't buy into the idea that the goal of life was to raise children, especially if you're a woman. My bad karma is: for years I made fun of people who had kids, and now I have to eat all those words! But after I turned 35, I started thinking, "I guess if I had kids, it wouldn't be the *worst* thing in the world." I was in a stable relationship that was financially solvent, which is important—baby wipes are damn expensive! Also, our fathers both died around that time, which makes you reassess your place in time, like: "I'm not the end product of history; I'm just a middle link between the past and the future." It's much more mystical than I would normally talk about—it was more of a change

Cover of SSQ&CPM Vol. 4 #3

Cartoon by Deborah Benedict, *Inside Joke #28* (1984). From Candi's collection.

♦ **V:** *In your zine collection you have issues of* **Bikini Girl**—

♦ **CS:** *Bikini Girl* was an early zine that dates back to the early '80s. Lynn Peril was interested in seeing my collection of them because people kept telling her that *Mystery Date* reminded them of *Bikini Girl*. However, it's more of a visual similarity than one of content. Just like *Mystery Date*, *Bikini Girl* was always done on pink paper, which was a New Wave or punk color back then—especially black and pink together. Bands would have pink in their names, like Pink Section, or have songs or album covers using pink. *Bikini Girl* deals with cultural images of "girlness" that in reality have little to do with us. These images repel us, but they also fascinate us in a snake-like way.

Bikini Girl was a zine about feminine (not necessarily feminist) imagery—women as depicted in the mass media. It's very New York-subculture, with a punk rock content, Andy Warhol people, Bettie Page, exploitation films, plenty of name-dropping, etc. It has lots of clippings from old magazines, and had a naughty-girl sexual tone to it—

♦ **V: [reading] "What do soiled panties really smell like?"**

♦ **CS:** Right—Lynn Peril would never put that in her zine. At this point in time, Bettie Page imagery and articles about exploitation films were quite rare, so this is somewhat ground-breaking. (Now every magazine you pick up features Bettie Page.) I believe *Bikini Girl* is still published sporadically. The thing about doing a zine is: nobody really quits as a formality; the gap of time since the last issue just becomes so huge that you have to confess you're not doing a zine anymore.

of f*eelings.* Also, our life seemed so settled-down and pleasant ("Let's go out for Thai food and then see a Hong Kong movie at the Roxie . . . *again*")—maybe we needed a little stress to shake it up!

Now we have one daughter, and all the old routines in our lives have been overturned. I have to be really serious now in order to continue doing zines at all. When Nicola was born, I had to decide whether I was going to stop publishing forever, or whether to continue doing zines but be a bit more serious and committed in my approach to the effort involved. I started keeping my desk and files in much better order, and set up a home office that could be closed off from the grabby little hands of a three-year-old. And for the first time in my life I learned how to use my limited free time productively.

♦ V: *Let's summarize some of the motivations for doing zines—*

♦ CS: As a shy person, zines, letters and mail are good formats for me. I can control what I'm saying and control the response. I hate talking on the telephone, but I love getting and sending letters. Zines let me hear from a lot of people and get a lot of fertilization of ideas. Doing a zine satisfies your *communication needs.* And as a person who started life kind of shy and filled with low self-esteem, zines have been a good thing in terms of putting me in contact with people. I was not the kind of personality to go, "Here, world, fuck you—here's what I do and who I am!" I had to start modestly, with something that only went out to a handful of people.

Doing a zine satisfies your *communication needs.*

Actually, in give or take a few billion years, everything will be gone, anyway. Someday the sun will go nova and we'll all fry. Everything, whether it's Picasso paintings or little grubby zines, will all be ashes someday. We don't know why we do anything we do, except that we're just driven to do it. Art doesn't make a lot of sense, but there you are. It's a *drive*, otherwise why would we put so damn much work into it? Ⅴ

Cover of Nancy's Magazine

Inspiring Candi

Reading

The Dreams of Donald Roller Wilson

The style grabs you first; this fellow has a very polished ultra-realistic technique, and he seems to be constantly challenging himself by seeking new textures to incorporate into his work—velvet drapes, oriental rugs, lace, bark, steam, corrugated cardboard, raw chicken skin. Later—about one nanosecond later—you notice *content*. Many strange objects and images recur . . . He paints a self-contained dream world, a phantom zone with occasional human visitors, though its primary inhabitants are lady chimpanzees in full Victorian dress and a horde of cigarette-smoking cats. Olives, pickles, jack-o-lanterns, skulls, shoes, roasts of beef, bell jars, sock monkeys, watermelons, hats . . . it's the stillness of endless dream, always with that glow against oncoming early evening. (Hawthorn, New York 1979)

Quotology

"Laura had only a corncob wrapped in a handkerchief, but it was a good doll. It was named Susan. It wasn't Susan's fault that she was only a corncob."—Laura Ingalls Wilder, *Little House in the Big Woods*

"I like factories . . . just to look at people working in machine rooms would be pretty much a thrill. Hospital basements I like. You find things in them, machines, that were real necessary about 10 years ago and then just started getting dusty."—David Lynch

"Living below your means is a cheap way to be rich. It's the only easy way to be rich."—Stewart Brand

"THE MOST IMPORTANT THING IN ART IS THE FRAME. For painting: literally; for other arts: figuratively—because without this humble appliance, you can't know where The Art stops and The Real World begins."—Frank Zappa, *The Real Frank Zappa Book*

"The most exciting phrase to hear in science, the one that heralds new discoveries, is not 'Eureka!' (I found it!) but 'That's funny . . .'"—Isaac Asimov

"The lesson of flea markets is that specific desire will be disappointed and alert curiosity rewarded."—Joan Juliet Buck

The Laws of Thrift Store Karma

1. Don't buy things you don't really want just because you've heard they're things that other people want. Leave the mugwumps for the mugwump collectors, etc.

2. If you pull something interesting from the bottom of the stack or the back of the shelf, but then decide not to buy it, *leave it on top or in the front.* Surely the qualities that made it intrigue you will intrigue the next clever person who comes by, making a sale for the thrift store and helping keep them in business for you.

3. Don't tear the pages with thrift store addresses out of the telephone books at public phones!

4. When the salt shaker is in one part of the store and the pepper shaker is in another, put the two together!

5. Beware of unpriced objects at garage sales and estate sales. The very act of your asking for a price irreversibly alters the seller's perception of its value, thus demonstrating the Heisenberg Uncertainty Principle.

See zine reviews by Candi on page 137

Murder Can Be Fun

One of the best-known zines is *Murder Can Be Fun*, a death-and-disaster journal published by John Marr since 1985. Meticulously researched at libraries and from his own collection of over 10,000 books, *MCBF* presents the choicest and weirdest anecdotes to a bemused and often goggle-eyed readership. Back issues of *MCBF* (most are still available) include "Naughty Children," "Death at Disneyland," "Zoo Deaths," "Please, Mr Postman: Don't Shoot!," "I Love Disasters," "I Hate Sports" and the classic "(Anti-) Sex Tips for Teens." For the latest issue send $3 cash to John Marr, PO Box 640111, San Francisco CA 94164.

♦ *VALE: What's your background?*

♦ JOHN MARR: In 1961, I was born in Oakland, California, a seriously under-appreciated city. When I was about seven, my parents moved to a new housing tract in Moraga. Our house cost something like $28,000. My parents could afford to buy it on my father's salary as an Oakland motorcycle cop. Now the whole area's gone completely chi-chi and upscale.

My parents met in the '50s when my father was in the Army and stationed in West Germany—technically my mother was a war bride! She was originally from East Germany but had sneaked across the border a few years earlier, one jump ahead of the guards.

Lots of people think, given my interests, that I must have been raised on a steady diet of cop "war stories." Actually, my father was pretty good about leaving his job down at the station. He'd tell us some of the good stories, like the time he found a tiger in East Oakland (it was someone's pet that had gotten loose!). And me and my sister learned to spot drunk drivers and hookers at an early age. We may not have been too clear on what the hookers were up to, but we knew they weren't waiting for the bus. My father

enjoyed being a cop. It's the kind of job where when you work, you work really hard, but you don't have to work very much. He eventually earned a law degree by attending night school, and retired to go into practice.

In all, my childhood was really normal.

♦ *V: When did you learn how to read?*

♦ JM: In the first grade, just like everyone else. But even before I could read, I was always looking at picture books. One of my favorites, *Der Strummelpeter*, belonged to my mother. This was a very formative book. It's a collection of illustrated poems by Dr Heinrich Hoffman, written in the 1830s. The title character, "Slovenly Peter," never cuts his hair, has incredibly long fingernails and is dirty and smells bad. There are other cautionary tales, like "The Sad Story of the Matches" (about a girl who sets herself on fire playing with matches). Probably the best-known is "The Story of Little Suck-a-Thumb." Little Conrad's mother is going out, and as she leaves, her last words are, "Don't suck your thumbs." Naturally, as soon as mom is gone Conrad starts sucking away. Suddenly a tall, long-legged "scissor man" leaps into the room and cuts off Conrad's thumbs with an enormous pair of

"His name was Johnny Marr, and he looked like—Johnny Marr. Like his given name sounded. Like any Johnny, anywhere, anytime."—Cornell Woolrich. Photo: Robert Waldman

Cover of *Der Strummelpeter*

scissors. The last picture shows little Conrad looking really sad, with bloody stumps where his thumbs used to be.

♦ **V: *That's really frightening!***

♦ JM: Another favorite book featured Max and Moritz—two roly-poly, devilish German kids who would do things like pack the local parson's tobacco-pipe with gunpowder. (The author, Wilhelm Busch, arguably invented the comic strip in the 1860s. Recently, the University of California Press published *The Genius of Wilhelm Busch*.) In their final sequence, Max and Moritz break into a bakery by tumbling down the chimney. They fall into a vat of pretzel dough and the baker rolls them up and bakes them. They manage to eat their way out. Then they break into a grain mill and cut open bags of grain. The miller catches them, tosses them into a bag and throws 'em into the mill. They get ground up into goose food, and the geese eat them. [laughs]

♦ **V: *Wow, what a privileged childhood—***

♦ JM: Those were my mother's books when she was a girl in Germany. Naturally, they were all in German, but that didn't make any difference since I couldn't read anyway. When I did learn to read, I tracked down English translations for the better ones. There were others I liked that were never translated into English, but they weren't as sadistic. You've just gotta love German children's literature!

♦ **V: *When you grew up, was the TV on eight hours a day?***

♦ JM: No. Actually, one of my more formative child-hood experiences occurred when I was in first grade:

our picture tube blew up. [laughs] I still remember the picture cutting out in the middle of "Stingrays" and smoke pouring out the back of the set! We were without a TV for a year, and this just intensified my reading ha-bit. Fortunately, our home had a lot more reading mate-rial than normal households; the average American family has, like, ten books! [laughs] And I quickly accu-mulated more books than the rest of my family!

At an early age my parents took me to library book sales, and by the time I was in fourth grade, they had become the highlight of the year. My parents would give me five or ten dollars and I would come home with a big box of books.

A lot of our family's books also came from flea mar-kets—there was a particularly great one in Alameda at the Island Drive-In. I was also a heavy user of the school library. One of my favorite childhood books, that made a deep impression on me, was Thomas Bailey Aldrich's *The Story of a Bad Boy*. It's about boy-hood in the 1830s in New Hampshire, and all the wild pranks the main character gets away with (he never seemed to get punished). One of his best pranks was rigging a dozen War of 1812 cannons to fire at mid-night. Not only did they manage to wake up the whole town, but the stunt destroyed the cannons and did a fair amount of other damage besides. Ah, the joy of readily available gunpowder . . .

Of course, I loved all the classic stuff—Mark Twain, Sherlock Holmes, Dracula, Pinocchio, H.G. Wells. But I also had a thing for archaic kids' series books from the '20s and '30s, like "The Flying Machine Boys," Ted Scott, Poppy Ott, the "High School Boys" and dozens of others.

In the early books, the Hardy boys commonly carried guns, and it wasn't unusual for someone to get killed.

One of my favorites was "The Motor Boys." They had their own cars, a motorboat and an airplane (in 1915!), and seemingly unlimited freedom and funds to go all over the world having amazing adventures. Most of their escapades revolved around helping an ento-mologist friend track down weird species of bugs. It was great stuff.

Did you know that the Hardy Boys series, original-ly written in the '20s, was rewritten in the '50s? The revisionists eliminated a lot of racism and stereotyp-ing. Plus, they made the characters far less violent. In the early books, the Hardy boys commonly carried guns, and it wasn't unusual for someone to get killed. Also, they were portrayed as the smart mystery-solvers while the cops were dumb bunglers; in the rewrites "our fine modern police force" was working closely with them. One moronic bungling policeman was retained, but instead of him being a cop he's a *cop wannabe* who's trying too hard to ever get hired!

Another series I enjoyed starred Freddy the Pig.

Most people wait until a book comes out in paperback, but I wait until it comes out in *used* paperback!

Freddy was quite the talented pig: he could talk, he founded a bank, played football, went to the North Pole, ran for President, and was quite an accomplished detective. I'm not the only one obsessed with Freddy. There's a whole group of adult collectors who put on Freddy the Pig conventions! I only need one more, "The Story of Freginald," to complete my set. I've been working on that collection now for more than 25 years!

Believe it or not, the *Reader's Digest* was another big influence. The issues from the '50s and '60s contained articles that were quite unsuitable for children. People laugh a lot at the *Digest*, but it was definitely a source of childhood amazement—as well as trauma. Their car safety article, ". . . And Sudden Death" still gives me nightmares. It was written before cars had any safety features at all; it's filled with imagery of people being skewered by steering columns and decapitated by windshields. I still get a little nervous when I'm over the speed limit!

The *Digest* also turned me on to a few good writers, including Daniel P. Mannix. They ran his stuff from time to time. I first read *Memoirs of a Sword Swallower* (also known as *Step Right Up!)* in the *Reader's Digest* condensed version, and then found the unabridged original at a book sale. I must have read that book 20 times; it's still one of my favorites. Now it seems that every "carny" book is coming back into print.

♦ *V: So you were never a television addict?*

♦ JM: Not at all. I liked "Leave It To Beaver," "The Three Stooges" and "The Little Rascals" (as well as some cartoons), but I was never a habitual TV watcher. I always preferred sitting in my room with a book. My childhood was spent going crazy at library sales, buying bags of books!

I also started hanging out at used bookstores. I remember the first time I went to one. It was Holmes Books [in Oakland, now out of business]. My father just dumped me out at the store and came back four hours later—he knew I would stay out of trouble *there*.

By the time I was in high school, I was not only a book collector but a book *dealer*. I would go around to thrift stores, flea markets and garage sales buying books cheaply and sell them through the mail. Now I had an excuse to spend even *more* time in those dusty emporiums—plus I had more money to spend there as well.

♦ *V: Where did you get your mail order customers?*

♦ JM: I put small classified ads in mystery fanzines as well as the more established *Alfred Hitchcock's* and *Ellery Queen's Mystery Magazines* (both of which are still being published). They're the last major mystery genre magazines left, although a few semi-professional ones like *Mystery Scene* are available.

♦ *V: Is this when you began to focus on the mystery and true crime genres?*

♦ JM: Mysteries, yes, but I didn't become seriously interested in true crime until years later in college. For one thing, there weren't a lot of good true crime books published until the '60s or '70s. My main interests at the time were mystery books and some science fiction. Books like Herbert Asbury's *The Gangs of New York* were great, but still hard to find. At that time there wasn't much demand for gory true crime books.

♦ *V: But true crime detective magazines were flourishing in the '50s and '60s—*

♦ JM: They were—I just didn't buy them, even though they were much better than the ones published today. The writing was better, the pictures were better—everything about them was better. I think it's because those magazines still pay the same rates now as they did back then: three to five cents a word. In the '50s you could make a living doing that; today, you'd starve to death.

The first true crime books I bought were from

John Marr library: *The Dancing Detective* by William Irish (Cornell Woolrich)

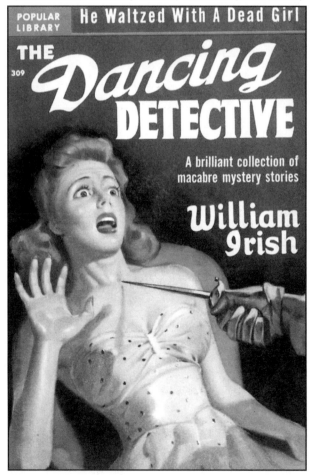

POPULAR LIBRARY

He Waltzed With A Dead Girl

THE
309 *Dancing* DETECTIVE

A brilliant collection of macabre mystery stories

William Irish

Scholastic Book Services, a company which had an exclusive monopoly arrangement with the public school system. They operated like a book club; each month the students would receive catalogs. You'd place your order and two weeks later there would be a pile of books sitting on your desk. In elementary school they occasionally offered books on famous criminals and "Great Human Monsters"—I *always* ordered those! I also ordered all their books on disasters; that has continued to be a strong interest.

♦ **V: What are some early favorites?**

♦ JM: My earliest favorites were train disasters, and one that really stuck with me happened in the '40s. An Italian diesel train loaded with hobos was going slowly through a tunnel in the Alps when it stalled, filling the tunnel with smoke. When the rescue team finally got the train out, they discovered hundreds of dead bodies—all the hobos had died of carbon monoxide poisoning.

The other one that has stuck in my mind happened during World War I. Thousands of French soldiers stationed near France were long overdue for a furlough home. But when the train finally arrived, it could only take a fraction of them. There was a near-riot when everyone tried to squeeze onboard, causing a severe overloading. The conductor refused to give the order to depart, but was forced to do so at gunpoint. The train began descending this steep mountain pass and—you

guessed it, it derailed and about 500 soldiers were killed. This story was suppressed for many years because it made the army look bad; the officials were afraid it would generate low morale.

> ## I took BART to see the Ramones . . . I remember how they impressed everyone by keeping their leather jackets on, even though it was 90 degrees!

♦ **V: That's a lot of people . . . When reading about disasters, there are usually details that stick in one's mind. I remember reading about a '70s PSA flight that crashed shortly after takeoff in San Diego. The ground was littered with bodies and colorful debris, and one of the artifacts was a pair of feet standing upright, still in shoes, with the legs snapped off above the ankles . . . Do you still have all those books?**

♦ JM: Yes . . . Back then there weren't that many disaster books; any time a book like *Ten Great Disasters* or *Volcanoes of the World* was offered, I'd snatch it up!

In high school I read everything by Dashiell Hammett and Raymond Chandler. I had just started book dealing when I noticed that a lot of people had Jim Thompson on their want lists. At a flea market I found *The Kill-Off,* and after reading it I went, "Whoa!" and started searching for the rest of his titles.

I also became interested in Harlan Ellison, Fredric Brown and Cornell Woolrich (I think the last two are still my favorites). I was always looking for new interesting writers to read—more specifically new *old* interesting writers. I went for *years* without buying any brand-new books, especially hardbacks. Most people wait until a book comes out in paperback, but I wait until it comes out in *used* paperback!

Even earlier, in my elementary school library I found and read a whole series of books edited by Alfred Hitchcock. These were all large-format hardbacks containing a lot of good stories. That's where I first discovered Fredric Brown. Then I was at a garage sale and found *Martians Go Home*—the first Brown novel I read. It was completely insane and totally addicting.

♦ **V: The publisher Dennis McMillan reprinted a lot of Fredric Brown books in limited editions—**

♦ JM: Right; it seems like almost everything great that was out-of-print is being reprinted now. I buy more new books than I ever did in the past. Dennis McMillan published an 18-volume set of hardbacks titled *Fredric Brown and the Detective Pulps*, which included virtually every piece of short fiction that Brown ever wrote. (He also issued some of them in quality paperback format.) That *Fredric Brown and*

John Marr library: *The Indiana Torture Slaying* by John Dean

A BEE-LINE SPECIAL 131   75c

THE INDIANA TORTURE SLAYING:
SYLVIA LIKENS' ORDEAL AND DEATH!
BY JOHN DEAN

SYLVIA LIKENS   MRS. BANISZEWSKI

Here, step by step—from discovery of a pretty teenager's abused body through the long, agonizing trial—is *the Detective Pulps* series almost bankrupted me. They were about $40 apiece, and there was a new one every three months—it was like, "When is this going to *end?!*"

Fredric Brown wrote several books in carnival settings, like *The Dead Ringer* and *Madball.* Dennis McMillan reissued a short story collection titled *The Freak Show Murders,* and naturally, the lead story is about murders in a freak show. Nothing like good *carny noir!*

♦ **V: When you were an engineering student at U.C. Berkeley, did you stay up late reading?**

♦ JM: Not only reading, but going to punk rock shows. That sort of made me an anomaly in the department; most of the people in my classes preferred to argue about physics over pizza and beer at La Val's. And none of them bought their clothes in thrift stores.

I got hooked on punk rock in high school when I saw DEVO perform on "Saturday Night Live"—I loved the music, the films and the funny little outfits. Underneath I sensed a really ominous subtext with an apocalyptic feel; unlike some people, I didn't think they were just a silly joke band. A few months later, the Dead Kennedys played a "dance" at my high school—under an assumed name. That was in 1978.

♦ **V: I was at that show! There were other groups that played—**

♦ JM: The Zeros and the Liars. It was a great event: a handful of San Francisco punks mixed with a large audience of young high school kids in earth-tone clothes, half of whom left as soon as the music started. It was, after all, the heyday of Pablo Cruise and Journey. But the half who stayed had a great time, dragging Biafra all over the cafeteria as the band played on. I remember the guys who put on the show got the San Francisco/Berkeley crowd in by telling the chaperons that they were on the basketball team—non-high school students at a high school dance were strictly *verboten.* After that, I started going to as many punk shows as possible, although it was hard to get a ride into the city. I took BART to see the Ramones when they played in front of S.F. City Hall one summer afternoon. I remember how they impressed everyone by keeping their leather jackets on, even though it was 90 degrees!

♦ **V: That was the first time I saw Joey Ramone wear that rubber pinhead hat . . . There's something in you that was drawn to an "alternative" way of life, yet you went straight to college and got a job—**

♦ JM: After graduating from college I got the brass ring: an environmentally-correct, well-paying job in San Francisco regulating pollution. [laughs] These days you have to *work* to be able to afford rent. Used books may be cheap, but they're not free. And you know you can never have enough!

♦ **V: After you worked for a while, you started publishing Murder Can Be Fun—**

♦ JM: The first issue came out in '85. By then I had some extra money—it wasn't so much the money, but

finally I had the time and the space to do something. In college, I lived in the dorms and there wasn't much room.

♦ **V: How did you come up with the title Murder Can Be Fun?**

♦ JM: Actually, I had an earlier title that was really brilliant, but I *forgot* it—as soon as you think of something, you have to immediately write it down! *Murder Can Be Fun* was one of Fredric Brown's lesser books, but it's a catchy title and catchy titles will get you far in this world. Would the Dead Kennedys have gotten where they did without that name? They were also a great band with a lot to say, but their name was just *inspired . . .*

♦ **V: Beyond the D.I.Y. context, obviously you wanted to achieve something beyond your 9-5 job—**

♦ JM: Specifically, I've always wanted to write. It's normal: if you read a lot, sooner or later you'll want to try your hand at writing. A couple years earlier some friends were working at *Maximumrock'n'roll* and I drifted there myself and volunteered to do layout. I learned what little I know about graphic arts there: what border tape and transfer lettering are, and how to get something ready for the printer.

John Marr library: *Bimbos of the Death Sun* by Sharyn McCrumb

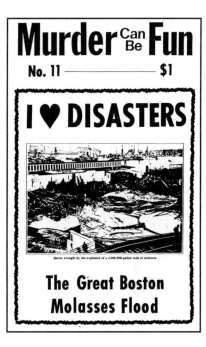

Murder ^Can_Be Fun

No. 11 ——————— $1

I ♥ DISASTERS

Havoc wrought by the explosion of a 2,000,000-gallon tank of molasses

The Great Boston Molasses Flood

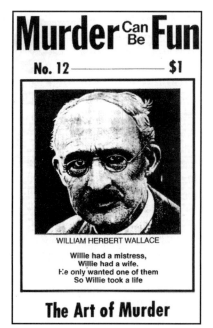

Murder ^Can_Be Fun

No. 12 ——————— $1

WILLIAM HERBERT WALLACE

Willie had a mistress,
Willie had a wife.
He only wanted one of them
So Willie took a life

The Art of Murder

Murder ^Can_Be Fun

No. 14 $1⁵⁰

Please Mr. Postman

Don't Shoot!

♦ *V: Along the way you learned how to type—*

♦ JM: That was a survival tactic—my handwriting is illegible! In junior high school I learned on a huge old black Underwood noiseless typewriter. I typed the first *MCBF* on a manual typewriter and laid it out using rubber cement. I didn't even use press-on type, but just clipped out headlines in the punk rock tradition of ransom-note graphics. When all else failed, I typed a headline and enlarged it several times on a copy machine. The first issue was 16 pages: four sheets folded in half. I printed 100 copies at the cheapest self-service place in Berkeley and sent it out unstapled. I didn't have a saddle-stitch stapler; I bought that later for $50—that was a heavy investment!

♦ *V: Who did you send it to?*

♦ JM: Various friends and a few other publications including *Flipside* and *Factsheet Five,* back when it was much smaller and printed on crude offset. I got some orders and a few letters but the world didn't exactly beat a path to my door. Nevertheless, I went ahead and published the second issue, the third, and so on. Each issue generated more and more mail—not enough to notice on a daily or weekly basis, but when you totaled it up at the end of the year you realized how much you'd gotten. My entire inventory of back issues used to fit on top of a chest of drawers in my closet, but now I have a storage room filled with boxes—if I hadn't gotten it, there literally wouldn't be any room in my apartment.

♦ *V: Did the first issue have a theme?*

♦ JM: No. *Murder Can Be Fun* started off as a grab-bag; I just wrote about anything I was interested in. I included a story about a cheerleader killing that happened near my high school—that's still one of my favorite cases. It was recently filmed for TV as "A Friend to Die For," starring Tori Spelling as the cheerleader! I also wrote about one of my favorite sub-gen-

res: teenage guilt novels, in which teenagers go out and crash the family car and kill someone or have a hideous hit-and-run accident. (I really appreciate "young adult fiction.") Also, a few book reviews were included. I used to say that part of the reason I started publishing was so I could write about *Memoirs of a Sword Swallower* and quote the first line: "I probably never would have become America's leading fire-eater if Flamo the Great hadn't happened to explode that night." [laughs]

My first review was in *Factsheet Five* and they got the title wrong. [laughs] They called my zine *Sex, Drugs and Death,* but that was the title of one of the articles— I guess they just got confused. I got letters from friends, enemies, and strangers sending me stamps.

♦ *V: You just asked for stamps?*

♦ JM: Yes; 50 cents or two stamps. It was a real shoestring operation. I figured one stamp would cover the postage and the other would cover the cost of printing the zine. [laughs]

♦ *V: Now you have **MCBF** offset printed—*

♦ JM: Offset is cheaper; if you order enough copies, they practically give 'em away. It also doesn't stick to vinyl furniture! I printed 7,000 copies of my last issue, roughly a two-year supply. To make the per-copy cost affordable, at least 2,000 have to be printed. Most of the first 12 issues will go out of print in the next two years, so eventually I plan to put out some kind of hefty anthology.

♦ *V: How did you do the research for issue #14 on post office shootings?*

♦ JM: A friend's sister who works for a local TV station had access to the *AP* wire databases and she provided the basic outlines. I also went to the local newspapers and tracked down the local news coverage. I realized I had to do the story in 1991, when there were two post office killings within a month of each other—one in

Yoo hoo, Mr. Bear!

ZOO DEATHS

Wanna play, Buster?

NAUGHTY CHILDREN

OBSCURE CRIME BOOKS

Covers of MCBF #11, #12, #14, #16, #17 and the "Obscure Crime Books" issue

New Jersey and the other in Michigan. And right after the issue came out, there were two on the same day!

Once the media gets an idea, even minor incidents get hyped to boost their theory. With each new incident, they'll print a sidebar showing "A History of Post Office Murders." Before the Oklahoma mass shooting in 1986, periodically some postal worker would go nuts and shoot a couple co-workers and it was no big deal. It might get strong local coverage, but that would be about it. After Oklahoma, mass shootings became synonymous with the post office—they went together like peanut butter and chocolate. Meanwhile the postal PR people are saying things like, "Well, we're the largest employer in the country; what do you *expect?!*"

After Oklahoma, mass shootings became synonymous with the post office—they went together like peanut butter and chocolate.

♦ *V: I didn't know that—*
♦ JM: They're the single largest civilian employer. When you ask them about postal shootings, their PR people give you this two-page sheet where they list the major postal shooting rampages interspersed with other major workplace shootings, like, "Hey, it's not just *us!*" [laughs] If you want a copy, just give 'em a call. They're trying to put a positive spin on it, or at least take some of the negativity out. Although . . . have you read Charles Bukowski's *Post Office?* That book makes you wonder why there aren't *more* shootings! [laughs]
♦ *V: As a substitute driver for a few months, I drove a truck picking up mail from those blue boxes, and there was no way I could collect from all the boxes*

in the time allotted—I needed at least another hour. I have no idea how the "regular" drivers could possibly have met their schedules.
♦ JM: That sounds like some punishment in the lower circles of Dante's hell! I love to dig out information and present it in-depth in a way you'll never find in mainstream media. My two favorite back issues are "Zoo Deaths" and "Death at Disneyland." "Zoo Deaths" was a lot of fun to research, but actually it was quite difficult because media coverage of these events has been minimal, to say the least. This is not seen as some sort of *national trend,* so the newspapers never present a sidebar with a condensed history or listing.
♦ *V: How do you research topics like that?*
♦ JM: You go through newspaper indexes, read books, ask librarians, and sometimes you get lucky. There are a lot of great zoo death stories that I'll never know the details of. I'll be reading a book and there will be a brief parenthetical mention of a woman being crushed by a rhino in Zurich in 1936. Since I don't read German and lack access to Zurich newspapers, I'll probably never find out more.
♦ *V: What are the causes of most zoo deaths?*
♦ JM: Stupidity, drunken stupidity, suicidal tendencies, outright insanity and, of course—the follies of youth. Most incidents involving bears and jungle cats are caused by zoo-goers sticking their arms inside the bars, or climbing into cages. You can hardly call them accidents.

A fine example of a recent zoo death caused by insanity happened in Washington, D.C.'s National Zoo. Margaret King was a paranoid schizophrenic with strong religious delusions—she thought she was Jesus Christ. Since the zoo had tightened security after a "mishap" over 35 years earlier, Ms. King really demonstrated her religious fervor by climbing a 3-1/2 foot fence that dropped 9 feet to a moat, then

DIET OR DIE

THE DOLLY DIMPLES WEIGHT REDUCING PLAN

by CELESTA "DOLLY DIMPLES" GEYER
and SAMUEL ROEN

John Marr library: *Diet or Die* by former circus fat woman, "Dolly Dimples"

swimming 26 feet before reaching the lions. Her death was ruled a suicide, but I think it was an attempt at sainthood—perhaps she was re-enacting a past life as a Christian martyr who was thrown to the lions. She also had nail holes in her palms . . .

But of course, there are exceptions to the usual causes. The story of Harold Cannon brings to mind Aesop's fable about not being able to change an animal's nature. Harold worked for several years at the Seneca Park Zoo in New York and befriended an Indian elephant named Sally. She was known for being a little "high-strung" and resistant to handling by strangers. Cannon took a year's leave of absence from work, and upon returning he entered Sally's pen to say "Hi!" to an old chum. His body was found horribly trampled to death—apparently he learned the hard way that elephants *do* forget!

One of the strongest arguments against media oversimplification is zoo deaths. Ferocious creatures like polar bears and wolves are portrayed as harmless fuzzy things to be cuddled and played with. There are numerous cases of children being torn apart by an animal they were only familiar with from Saturday morning cartoons, whom they only wanted to pet. Children's zoo mishaps tend to be caused by kids innocently waving peanuts or popcorn a bit too close to the animals' cages, not realizing that the animal is eyeing *them,* not just their fistful of Nutter Butters . . .

♦ *V: So the "Zoo Deaths" research was tough—*

♦ JM: Anything that happens in New York City, you're not going to have any trouble finding information on it. But incidents that happen in the provinces are more problematic. You just don't get that kind of media saturation/trend spotting with zoo deaths. A good example was the 1970 Portland (Oregon) lion killing. Some stupid teenager got himself killed when he dangled from the rim of a lion pit on a dare—he learned the hard way just how high lions can jump! The next night, someone sneaked into the zoo and shot and killed the two lions. That was all covered in the *New York Times.* But to find out who did it, I had to go digging through the Portland library when I was up there on a book-shopping vacation. (Incidentally, Portland is a great town for used books!) Turned out (surprise, surprise) one of the dead teen's buddies had confessed a few years later.

Even San Francisco research was difficult. I don't think anyone has ever actually been *killed* in the San Francisco Zoo, but a few guys have gotten chewed up (no women, as far as I know). One guy got his arm chewed up (but not off) by a polar bear when he tried to feed it some sugar. Another guy—some drunk—climbed into the lion cage, screaming at the lion and waving around a wine bottle. The only reason he didn't get killed was because the zookeeper was right there and had a rifle; it took just a single shot to kill the lion. The *Chronicle* printed a great photo of this old wino all chewed up and covered with bandages in a hospital.

While researching the "Zoo Deaths" issue I was at a cafe on Polk Street, and some of the zoo victims lived like three blocks from where I was sitting! Newspapers routinely used to publish everyone's address, through the '60s at least. I guess it was so G.B. Jones of Market Street wouldn't be mistaken for G.B. Jones of Broadway!

♦ *V: Wasn't the "Death at Disneyland" issue also hard to research?*

Nobody expects to meet the Grim Reaper at "The Happiest Place On Earth"!

♦ JM: There wasn't any convenient place where you can just look up a list of all the people who have been killed at Disneyland, and needless to say, the park is of no help *whatsoever.* By going through newspaper indexes I got the more recent stories. If a guy got squashed at the Matterhorn ride and reporters are present, you can just imagine the Disney rep saying, "Come on into the office, boys. Yeah, it's real tragic. He was probably drunk; we're investigating it. It doesn't look like there was any *ride* malfunction—back in '63 someone else got killed in the same way."

I might read this and scribble down, "Matterhorn,

Waiting in Line to Die

Disneyland has often been called "the happiest place on earth." Since its opening in 1955, hundreds of millions of people from all walks of life have flocked to this American Mecca and been swept up in the fantasy world envisioned by Walt Disney. From the park entrance on "Main Street USA," recreating turn-of-the-century small town America at 5/8 scale, to the top of the faux Matterhorn, complete with imitation bobsled runs, Disneyland evokes images and fantasies of life in happier, more pleasant and more exciting worlds.

But, beneath this glittering facade lurks something malevolent, something lethal. In the Magic Kingdom, life is not all pixie dust and happy, fairy tale endings. Behind the mouse's perpetually forced grin, there is more than a trace of the death head's grimace. For not all of the millions of "guests" (never visitors, patrons or suckers) entering the park in search of fantasy and pleasure survive to see the Electric Parade. They will leave the park in body bags, struck down by fantasy "attractions" run amok.

Reactionary pundits and defenders of the All-American Way of Life, Orange County-style, will immediately spring to the defense of the pride of Anaheim with the old transportation argument. "Why, you're more likely to die on the way to the park than inside." And right they are, *especially* in the case of Disneyland. History does not record the number of young Disneyland-bound families wiped out in fiery holocausts on the Santa Ana freeway. But other modes of transport do demonstrate the dangers. In 1968 alone, the Disneyland/LAX helicopter service suffered two of the worst civilian chopper crashes in U.S. history. In May, a helicopter carrying 23 people lucky enough to leave the park alive disintegrated in mid–air and crashed near Paramount. There were no survivors. Less than three months later, a Disney–bound chopper crashed on a Compton playing ground, killing 21 would-be "guests" and crew on board. Even the stroll from the parking lot to the park entrance is not without its risks. In 1987, after a Mormon party at the park, a gang fight in one of the lots erupted in gunfire, leaving one youth dead and a bystander injured.

But this is beside the point when it comes to discussing the hazards awaiting the unwary inside Disneyland. You're just as likely to die en route to such traditional mid-American amusements as tractor pulls or Bon Jovi concerts. Once inside, you're safe. But, to place yourself at the mercy of Disneyland is to risk mangling, mutilation and even death.

From 1955 through 1963, Disneyland's safety record was flawless. Not all of their "guests" may have left happy, but they did leave alive. Tragically, this perfect record ended in May of 1964, instituting the era of carnage that continues even today.

—introduction from *MCBF #13*, "Death at Disneyland" issue

1963" and then go through the Orange County newspapers day by day for that year. The U.C. Berkeley library microfilm room used to receive newspapers from every county in California. I have an Alumni Association lifetime membership which I got just for the library card, but anyone can get a U.C. library card just by paying money.

♦ **V: "Death at Disneyland" and "Death at the Zoo" seem like related topics—**

♦ **JM:** But they're different. With caged, frustrated and ferocious animals, the intimation of violence and danger is always present, but nobody expects to meet the Grim Reaper at "The Happiest Place on Earth"! [Disneyland motto] This lack of expectation may be due to the efficiency of Disney's spin-doctors, who by any means necessary suppress or minimize bad publicity.

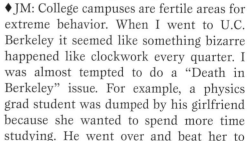

With its speeding bobsleds and Abominable Snowman, the Matterhorn quite rightly has earned its reputation as one of the deadliest rides at Disneyland. The two victims on record were a lovelorn teenager and a middle-aged matron—the latter was dragged along the tracks, pinned beneath the bobsled. Much like the way government agents operate, the park quietly closed the ride "Due to Technical Difficulties" and covertly unloaded the remaining riders through a hidden elevator.

But what's even more amazing than the two deaths on the Matterhorn is the pair on the People Mover, which proceeds at two miles per hour. One corpse was so tightly wedged between cars that workers had to dismantle everything to extricate the victim's remains. I guess looks can be deceiving!

♦ **V: Another future-issue theme that comes to mind is "Death on College Campuses"—**

♦ **JM:** College campuses are fertile areas for extreme behavior. When I went to U.C. Berkeley it seemed like something bizarre happened like clockwork every quarter. I was almost tempted to do a "Death in Berkeley" issue. For example, a physics grad student was dumped by his girlfriend because she wanted to spend more time studying. He went over and beat her to death with a bottle and then doused her with flammable liquid and lit her on fire. He wound up trying to commit suicide by jumping off a freeway overpass, but failed. In jail, he ended up being brutally raped and having a total mental breakdown. So much for his PhD!

Another day some guy climbed over the suicide

barrier of the Campanile [high tower] and stood on the ledge for hours, threatening to jump. Every other high viewpoint on campus was crowded with people watching the guy. [laughs] Other incidents: somehow a freshly killed deer's head wound up in a dorm one night; a street person committed hara-kiri in Sproul Plaza; a street person plucked his eyes out on Telegraph Avenue; someone jumped off the roof of Eshleman Hall and died. In the only all-girl dorm on campus, a student woke up at 4 A.M., went to the bathroom at the end of the hall, gave birth, threw the kid out the window, and went back to sleep. No one had known she was pregnant; she was chunky and always wore loose clothing. Someone coming back from a date heard the baby crying—the mother lived on the second floor and the baby had landed softly in some bushes. The police quickly figured out who the mom was.

In another incident, some guy who got pulled over by the police in downtown Oakland pulled out a gun and shot the officer (obviously, he didn't want a ticket). He came tearing up to Berkeley and stopped at the Cafe Med, dashed inside and the police showed up and shot him. The next day there were all these flyers posted around: "Must we tolerate all this violence in Berkeley?" There was no mention as to *why* the police were after the guy.

Berkeley will always be a fertile source of material; there's definitely no shortage of crazy people there.

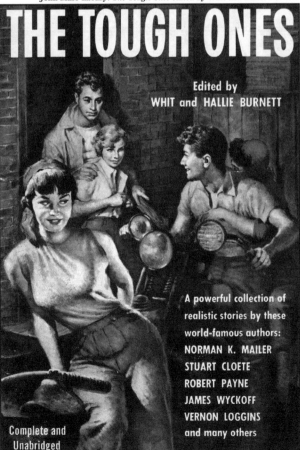

John Marr library: *The Tough Ones* edited by Whit and Hallie Burnett

THE TOUGH ONES

Edited by
WHIT and HALLIE BURNETT

A powerful collection of
realistic stories by these
world-famous authors:

NORMAN K. MAILER
STUART CLOETE
ROBERT PAYNE
JAMES WYCKOFF
VERNON LOGGINS
and many others

Complete and
Unabridged

College provides a high-pressure environment; a lot of people have their self-image tied up with academic success, and when things start going bad they can easily go berserk.

> **A lot of people think of *Murder Can Be Fun* as this violence-obsessed, sick, *noir* publication, but I do have my lighter side . . .**

♦ **V: Berkeley also hosted that infamous rapist, "Stinky," who was never caught. He got his moniker from a peculiar smell that was described as "overwhelmingly noxious." What other themes have you developed?**
♦ JM: A lot of people think of *Murder Can Be Fun* as this violence-obsessed, sick, *noir* publication, but I do have my lighter side, like when I did "Anti-Sex Tips for Teens." That was my first 36-pager; earlier publications were 20 pages or less. It was about those wonderful teenage advice manuals from as far back as the 1890s. I had been buying these at thrift stores and book sales for years, and one day I thought, "These would make a good subject for a future issue—plus, this would give an excuse to actually read them." I went through my collection of about 40 books and summarized and discussed them, reprinting choice bits. In many ways, this is actually my sickest issue. Since then I've picked up a bunch more good ones, but the person who has the really definitive collection is Lynn Peril of *Mystery Date.*

One book from the 1890s was part of an entire series which purported to advise people throughout their entire life: "What a young man ought to know," "What a young husband ought to know," "What a man of 45 ought to know," etc, with a corresponding set for women. I finally got all eight of them. The books contain the most twisted stuff imaginable: advising women against reading novels, saying everyone should sleep in open sleeping porches (like, on the East Coast in the dead of winter?!), etc. And these books are not written by your garden-variety crackpots but by *doctors!*
♦ **V: I'm sure masturbation was a popular subject—**
♦ JM: Yes, but only by innuendo. I think the proper term was "self-pollution." They advised: "Cross yourself! Bite your tongue! Take cold showers and plenty of them!" [laughs] "Do lots of athletics. Avoid tight-fitting bedclothes." Of course, if you're sleeping on an open porch in midwinter you don't have to worry about that kind of thing—you're too busy shivering. [laughs]
♦ **V: How do you compile the MCBF Datebooks?**
♦ JM: That was one of my favorite things to do. I produced 10 years of entirely different datebooks but have decided to stop; 1997 was the final one—I won't

be doing them anymore. When I read, I have 3x5" index cards at hand, organized by date. Like a lot of my projects, the datebook gave me an excuse to read books I probably wouldn't have read. Over the years I've acquired a fairly broad overview of the history of death, disaster and violence in general.

One reason I started *Murder Can Be Fun* was to provide an excuse to do research. Going to the library to track down every death at Disneyland, and looking through the 1963 *Orange County Register* day-by-day—just for your own personal curiosity, is a little pathological. [laughs] But if you're writing an *article,* you can spend all the time you want; you're doing this for your "art" or as a service to your readers . . . you're not merely wasting your time and eyesight staring at microfilm for days.

Cover of the *MCBF* inspired comic book

♦ V: *How about researching through the Internet?*

♦ JM: The Internet is great if what you want to know has happened in the last ten years or less. When the *New York Times* makes all their back files available electronically, *then* you'll be able to do some serious research. Meanwhile, most electronic newspaper archives only go back to 1980, if that—most don't go back before *1990!* People get so excited about the "Digital Revolution" and forget about all the information that remains only on analog media. With the CD takeover, a lot of the music that isn't necessarily "the best" but is still "pretty damned good" is going to be lost to people who've scrapped their turntables. Also, people like to say that one of the great things about the Internet is: anyone can publish. Well, the downside is that everyone *has*—especially the nuts, crackpots and lunatics with axes to grind. As Jerod Pore from *Factsheet Five* likes to say, "The Internet is the sum total of human opinion." I really find it frightening when people have this over-reliance on the Internet.

♦ V: *The* **New Yorker** *printed an article about how major libraries were junking their card catalogs. Yet these card catalogs bear millions of hand-written notations and comments by generations of librarians; they're history themselves. Whoever authorized discarding them obviously hasn't read historians like Fernand Braudel.*

♦ JM: It's terrible. I don't consider myself a Luddite by any stretch of the imagination, but I think those card catalogs should be saved, or at least scanned into some

massive database so they can be accessed electronically. All those handwritten notations need to be preserved! Besides, "analog" research offers the added advantage of serendipity. I always get sidetracked by other stories of the day. Just last week, I was poking around in some turn-of-the-century San Francisco papers and got completely sidetracked by stories about this guy running around the city throwing acid on women's dresses. Apparently, he was never caught.

Orange County had an organization titled "Young Americans for Nixon" (really creepy). During the height of the surfing craze, one member decided to paddle his surfboard from Santa Cruz to Orange County. [laughs] He'd go into the Pacific Ocean and paddle away, then come ashore every night. His girlfriend was following via car on the Pacific Coast Highway and she would pick him up. The newspapers were going crazy, insinuating all these things about the relationship because they seemed to be spending the night together, and this was scandalous. He made it in time to register for his community college classes. This was one of those cornball human-interest stories where the moral viewpoint seems really quaint today.

♦ V: *Hasn't sex advice gotten more liberal over the years?*

♦ JM: Of course; advice columnists have to eat. And these days, not too many people outside of the lunatic fringe are going to take a columnist seriously who pushes wisdom like "men expect to marry a virgin." Even "Dear Abby" and "Dear Ann Landers" have gotten comparatively liberal compared to what they used to be. Whereas "Ask Beth" seems to have gotten more puritanical. That used to be my favorite part of the Sunday paper; it seemed like once a month a guy would write in asking, "I was taking a shower with my friend the other day and we got to fooling around. Am I gay?" [laughs] Or, "My friend and I *did* something," but they never say what they did! She doesn't print letters like that anymore; now it's "I'm flunking out of school," or "One of my breasts is bigger than the other," or "I only seem to have one testicle." It's not as twisted.

There's all this rhetoric today about how depraved popular culture is, but I think popular culture was much more depraved during the '70s.

♦ V: *What do you mean?*

♦ JM: Things were a lot more sexually explicit back

then. I have a book from the '70s called *The Beginner's Guide to Group Sex.* It's a sober, straightforward guide about who does what to whom—orgy etiquette, if you will. Now, I don't doubt that you can get something similar today from some small press. But this book was published as a mass market paperback by Pocket Books! Talk about being aimed at a mainstream audience . . .

♦ *V: That's because the '60s had happened. It just took a little while for the straight media to catch on—that's all.*

There's all this rhetoric today about how depraved popular culture is, but I think popular culture was much more depraved during the '70s.

♦ JM: Exactly. It was sort of like the '60s were the theory, the '70s the mass practice. People are continually ranting that there's this wave of pornography about to engulf the nation's schools, but if it didn't happen in the '70s, it's not going to happen now.

I used to read all the anti-sex education hysteria articles in the *Reader's Digest* and other far less reputable publications. By the time I was ready to take "Family Life" class in high school, I was primed. I was expecting to see some explicit stuff! Needless to say, I was completely disappointed. The hokey anti-drug film strips were much more fun.

Young adult fiction has also changed. Back in the '70s when it started getting big (ironically after I had

graduated to the adult side of the library—I read very little modern Y.A. fiction as a teen), the stories were much more explicit, sexually and otherwise. Now, things are much milder and more conservative. I doubt Judy Bloom could get published as a new writer today—it seems like the country's full of bluenoses who want to ban her books.

On a Usenet children's books group, I followed a thread about "What Young Adults Shouldn't Read." One series they discussed was "Bloodlust." One woman with nothing better to do than to pre-screen kids' books was complaining about this series, so I went out and found one entitled *Body Parts.* An undertaker at a mortuary creates a zombie from assembled parts; the zombie turns out to be a cute teenage girl. The young boy protagonist of the story winds up having sex with her in a coffin, not realizing she's a zombie. [laughs] He eventually realizes what she is when he recognizes her hand as belonging to one of his neighbors who had gotten her hand chopped off in a grisly, unexplained crime! Great stuff.

♦ *V: Who buys these?*

♦ JM: Teenagers. The young adult market has boomed over the years; it barely existed when I was in high school. This particular series is quite perverse; maybe that's why the books are hard to find. Teenage horror is the biggest thing going in the young adult publishing world; if you go into a bookstore, you see shelves overflowing with them. A few years ago the "hot" genre was teenage murder stories, and some of them weren't bad . . .

♦ *V: This is an amazing market: teenagers who read—*

♦ JM: Actually a lot of them are so mindlessly written

Terms Every Teen Should Know

Abortion: Murder for it, suicide for you.

Anal Sex: Did not exist prior to 1985.

Cars: When they're not getting you around, they're getting you in trouble.

Chastity: The ideal mode of conduct for boys and girls alike.

Contraception: Only works for married people.

God: Your personal friend.

Going Steady: A popular practice that is not recommended.

Hymen: A girl's single most precious possession.

Intercourse: A mysterious act which only married couples may perform, and then only for procreation.

Jesus Christ: The answer to any and all of your problems.

Kissing: Something a girl may do with a boy after a very super-special prom.

Lewd Women: Only two types exist: those that are diseased *some* of the time and those that are diseased *all* of the time.

Masturbation: A frightful practice that saps vitality,

softens the brain and eventually drives one insane.

Marijuana: A vile narcotic noted for driving its users into a sexual frenzy.

Novels (reading of): A major cause of sexual infirmity among women.

Necking: A controversial activity.

Oral Sex: See **Anal Sex**

Petting: A mysterious, undefined practice which, while indulged in by many, will wreck your reputation, if not your life.

Reputation: A girl's second most precious possession.

Teachers: Sincere, dedicated professionals who only want to help you learn to the extent of your abilities.

Venereal Disease: A horrible, but just punishment for those who defy the laws of God and Man; oddly enough, also readily communicable via combs, doorknobs, toilets, and glasses.

—from *MCBF,*
"(Anti-) Sex Tips ForTeens" Issue

that any teenager can read them—even teenagers who *can't* read! [laughs] Actually, I just think it means that kids read more Y.A. books and less of other stuff, like adult fiction and magazines.

♦ *V: You also did an issue called "I Hate Sports"—*

♦JM: Yes, although I really don't hate sports—it's just the players, fans and owners I can't stand. In retrospect, I wasn't too happy with how that issue turned out. I did cover some good stories like the World Series that got fixed, or the woman who attempted suicide in the middle of the NCAA track-and-field championships. She was only third place in the 10,000 meter race. At the end of one straightaway instead of going around the curb, she kept going straight, climbed over a fence, ran out onto a bridge and jumped off. She survived, but was paralyzed. I think she's now a missionary.

All sorts of bizarre events have happened in the history of sports. During off season, a player from the Canadian Football League came home and helped his brother rob a liquor store. There was gunplay, someone went through a window and he got killed—I guess they don't pay them too well up North! [laughs] One of Herb Caen's [late S.F. *Chronicle* columnist] readers wrote in to say that O.J. Simpson is the biggest sports figure to be indicted for murder since somebody who won the Wimbledon singles championship in 1890. I took that as a personal challenge and set out to refute it. It turned out that a '70s world middleweight boxing champion, Carlos Monzan, had thrown his girlfriend off a balcony. She died and he was quickly convicted. There are a lot more sordid sports stories that you don't hear much about.

♦ *V: Somebody gets killed in the boxing ring fairly regularly—*

♦JM: As far as I'm concerned: if you box, you're insane. It's the only sport where you win automatically (not by forfeit!) if you kill your opponent. There used to be intercollegiate boxing, but that stopped after too many guys got killed. There was a case several years ago where the winner of a bout later collapsed and died.

♦ *V: Is that covered in your sports issue?*

♦JM: No, but I'm working on another sports issue now. One totally obscure story I just finished research-

John Marr library: *Hungry Men* by Edward Anderson

ing is especially bizarre. A bunch of people tried to watch a college football game from the roof of a building across the street. Unfortunately, it was a glass factory. The roof collapsed and a bunch of people landed on a red-hot glass furnace! Twenty-two people were killed. It's probably the worst (and easily the most painful) disaster to befall spectators at an American sporting event.

♦ *V: How do you decide on topics for* MCBF?

♦JM: It's pretty random. Usually I start with information that's not widely available, like an out-of-print book or an old obscure magazine article. If it's something that I like enough, I start digging—I'm not about to do all that work just to write something boring!

Sometimes I start at ground zero with a phrase I can't resist, like "Zoo Deaths," and take it from there. I like *MCBF* to be fresh; to be about incidents most people haven't heard about, or at least don't know all the gruesome details. It's a lot more interesting to write about "The Boston Molasses Flood" rather than tired old war-horses like the San Francisco Earthquake of 1906 or the sinking of the Titanic. I try to write about subjects you can't just go down to the library and pick up a book on.

That's why I'll never do an article or issue on Charles Manson. People have been pestering me for years to do something on "The Family"—I could probably triple my circulation if I put Manson on the cover of every issue. Well, it's not going to happen. First, I'm

---

One of my favorite sub-genres: teenage guilt novels, in which teenagers go out and crash the family car and kill someone or have a hideous hit-and-run accident.

---

not nearly as enthralled with the guy as most other true crime buffs. When you get right down to it, he didn't do anything the U.S. Army hasn't been doing for the last 200 years! But I do admit he was a wacky guy who was always ready with a great quote. Besides, the books out on him (*Helter Skelter, The*

Family, and Amok's recently-reprinted *The Garbage People)* are all great. They tell you pretty much everything you would ever want to know about Charlie & the gang.

♦ **V: "Naughty Children"?**

♦ JM: That was my last issue (#17) and it's about naughty children before 1960. Like most people, I thought that juvenile savagery was pretty much a new thing. I got to digging around and found plenty of dirt on kids from bygone days wrecking trains, drowning playmates, setting each other on fire—it's amazing! Most of this happened before there were even comic books, much less violent TV shows. There was even a teenager in Pilgrim-era Massachusetts that they hung for having sex with a horse!

The naughtiest one was easily Jesse Pomeroy, a youngster who terrorized Boston in the 1870s. When he was 12, he started luring small boys to remote places. Far from prying eyes, he'd force them to strip, tie them up and torture them. He got away with this seven or eight times before he was caught. He didn't kill anyone, but several of his victims were scarred for life. After being caught, he was sent to a reformatory for two years; he won early release by being a model prisoner. Not too long after he got out, he murdered and sexually mutilated a boy and a young girl. This made people really angry. He was sentenced to death, but because of his tender years, his sentence was later commuted to life in solitary confinement. He even set a record of sorts by spending almost 60 years in

prison, the first 42 in solitary.

♦ **V: Do you do all the writing yourself?**

♦ JM: Usually I'm the one to blame. The only time I've run contributions is after I've added pages. Craig and Jane Taatjes (of the late lamented zine *End Times*) did a great article on Bible deaths back in issue #5, and *Thrift SCORE* Al did a few pieces for me until she got busy with her zine. But right now, I don't have any problem filling the zine with my own writing; my real problem is cutting it down to size.

> ## I could probably triple my circulation if I put Manson on the cover of every issue. Well, it's not going to happen.

♦ **V: What other kinds of books do you read?**

♦ JM: Well, I'm a big fan of books about bums, hobos and general urban sleaze. One of the best authors is Henry Mayhew. He was one of the sources that Dickens used. In the 1830s he went around the slums of London interviewing people, and you would not believe how people lived back then. There was a class of people called "Pure Finders" who went around picking up dogshit, which was used in tanning leather. There was a controversy in the profession as to whether or not you should use a glove. You might want to use a glove for the obvious reasons, but on the other hand, it's easier to get your hand clean than to get a glove clean. There were public rat pits where people could watch dogs kill rats and bet on it. The author also wrote in detail about how the street kids lived. Reading Mayhew makes you think that things really *have* gotten better. [laughs]

And of course there's always camp. One of my favorite writers is Ed Wood. I recently found this book by him titled *The Bloodiest Sex Crimes in History.* You know, Ed Wood thought of himself as a writer first and a filmmaker second.

♦ **V: How did you know he wrote this? The cover credits "Spencer and West."**

♦ JM: *Nightmare of Ecstasy,* which was the basis for Tim Burton's *Ed Wood* movie, contains an Ed Wood bibliography listing that title. When I bought this, I thought it was just another pornography book masquerading as true crime (or vice versa)—another of those poorly written books written to titillate the reader and marketed by porn houses. Often, they're written by "doctors" who have probably never been within a 20-mile radius of a medical school. And they're *always* great!

♦ **V: And often they have nice moralistic introductions like: [reads] "Attempts to liberate ourselves from the shackles of hypocrisy are being made. The process is slow and at times confusing, but man's**

John Marr library: *Fighting the Traffic in Young Girls or War on the White Slave Trade*

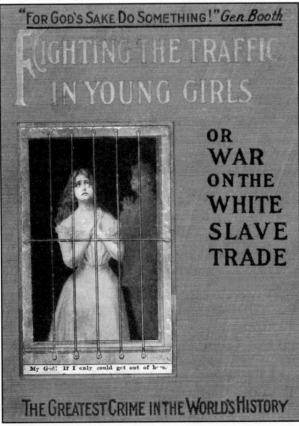

The Wit and Wisdom of Naughty Children

I am tired of home, sick of school, and bored with life.
—*14-year-old boy explaining why he robbed a store at knife-point circa 1960*

I won't do it again.
—*Welsh boy, 9, after drowning 4-year-old boy, 1947*

I took the pram from outside the shop. There was a baby in the pram and I threw it in the water. I just wanted to do it.
—*English boy, 9, 1947*

I'd like to be a nurse because then I can stick needles in people. I like hurting people.
—*Mary Bell, 11, 1968*

Murder isn't that bad. We all die sometime.
—*Mary Bell, 11, 1968*

They were floating about like two drowned puppies.
—*William Wild, 13, describing the aftermath of drowning two toddlers, England, 1835*

That's where I shoved him in.
—*James B. pointing out where he drowned a 7-year-old boy for "being a sissy," Philadelphia, 1937*

I was tired of walking. I thought I would stop the train and ride awhile.
—*Harry Scherer, 16, explaining why he put a railroad tie across the tracks, Tulsa, OK 1943*

Just to see what would happen.
—*11 & 12-year-old boys explaining why they piled bricks on a railroad track, Bayonne, NJ 1934*

We just wanted to see what would happen.
—*boy, 15, after pushing a 55-gallon drum of tar 50 feet uphill to put on train tracks, Atlanta, GA 1955*

When it hit it flashed through my mind, "What if it wrecks the train?" I hadn't thought of that before.
—*same boys*

If I killed one they would just send me to reform schools again, but if I killed them both they'll send me to the chair.
—*14-year-old boy explaining why he had to kill two playmates, Arkansas 1960*

I hated to kill but I had to—I'm insane.
—*note left by 14-year-old Ohio boy who shot his father circa 1957*

I did not try to rob the Dobrindts, for what do I care for the 2 or 3 more you are able to give?
—*"Cry Baby Bandit" Karl Müller, 15, denying robbing a family of 3 he killed, Germany, 1927*

Ain't dead yet, is you? I'll make you dead.
—*Hattie, 9, while hitting 2-year-old with an ax circa 1896 for biting her*

Because she would not let me go to the picture show.
—*boy's reason for shooting and killing his stepmother, Fort Myers, FL 1940*

I appreciate the kindness shown to me and I want to thank everybody.
—*George Rogalski, 14, to court after being sentenced to 10 years in prison for a kidnap/murder of a small girl, Chicago 1943*

So I could see the fire engines roll!
—*Thomas L., 15, explaining why he'd set fires in 10 Manhattan apartment buildings, 1925*

I don't know.
—*the classic excuse*

—MCBF #17, the "Naughty Children" Issue

---

insatiable thirst for knowledge prods him forward. We gather our strength and move forward toward a better understanding of the greatest mystery on earth . . . man."

♦ JM: Stuff like that can come in handy if you have to prove "redeeming social value" in court! The book includes a glossary of sex terms like "auto-fellatio" (self-explanatory) and "amastia" which means "ultra-erotic." I get the feeling that Ed Wood made up some of these words. [laughs] Anything that Ed Wood has written is certainly a must-have, like *Killer in Drag* which has recently been re-released.

All these books are coming out now. With true crime books selling so well these days, it seems like anyone who has ever committed any sort of murder is getting a book written about them, and they're all terrible. There's an unfortunate trend in publishing: if you look at that shelf of true crime books, you can probably pick out the most recent books by their thickness.

♦ V: *Why is this?*

♦ JM: The publishers want them longer and longer. My theory is: the only time the average person reads these days is when they're riding public transit from their jobs in the city to their increasingly distant homes in the suburbs. If you have a thick book, you don't have to worry about running out of reading or having to decide which book to read next. When I got my job in the city and was still commuting from Berkeley, everyone on the train would be reading these thick paperbacks. It seemed that they were all reading the same five or six books, too.

These days, most of my crime reading is strictly the older stuff—it's much better written than the books being dashed out today. Also, there's been a format change; in the past, each chapter would cover a separate case. A good writer can take any crime, no matter how boring or stupid, and write a good 5,000 word chapter about it. Today's writers are taking crimes that are pretty boring to begin with, and then padding the text out to a 300- or 400-page book. They discuss the family history of the prosecutor, beginning with his grandparents coming to America, and finally get to the noble young son. They completely kiss the informant's ass (usually a prosecutor or defense lawyer) paying him back for

supplying the information. But who wants to slog through all this fluff?

Another one of my pet peeves is: ever since the movie *Pulp Fiction* came out, the whole concept of what "pulp fiction" is has been distorted. I grew up reading what I consider to be *real* pulp fiction: fiction that was published in serial form in the pulp magazines of the '30s. When people talk about pulp fiction today, they are referring to the paperbacks of the '50s. Stylistically the genres were much different: the '30s were pre-noir and the '50s were post-noir. The pulp stories were written like serials and the paperbacks were written as novels. I consider them to be two completely different kettles of fish. Of course, I realize that I'm guilty of this myself. I just found out that a lot of the books I've been calling "dime novels" (the unbelievably bad 1890s equivalent of pulp fiction) are actually "nickel libraries" or "schoolboy weeklies" to real dime novel purists!

The *real* pulp fiction is great in a fun way. One of my favorite series featured *Doc Savage,* a do-gooder fighting all these bizarre criminals. In one book, the criminal had this mysterious weapon which he would turn on someone walking down the street; all of a sudden they'd be screaming and their eyeballs would be popping out of their sockets! Contrast that to some-

John Marr library: *Snake Handlers: God Fearers or Fanatics?*

thing written by Jim Thompson, or any of the other paperback writers of the '50s. They're great, but they write in an entirely different style: not as sensational, not as episodic, much more realistic and much more cynical—very post-war.

Ted Bundy was interesting because he was intelligent and imaginative; it's just that once in a while he was driven by an uncontrollable urge!

♦ **V: Now we're in the '90s, where anything to do with mass murder and killing has become "hip" in the past few years. These days frat boys wear T-shirts celebrating serial killers—**

♦ JM: Do you want to know the big audience for that kind of material now? Middle-aged women and housewives, and Ann Rule is their hero.

♦ **V: She's the Danielle Steele of the true crime world.**

♦ JM: It's amazing. Who'd think so many women love to read about other women getting sliced and diced? Now, in a lot of ways, I'm tired of the whole serial killer fad. There are only a few really interesting serial killers—most of them are losers and drifters killing prostitutes and hitchhikers. They're just lowlifes killing the easiest, most accessible victims. All you have to do is offer a hooker money and she'll get in your car and let you drive her anyplace.

I remember being at a CRAMPS' show in the early '80s where Lux Interior joked how he used to hitchhike in Sacramento and pretend that Ted Bundy was after him; I was the only one in the audience who *got* it. No one else seemed to know who Ted Bundy was, and that's a crime! With the punk D.I.Y. spirit in the air, I decided to start a zine to fill this shocking void of knowledge. Now, you see serial killers on the Movie of the Week. It's time to move on to something different.

Most serial killers are really boring people and their crimes are boring. Ted Bundy was interesting because he was intelligent and imaginative; it's just that once in a while he was driven by an uncontrollable urge! Near the University of Washington campus in sorority row is a well-traveled alley lined with buildings with windows. One night some friends dropped a woman off at one end of this alley; she lived at the other end. Somewhere in between, Ted Bundy met her and talked her into going with him, and she was never seen again. This wasn't some deserted alley; there were a lot of people around. Compare this to driving down to the Tenderloin and waving a $20 bill at a hooker. So, I don't follow this serial killer thing very closely anymore. I hate it when things become trendy and get overdone. You always have to stay one jump ahead! **V**

John Marr's Recommended Reading

This is not a "best of" list, but an arbitrary selection of books I've enjoyed on one level or another over the years.

FICTION

CHILDREN/YOUNG ADULT

Aldrich, Thomas Bailey *The Story of a Bad Boy*
Andrews, V.C. *Flowers in the Attic*
Brooks, Walter S. *Freddy the Detective*
Christopher, John *The White Mountains*
Cleary, Beverly *Ramona the Pest*
Collier, James Lincoln *The Teddy Bear Habit*
Collodi, Carl *Adventures of Pinocchio*
Cormier, Robert *The Chocolate War*
Dahl, Roald *Charlie and the Chocolate Factory*
D'Aulaires, I. & P. *D'Aulaire's Norse Gods and Giants*
Felsen, Henry Gregor *Hot Rod*
Grimm, W. & J. *The Complete Fairy Tales*
Hatch, Richard *The Lobster Books*
Holm, Ann *North to Freedom*
Jordan, Hope *Haunted Summer*
Key, Alexander *Escape to Witch Mountain*
McCloskey, Robert *Homer Price*
Meader, Stephen *T-Model Tommy*
Pinkwater, Daniel *Young Adults*
Salten, Felix *Bambi*
Standish, Burt *Frank Merriwell's School-days*
Twain, Mark *Tom Sawyer*

CRIME/MYSTERY

Alexander, David *The Madhouse in Washington Square*
Brown, Fredric *The Deep End*
Bunker, Edward *Little Boy Blue*
Burke, Thomas *Limehouse Nights*
Crumley, James *The Wrong Case*
Chandler, Raymond *The Big Sleep*
Dahl, Roald *The Best of . . .*
Doyle, A.C. *Complete Sherlock Holmes*
Ellson, Hal *Duke*
Ellin, Stanley *Quiet Horror*
Fisher, Steve *I Wake Up Screaming*
Goodis, David *Street of No Return*
Grant, Maxwell *The Living Shadow*
Heard, Nathan *Howard Street*
Hammett, Dashiell *The Continental Op*
Highsmith, Patricia *Tales of Natural and Unnatural Catastrophes*
Himes, Chester *The Real Cool Killers*
Hopenstand & Brown (ed.) *The Defective Detective in the Pulps*
Karp, David *Brotherhood of Velvet*
Keeler, Harry S. *The Amazing Web*
Kerr, Philip *The Berlin Trilogy*
Lacy, Ed *Room to Swing*
Latimer, Jonathan *Solomon's Vineyard*
MacDonald, Ross *The Drowning Pool*
March, William *The Bad Seed*
Meredith (ed.) *The Best from Manhunt*
McCoy, Horace *They Shoot Horses, Don't They?*
McCrumb, Sharyn *Bimbos of the Death Sun*
Perry, Will *Death of an Informer*
Pronzini & Adrian (ed.) *Hard-boiled: An Anthology of American Crime Stories*
Raymond, Derek *The Devil's Home on Leave*
Ritchie, Jack *Little Boxes of Bewilderment*
Sapir & Murphy *Bay City Blast*
Sjöwall & Wahlöö *The Laughing Policeman*
Slesar, Henry *Death on Television*
Thompson, Jim *The Getaway, The Criminal*
Westlake, Donald *Jimmy the Kid*
Willeford, Charles *Cockfighter, The Burnt Orange Heresy*
Woolrich, Cornell *Nightwebs, Rendezvous in Black*

SCI-FI/FANTASY/HORROR

Brown, Frederic *Martians Go Home!*
Burroughs, E.R. *Tarzan of the Apes*
Coblentz, Stanton *Hidden World*
Collier, John *Fancies and Goodnights*
Disch, Thomas *The Prisoner*
Ellison, Harlan *The Essential Ellison*
Farmer, Philip Jose *Riverworld and Other Stories*. (ed.:) *Mother Was a Lovely Beast*
King, Stephen *Carrie*
Leiber, Fritz *Our Lady of Darkness*
Lovecraft, H.P. *The Tomb*
Robeson, Kenneth *The Vanisher*
Serling, Rod *Stories From the Twilight Zone*

MISCELLANEOUS

Aldiss, Brian *The Hand-Reared Boy*
Bukowski, Charles *Post Office*
Burgess, Anthony *A Clockwork Orange*
Burroughs, William *Junkie*
Defoe, Daniel *Robinson Crusoe, etc*
Dreiser, Theodore *An American Tragedy*
Frank, Jeffrey *The Creep*
Gardner, Leonard *Fat City*
Gorey, Edward *Amphigorey*
Grass, Gunter *The Tin Drum*
Henry, O. *The Four Million*
Jacobs & Jones *The Beaver Papers*
Jessup, Richard *The Cincinnati Kid*
Kohner, Frederick *Gidget*
Lehman, Ernest *The Sweet Smell of Success and Other Stories*
Levin, Meyer *Compulsion*
Lewis, Sinclair *Main Street*
Miller, J.P. *The People Next Door*
Moriarty, Florence (ed.) *True Confessions: 60 Years of Sin, Suffering, & Sorrow*
Norris, Frank *McTeague*
Orwell, George *1984*
Parsons, Tony *Platinum Logic*
Phillips, David Graham *The Fashionable Adventures of Joshua Craig*
Sillitoe, Alan *The Loneliness of the Long Distance Runner*
Schulberg, Bud *What Makes Sammy Run?*
Shulman, Max *The Many Loves of Dobie Gillis*
Stevenson, R.L. *The New Arabian Nights*
Tevis, Walter *Queen's Gambit*
Trumbo, Dalton *Johnny Got His Gun*
West, Nathanael *Miss Lonelyhearts*

POETRY

Busch, Wilhelm *The Genius of . . .*
Goodman, Jonathan (ed.) *Bloody Versicles: The Rhymes of Crime*
Graham, Harry *Ruthless Rhymes For Heartless Homes*
Hoffman, Heinrich *Slovenly Peter*
Homer, *The Odyssey*
Houseman, A.E. *Complete Poems*
March, Joseph Mancure *The Set-Up*
Masters, Edgar Lee *Spoon River Anthology*
Parker, Dorothy *The Portable . . .*
(various) *The Greek Anthology*

NON-FICTION

ACCIDENTS & DISASTERS

Benson, Ragnar *Fire, Flash, and Fury*
Benzaquin, Paul *Holocaust*
Bird, Michael *The Town that Died*
Cornell, James *The Great International Disaster Book*
Deighton & Schwartzman *Airshipwreck!*
Dobson, Miller & Payne *The Cruelest Night*
Eddy, Potter & Page *Destination Disaster*
Fuller, John *The Day of St. Anthony's Fire*
Gallagher, Thomas *Fire At Sea*
Kletz, Trevor *What Went Wrong? Case Histories of Process Plant Disasters*
Lawson, G. *Beverly Hills: Anatomy of a Night Club Fire*
Lyle, Kate *Scalded to Death by the Steam*
Perrow, Charles *Normal Accidents: Living with High Risk Technologies*
Reader's Digest, Editors of (ed.) *Drama in Real Life*
Reed, Robert *Train Wrecks*
Rolt, L.T.C. *Red For Danger: A History of Railway Accidents*
Serling, Robert *The Probable Cause*
Shaw, Robert *Down Brakes*
Weingarten, Arthur *The Sky is Falling*

TRUE CRIME

Allen, William *Starkweather*
Anderson, Scott *The 4 O'Clock Murders*
Asbury, Herbert *Gangs of New York*
Bartlett, Evan *Love Murders of Harry F. Powers*
Becker, Jillian *Hitler's Children*
Bolitho, William *Murder for Profit*
Boucher, Anthony (ed.) *The Quality of Murder*
Bowen, Croswell *They Went Wrong*
Bremer, Arthur *Assassin's Diary*
Brown, Wenzell *The Lonelyhearts Murders*
Buchanan, Edna *The Corpse Had a Familiar Face*
Burns, Robert *I am a Fugitive from a Chain Gang*
Collan & Sterling *I Was a House Detective*
Damio, Ward *Urge to Kill*
Dean, John *The Indiana Torture Slaying*
deQuincey, Thomas "Murder Considered as One of the Fine Arts"
de River, J. Paul *The Sexual Criminal*
Colander, Pat *Thin Air*
Farrell, Harry *Swift Justice*
Gaddis & Long *Killer: A Journal of Murder*
Gaskins & Earle *Final Truth: The Autobiography of Donald "Pee Wee" Gaskins*
Gaute & Odell *The New Murderer's Who's Who*
Gilmore, John *Severed*
Godwin, John *Murder U.S.A.*
Golden, Henry *A Little Girl Is Dead*
Goldfaber, Ed *Tracer: The Search For Missing Persons*
Graysmith, Robert *Zodiac*
Hazelwood *Autoerotic Asphyxiation*
Hearst, Patty *Every Secret Thing*
Hofstadter, Richard (ed.) *American Violence*
Holbrook, Stewart *Murder Out Yonder*
Howard, Clarke *Zebra*
Jackson, J.H. (ed.) *The Portable Murder Book*
Lamott, Ken *Chronicles of San Quentin*
Lentz, Harris *Assassinations and Executions*
Leyton, Elliot *Hunting Humans*
Lyons, Arthur *Satan Wants You*
Markham, Ronald *Alone With the Devil*
Martin, John Bartlow *Butchers Dozen*
Mast, Dexter *Six Gold Stars*
Masters, Brian *Killing for Company*
McComas, J.F. (ed.) *The Graveside Companion*
McDade, Thomas *Annals of Murder*
McDougal, Dennis *Angel of Darkness*
McGuire & Norton *Perfect Victim*
McKelway, St. Clair *True Tales from the Annals of Crime and Rascality*
Michaud & Aynesworth *The Only Living Witness*
Millett, Kate *The Basement*
Olsen, Jack *The Man With the Candy*
Pearson, Edmund *Studies in Murder*
Phelan, James *Scandals, Scamps & Scoundrels*
Pierrepoint, Albert *Executioner: Pierrepoint*
Radin, Edward *12 Against the Law*
Reiterman, Tim *Raven: The Untold Story of Jim Jones and His People*
Ressler & Shachtman *Whoever Fights Monsters*
Rosberg, Robert *Games of Thieves*
Schecter, Harold *Deviant*
Serency, Gitta *The Case of Mary Bell*
Sifakis, Carl *The Encyclopedia of American Crime*
Thorwald, Jürgen *The Century of the Detective*
Webb, Jack *The Badge*
Williams, H.A. *Bad Blood: The Story of Stanley Graham*
Wolfe, Linda *The Professor and the Prostitute*

CARNIVAL/FREAKS

Bogden, Robert *Freakshow*
Boles, Don *The Midway Showman*
Burchett, George *Memoirs of a Tattooist*
Caradec, Nohain *Le Petomane*
Carmichael, Bill *Incredible Collectors, Weird Antiques and Odd Hobbies*
Drimmer, Frederick *Very Special People*
Fiedler, Leslie *Freaks*
Gresham, William Lindsay *Monster Midway, Nightmare Alley*
Howell & Ford *The Illustrated True History of the Elephant Man*
Jay, Ricky *Learned Pigs and Fireproof Women*
Johnson & Varndell *Freaks, Geeks, and Stranger Girls*
Lewis, Arthur *Carnival!*
Mannix, Dan *Step Right Up! (aka Memoirs of a Sword Swallower), Freaks: We Who Are Not As Others*
McKennon, Joe *Pictorial History of American Carnivals*
Parker, Mike *World's Most Fantastic Freaks*
Rose, Jim *Freak Like Me*
St. Claire, Stoney *Stoney Knows How*
Sorrows, Gene *All About Carnivals*
Tate, Celestine *Some Crawl and Never Walk*
Taylor, James *Shocked & Amazed* (several volumes available; also videos, POB 22262, Baltimore MD 21203)
Wallace, Amy & Irving *The Two: The Story of the Original Siamese Twins*

BUMS/URBAN SLEAZE

Black, Jack *You Can't Win*
Buryns, Ed *Vagabonding USA*
Byrne, Robert *McGorty: Story of a Billiard Bum*
DiPrima, Diane *Memoirs of a Beatnik*
Friedman, Josh Alan *Tales of Times Square*
Kinkedd, Gwen *Chinatown*
Littlejohn, Duffy *Hopping Freight Trains in America*
Love, Edmund *Subways Are For Sleeping*
Mayhew, Henry *London Labor and the London Poor* (four vols.)
Orwell, George *Down and Out in Paris and London*
Reitman, Ben *Boxcar Bertha*
Sante, Luc *Lowlife*
Wethern & Colnett *A Wayward Angel*
Willeford, Charles *I Was Looking for a Street*

PHOTOS/ART

Addams, Charles *The Dear Dead Days*
Goodrich, Lloyd *Edward Hopper*
Lesberg, Sandy *Violence in Our Times*
Lesy, Michael *Wisconsin Death Trip*
Keenes *Tomorrows Masters*
Nagler, Richard *Oakland Rhapsody*
Sante, Luc *Evidence*
Sloan, Manley & Van Parys *Dear Mr. Ripley*
Warhol, Andy *Death & Disasters*
Weegee *Naked City*

ADVICE

Boone, Pat *'Twixt 12 and 20*
Clark, Dick *To Goof or Not to Goof*
Ekoos, Carl *In High at Sexteen*
Francis, Connie *For Every Young Heart*
Landers, Ann *Since You Ask Me*
Peck, Ellen *How To Get A Teenage Boy and What To Do With Him When You Get Him*
Rose, Margaret *Rush: A Sorority Girl's Guide to Getting In*
Stall, Sylvanus *What a Young Man Ought to Know*
Shields, Brooke *On Your Own*
Weber, Eric *How To Pick Up Girls*

MISCELLANEOUS

Adams, Cecil *The Straight Dope*
Anger, Kenneth *Hollywood Babylon*
Baaker, J. & T. *Shower of Blessings*
Barth, Kirby, Smith & Wilkins *Roadside USA*
Berton, Pierre *The Big Sell*
Braun, M. *Differential Equations and Their Application*
Brodie, Fawn *No Man Knows My History*
Brunvand, Jan *The Vanishing Hitchhiker*
Bryant, Anita *My Eyes Have Seen the Glory*
Carmichael, Bill *Incredible Collectors, Weird Antiques, and Odd Hobbies*
Chaplin, J.P. *Rumor, Fear, and the Madness of Crowds*
Cohen & Jacopetti *Africa Addio*
Copjec, Joan (ed.) *Shades of Noir*
deFord, Frank *Five Strides on the Banked Track*
Davis, Steven *Hammer of the Gods*
Dundes, Alan *Cracking Jokes*
Feig, Konnilyn *Hitler's Death Camps*
Gaines, Stephen *Marjoe*
Gilbreath & Carey *Belles On Their Toes*
Goddard, Henry *The Kallikak Family*
Gordon, Mel *The Grand Guignol: Theater of Fear and Terror*
Greenburg, Dan *Scoring*
Herman, Gary *Rock'n'Roll Babylon*
Heuvelmans, Bernard *In the Wake of the Sea Serpents*
Howarth, David (ed.) *Great Escapes*
Huff, Darrell *How To Lie With Statistics*
Jordan, Pat *A False Spring*
Kobler, John *Afternoon in the Attic*
Leigh, Michael *The Velvet Underground*
Leslie, Edward *Desperate Journeys, Abandoned Souls*
Linkletter, Art *Drugs At My Doorstep*
Lopez, Enrique *They Lived On Human Flesh*
Lovelace, Linda *Ordeal*
Mardikian, George *Song of America*
Mitchell, Joseph *Up in the Old Hotel*
Morris, Desmond *The Soccer Tribe*
O'Neill, Cherry Boone *Starving For Attention*
Pearson, Edmund *Queer Books*
Pike, Jeff *The Death of Rock'n'Roll*
Pop, Iggy & Wehrer *I Need More*
Raabe, Tom *Biblioholism: The Literary Addiction*
Rentzel, Lance *When All the Laughter Died in Sorrow*
Rhue, Morton *The Wave*
Rosenthal & Geld *One More Victim*
Roueche, Berton *Medical Detectives*
Rozin, Skip *One Step From Glory*
Ryan, Elizabeth *Life is a Lonely Place*
Savage, Jon *England's Dreaming*
Scarne, John *Odds Against Me*
Scheinin, Richard *Field of Screams: The Dark Underside of America's Pastime*
Solanas, Valerie *The SCUM Manifesto*
Stang, Ivan *High Weirdness by Mail*
Stein, Harry *Tiny Tim*
Steinbacher, John *The Child Seducers*
Van Every, Edward *Sins of New York*
Wallace, Amy *The Prodigy*
Wallechinsky & Medved *Whatever Happened to the Class of '65?*
Waters, John *Shock Value, Crackpot*
Wertham, Fredric *Seduction of the Innocent*
Wolf, David *Foul!*

◆ ◆ ◆

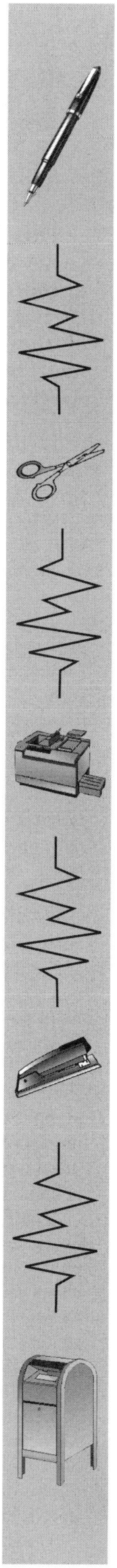

Proletarian Novels

This article was written by Stephen Schwartz (AKA Nico Ordway), a leading contributor to *Search & Destroy* and a founding contributor to *RE/Search*. He is a San Francisco *Chronicle* writer and secretary of the Northern California Newspaper Guild. His new book, *The Left Coast: California and the American Mind*, will be published in 1998.

Precursors of the current zine explosion include all publications classed as "proletarian": novels, nonfiction, short stories, magazines, pamphlets, poetry, plus related genres such as tough-guy, freak/carnival/sideshow books, writing by people of color, early feminist writing—in short, all the voices of the social underclass. The following essay focuses on the proletarian novel.

The "proletarian novel," as it is known in American literary criticism today, is almost entirely a product of the 1930s Communist milieu. A definitive account of the phenomenon is included in Walter B. Rideout's *The Radical Novel in the United States*, published by Harvard University Press in 1956. Why write novels rather than historical accounts? To quote Novalis, "Novels arise out of the *shortcomings* of history."

However, novels of working class struggle derive neither their original models nor their finest products from the Communist movement. Indeed, it would be hard to imagine better social or labor novels than such works of the French "naturalist" writer, Emile Zola, as his magnificent *Germinal* (1885), perhaps the greatest strike novel ever written, or *L'Assommoir* and *La Bete Humaine* (the latter produced as a brilliant film in 1938). As a story of starvation and Bohemian striving in the great modern cities, nothing can touch *Hunger* (1890) by the Norwegian novelist Knut Hamsun.

In the somewhat different genre of novels about revolutionary movements, the Russian Maxim Gorky produced a classic in his *Mother*. But for me, the greatest 20th century fictional narrative about radicals remains *Seven Red Sundays* (1932) by the Spanish author Ramon Sender, an amazing account of anarchists and communists in the years preceding the Spanish civil war. The best novel written in English about 1930s Communism as a temptation is Lionel Trilling's *The Middle of the Journey*.

The Russo-Belgian anarchist and communist Victor Serge produced a cycle of marvelous revolutionary novels, beginning and ending in captivity: the first, *Men in Prison*, tells the story of anarchists jailed in France just before World War I, while the last, *Midnight in the Century*, describes anti-Stalinists and other dissenters in the Soviet gulag. The works of the German-Mexican author B. Traven are probably the most popular social novels read today. They deal with footloose rebel workers traveling across the Rio Grande (*The Cotton Pickers*, originally titled *The Wobbly*), the Mexican oil industry (*The White Rose*), ill-fated sailors (*The Death Ship*), gold-hunters driven insane by greed (*The Treasure of the Sierra Madre*), and, of course, his monumental cycle of "Jungle" novels, describing the outbreak of the Mexican Revolution of 1910.

Outstanding social and populist works of fiction had previously emerged in American literature at the turn of the 19th century, typified by Frank Norris's *The Octopus*. This classic of California liter-ature describes an armed conflict between settlers and railroad interests in the 1880s. Upton Sinclair's career as a social author began in 1906 with *The Jungle*, which was intended as an epic of socialist organizing among Lithuanian immigrants in Chicago, but became imperishably famous for its expose of the horrible conditions of the meat-packing industry.

In 1908 Jack London published *The Iron Heel*, an account of an anti-socialist counter-revolution in a future America that not only brilliantly anticipated the rise of fascism in Europe 20 years later but also offers a warning, totally relevant today, of the rise of an oligarchical state and the crushing of all popular liberties. Endorsed by the brilliant Bolshevik theoretician Nikolai Bukharin, and still in print, it continues to attract new readers of varying ideological orientations.

The "proletarian novel" of the 1930s, however, represented something different from these predecessors. The "proletarian" genre as a study of the life of the poor was already established in the United States, in stories and books by Stephen Crane and Theodore Dreiser, among many others. John Dos Passos incorporated Wobblies and other labor figures into his successful "camera eye" narratives (*U.S.A.* trilogy), and an author of considerable talent, James T. Farrell, a communist and Trotskyite, wrote perhaps the best of all the "proletarian" works of that era, the *Studs Lonigan* trilogy. But Dos Passos and Farrell were writers first and "proletarians" second.

Beginning with Michael Gold's *Jews Without Money*, published in 1930, a new trend was detected in American letters. Gold, born Irwin Granich, was a former anarchist who had converted to Communism under the influence of, among others, Leon Trotsky. Gold's work was viewed as a parallel to the "proletarian culture" writings then produced in the Soviet Union. These works concentrated single-mindedly, and often dully, on the details of industrial life, were told from the point of view of the rank-and-file worker, and were usually written in simple language, utilizing obvious, dramatic plot devices and symbolism.

Trotsky, for his part, opposed the concept of a "proletarian culture." As a Marxist, he argued that whereas "bourgeois" literature reflected a long period of capitalist domination over society, the rule of "proletarian dictatorship" would be too brief to produce lasting artistic or literary achievements. With the mentality of a 19th century popular enlightener, Trotsky also warned that "proletarian literature" was based on the fallacy that workers could not understand the classics, and noted that few of the "proletarian" writers had real talent.

Nevertheless, "proletarian culture" became a catch-phrase of the new Communist dispensation, and many attempts to imitate Soviet fiction were written and published (if seldom read) in the U.S. during the 1930s. Gold's *Jews Without Money* was among the best; a highly readable, entertaining, and moving description of Gold's own Jewish immigrant origins. It is an infectious book, beloved in unpredictable places; the famous anti-Castro Cuban poet Heberto Padilla, for example, is known to have memorized some of it and to quote it passionately when inebriated.

Gold's book sold well in its first edition, and seemed to promise the beginning of a golden age of Communist fiction in America. However, it had a major flaw from the viewpoint of party cultural commissars: its protagonist's best friend is a Jewish street child who, because of his dark complexion, is nicknamed (like thousands of other Jewish immigrant boys of that era) "Nigger." In an instance of "political correctness" avant la lettre, the book became scandalous in the Communist bureaucracy for this *Huckleberry Finn*-like concession to the reality of popular speech, and was not republished until many decades had passed, at the end of Gold's life. Gold wrote no more novels—although a good deal of the Stalinist journalism he produced in the succeeding years could with justice be described as fictional. (Gold, who with most of his siblings became deeply involved in the defense of Stalin and in Soviet espionage, died in isolation and disillusion.)

Jews Without Money, however, was far outshadowed, in terms of literary quality, by a volume deservedly considered an outstanding classic of 20th century fiction, Henry Roth's *Call It Sleep,* which appeared in 1935. This beautiful, shocking, and highly-experimental account of an immigrant childhood on the Lower East Side of New York was widely hailed at publication as an achievement comparable to Joyce's *Ulysses,* and was praised by the critic Robert Alter, in 1988, as "among the few great American novels of the 20th century." The critic Irving Howe similarly declared it to be "one of the few genuinely distinguished novels written by a 20th-century American."

Yet its author's fate further illustrated the traps facing writers of outstanding talent in the Communist movement. Roth was prevailed upon to abandon his literary work by party functionaries who argued he could do more for "the Revolution" by serving as a rank-and-file union member in industry, and he worked in many simple trades, ending up in a foundry, and remaining silent as a writer until years after his break with the Communist party in 1967. The second edition of *Call It Sleep,* issued in the mid-'60s, has sold one million copies. Roth, who died in 1995 at 89, resumed publishing novels toward the end of his life, but any observer of his case must despair at the colossal loss to literature represented by this party-dictated ascesis.

As the Depression wore on, "proletarian literature" became a significant fad, and even briefly dominated the American fiction scene. John Steinbeck and William Saroyan both published works of a pro-Communist or radical nature, if not fully congruent with the "proletarian" pattern. Of the full-fledged "proletarians" the most successful, in terms of a longer career, was undoubtedly the Chicago writer Nelson Algren, whose *Somebody In Boots* (1935) is unread today except by experts, but who followed that first effort with his masterful *Man With the Golden Arm* and *A Walk on the Wild Side.* The critic and philosopher Edward Dahlberg published a harrowing account of adolescent life among tramps, *Bottom Dogs.*

Communist polemicist and later Soviet spy Whittaker Chambers wrote a popular short story, "Can You Hear Their Voices?" about radical farmers, and saw it produced as a play throughout the country. Chambers' work was intended explicitly as fiction in the service of agitation; similarly, a well-known early "proletarian" novel, *S.S. Utah* by "Mike Pell," was a barely-disguised manual for organizing Communist mutinies in the navies of the capitalist nations.

Jack Conroy's *The Disinherited,* published in 1933, has survived as an exemplar of the "proletarian" style. Conroy was also well-known as an editor of *Anvil,* one of the most prominent radical "little magazines" (proletarian magazines such as *Anvil* were precursors to today's zines) which also published Gold, Farrell, Algren, Erskine Caldwell, Jesse Stuart, and the Black writers Langston Hughes and Frank Yerby, who ended up successful, as well as more obscure and primitive Communist authors like Meridel Le Sueur.

Waiting For Nothing, by Tom Kromer, appeared in 1935, from Alfred Knopf, sponsored by the California-based Soviet advocate Lincoln Steffens. Like Dahlberg's *Bottom Dogs,* it is a disturbing firsthand account of a youth spent wandering around the country. Its jacket copy noted, "Parts of this novel were scrawled on Bull Durham (cigarette) papers in boxcars, margins of religious tracts . . . and on a few, very few occasions actually pecked out on a typewriter." The author was described as a 28-year-old, born in West Virginia, who graduated from college and was employed as a rural teacher after working in the glassblowing industry, where his father died of cancer, and serving as a night newspaper proofreader.

His book has attracted enduring attention for its intensity,

Tom Kromer, author of *Waiting for Nothing* (back cover of 1st edition dust jacket, 1935)

although it is rather narrow in its focus, particularly when compared with a book like *Call It Sleep.* It was, however, daring for its time, in that it included a description of a homosexual pickup to which the narrator submitted himself to get a decent meal. (James T. Farrell shared a "proletarian" interest in homosexuality.)

Other "proletarians" who attracted attention in the '30s, and who then were forgotten (except in the academy) include "Fielding Burke" (Olive Dargan), John Herrmann, Grace Lumpkin (*A Sign for Cain*), Josephine Herbst (*Rope of Gold*), Robert Cantwell (*Land of Plenty*), Albert Halper (*The Foundry, The Chute, Union Square*), Albert Maltz (*The Underground Stream*), William Rollins, Jr (*The Shadow Before*), Isidor Schneider (*Comrade: Mister*), Clara Weatherwax (*Marching! Marching!*), Leane Zugsmith (*A Time to Remember; The Summer Soldier*), and Edwin Seaver. Communist writers produced novels during the 1940s and 1950s, but most were unworthy of note. The Stalinist author Howard Fast produced historical potboilers that had little in common with the "proletarian genre," continuing to do so after his ambiguous break with the party. The only other writers of importance to emerge from the "proletarian" excitement were two Blacks, Richard Wright and Chester Himes.

Wright's *Native Son* (1940) remains a classic of American literature, but its unblinking account of urban Black criminality has tended to undermine its popularity in recent years. Himes' second novel, *Lonely Crusade* (1947) is the most accurate and devastating account of Stalinism ever written by an American. It led to a boycott of Himes' work and his departure for Europe, although he later gained considerable fame as a writer of comic novels such as *Cotton Comes to Harlem.*

Lastly, other proletarian novels include Thomas Bell's *Out of This Furnace,* Daniel Fuchs' *Williamsburg* Trilogy, Dalton Trumbo's *Johnny Got His Gun,* Josephine Johnson's *Jordanstown,* Tess Slesinger's *The Unpossessed,* Jack Black's *You Can't Win,* Ira Wolfert's *Tucker's People,* Mary Heaton Vorse's *Strike!,* the works of Nathanael West, Celine's *Death on the Installment Plan,* James Gould Cozzens' *Castaway,* Willa Cather's *Shadows on the Rock* and *Lucy Gayheart,* Ellen Glasgow's *Vein of Iron,* Thornton Wilder's *Heaven's My Destination,* Carlos Bulosan's *America Is In The Heart,* most of Katherine Anne Porter's stories, plus certain works by Carson McCullers, Henry Miller, Thomas Wolfe, Thomas Hardy, Charles Dickens, Daniel Defoe, etc.

Nonfiction works of relevance include Sherwood Anderson's *Puzzled America,* James Rorty's *Where Life Is Better: An Unsentimental American Journey,* Nathan Asch's *The Road: In Search of America,* Louis Adamic's *Laughing in the Jungle* (a memoir) and *Dynamite* (labor history), and Theodore Dreiser's *Tragic America.* Surveys and anthologies include Daniel Aaron's *Writers on the Left,* Harvey Swados' *The American Writer and the Great Depression,* Jack Salzman and Barry Wallenstein's *Years of Protest,* Malcolm Cowley's *Think Back on Us, Writers in Revolt: The Anvil Anthology 1933-1940,* and David Madden's *Tough Guy Writers of the Thirties* and *Proletarian Writers of the Thirties.* The last volume is indispensable.

Recently, proletarian writing also appeared from the "Beat Generation," particularly Allen Ginsberg, whose "America" poem (included in *Howl*) contains lines like, "America I feel sentimental about the Wobblies. America I used to be a communist when I was a kid I'm not sorry. My mind is made up there is going to be trouble. You should have seen me reading Marx."

Source for proletarian novels: Bolerium Books, 2141 Mission #300, San Francisco CA 94110 (415)863-6353. Catalog available.

JULIE PEASLEY'S ZINE REVIEWS

2% Homogenized

Do you like Wisconsin? Do you hate Wisconsin? Editor Phil investigates politics, shitty jobs, work hell, futurism and cheese-state culture in this humorous "Journal of Sex, Politics and Dairy Products." $1 to Box 260241, Madison WI 53726-0241.

Ain't Nothin' Like Fuckin' Moonshine

Extrapolating on the theme of "monkeys and bananas," Bwana Spoons has compiled an odd juxtaposition of music reviews, twisted comics, a live action photo essay and collectible toy worship into a format that careens into your brain through 11 circuits at once. Scratchy, heady, purdy blue printing with a shiny red and yellow cover. Winsome errata and issue #7 comes with a 7" single. $4 to Box 6645, Portland OR 97228.

The Assassin and the Whiner

Carrie draws comix about her beer-drinking hobby, crushes on girls at her job at an L.A. soundstage, loneliness and sexuality. They're presented as daily stories, complete with the date of event. Extremely funny and brutal, these images and words will strike a chord with anyone who has wondered, wept and wailed. Carrie also does *Beer Zine*—a compilation of drunken stories, many illustrated with hilarious comix. $2 to Carrie McNinch, Box 481501, Los Angeles CA 90048.

Cashiers du Cinemart

One of the best zines I've read about movies and the people who make them. It focuses on independent, cult, foreign and obscure films and the editor Mike is a veritable encyclopedia of cinematic knowledge. Issue #6 has articles on Jackie Chan, *The Omega Man* and a side-splitting exposé of the horrors of working at a movie theater ("I didn't mind the little old ladies who demanded a refund, despite my earlier warnings that they would probably not enjoy *Whore*"). Mike also has a self-made video available entitled *Who Do You Think You're Fooling?* which demonstrates how much Tarantino's *Resevoir Dogs* steals from Ringo Lam's *City On Fire.* $2 to Box 2401, Riverview MI 48192.

Guinea Pig Zero: A Journal for Human Pharma-

ceutical Research Subjects

Robert Helms, in the short span of about six months, has single-handedly made *Factsheet Five's* Editor's Choice and gotten himself major media coverage for his explicit zine about those who make a living by allowing their bodies to be prodded, dosed and scoped for money. A card-carrying guinea pig himself, Helms takes his profession quite seriously and has even provided a ratings chart for various hospitals as to their treatment of subjects (Hahnemann Hospital at the Medical College of PA gets an "F"). Negligent deaths, gruesome military medical experimentation, human guinea pigs throughout history, and a trip to the 1996 Bioethics Conference make this zine fascinating, especially for those who make extra money by participating in medical studies. $3 to 4728 Spruce St. Cage #369, Philadelphia PA 19139.

Last Prom: Eclectic Esoterica for a Better Tomorrow

Although I have only one issue of this, it is definitely a unique journalistic investigation into a single topic. Both filmmaker and reporter, Ralph Coon travels to Clarksburg, WV to research and uncover the mysteries surrounding UFO enthusiast Gray Barker. The life of this strange man is revealed in this zine through reconstructed fiction and Ralph's personal experiences visiting Barker's memorial room of UFO literature in the library. A must-read for any UFO dream warrior. Coon also did a film called *Whispers From Space* about flying saucers. $5 to Ralph Coon, 120 S. San Fernando Blvd. #243, Burbank CA 91502.

Life is a Joke

The grotesque tragedy and comedy of everyday life is illuminated through comix and parenthetical observations in Joe's hilarious personal zine about living in San Francisco, pet rats, revenge on ornery customers, getting maced and much more. Presented in a fragmented diary format, this zine is definitely more than the sum of its parts—gory, seedy and straight to the point. $1 to Box 423085, San Francisco CA 94142-3085

Plotz: The Zine for the Vaclempt

Be you Jew or gentile, you will enjoy this cultural investigation into the Jewish experience as told from the perspective of a woman who works temp jobs, goes to shows and reflects on what it means to be Jewish. All topics Jewish are covered including childhood memories, Yiddish glossaries, celebrities who are circumcised, Jewish wrestlers, interviews with Jewish members of the music and zine worlds as well as articles about racism, prejudice and romance. $2 to Barbara Plotz, Box 819 Stuyvesant Station, NYC NY 10009.

Silly Daddy
Joe Chiapetta's comix about his young daughter, past jobs, fantasy scenarios and the trials and tribulations of life. Illustrated in his realistic, candid drawing style, this zine is guaranteed to make you simultaneously laugh, cry and get pissed. Titles include: "Baked Barroom Romance" and "A Death in the Family." Send $3 to Joe Chiapetta, 2209 Northgate Ave., N. Riverside IL 60546-1339.

Static
A thick zine of scams, sabotage, pranks and work stories. Squeaky interviews the security guard who caught him shoplifting while waiting for the police to come (what a devoted zine editor!), the increasing hobby of sending prank letters to corporations to test their responses, interview with Jawbreaker's Blake on pranking. Karma, mail terrorism, comix and propaganda all under one roof. $3 to Box 420902, San Francisco CA 94142.

X: The Unknown
A somewhat tongue-in-cheek zine devoted to investigating the UFO phenomenon and related topics on conspiracies, vampires, Bigfoot, witchcraft, Satanism and weird science. This zine is worthy for its sheer variety and unpredictable forays into extraterrestrial eclecticism. $1.50 to Pat O'Donnell, Box 14, Matawan NJ 07747.

CANDI STRECKER'S ZINE REVIEWS

Duplex Planet
David Greenberger started publishing *Duplex Planet* back in the late '70s and has kept it going through the present. And he's prolific—he's done over 130 issues! His unique angle is that he goes to a rest home, asks the elderly patients some simple questions like "What is the moon made of?" and takes down their answers, which are often fairly surreal. There's now a book of some of the finest *Duplex Planet* moments. $2.50 each from David Greenberger, POB 1230, Saratoga Springs NY 12866.

X Magazine
Here's a good example of a kind of hybrid publication I'm seeing a lot more of these days: like a zine, it has an irregular when-I-get-around-to-it publishing schedule and an irreverent attitude, but it looks like a "real" magazine, with ads and a glossy cover. Maybe we could call it a "stealth" zine—those glossy covers confuse enemy radar long enough for it to sneak out into national distribution! This mag-or-zine contains a mix of music, pop culture and boyish humor that I really

enjoy. (For legal reasons, all future issues will be published under the new name of *Dryer.*) $3 each from Jeff Hansen, POB 1077, Royal Oak MI 48068-1077

Obscure Publications
Talk about your narrow niche—this newsletter is entirely devoted to zine-world news and gossip. $2 each from Jim Romenesko, 1305 Grand Ave, St Paul MN 55105.

Schmaga
A favorite zine that's a bit like a little literary magazine, but with an unpretentious down-home attitude. $2 from Jim Kern, POB 8062, Vallejo CA 94590.

Farm Pulp
A pretty-near-indescribable one-man mix of experimental fiction and art, with a lot of tampering with format—different-sized sheets of paper are folded and stapled in together into a sort of zine origami. I'm in awe of his creativity! $3 from Gregory Hischak, 217 NW 70th St, Seattle WA 98117-4845.

Ladies' Fetish & Taboo Society Compendium of Urban Anthropology
A quarterly personal zine from a single gal whose life seems to attract more than its share of weirdness. The things that happen to Kathy and her friends are so absurd that they're often followed by the notice "This Really Happened. No One Could Make This Stuff Up." $3 from Kathy Biehl, POB 542327, Houston TX 77254-2327.

Cheap Truth
Before he was a science-fiction writer, Bruce Sterling was a science-fiction fan who published two-page manifestoes titled *Cheap Truth*, in which he shredded various stick-in-the-mud sci-fi and fandom attitudes under a pseudonym. Clearly he was having a lot of fun doing it, and at times the fur would really fly. [No longer being published.]

Inside Joke
A crucial piece of 1980s zine history, Inside Joke was a huge monthly compilation of comics, humorous writing, and pop culture with contributions by almost everybody active in the zine scene at the time (including myself and Mike Gunderloy). Plus, editor Elayne Wechsler managed to put it together in her spare time on a brutally frequent schedule. A very inclusive (instead of selective) zine that welcomed newcomers and gave them a place to submit their first bits of writing or art. [No longer being published.]

Nancy's Magazine
A good example of a zine that has settled into a perfect personal groove over many years of publishing. *Nancy's* has what I think of as a "gal" sensibility, as opposed to political "grrrl" sensibility—an unpretentious doodle-y casualness that makes you lower your guard, then WHAM, out of left field you're struck by revelations of great depth. Only zine I know of that gets state arts council funding—a scam that more of us should be jumping on. $3 to Nancy Bonnell-Kangas, POB 02108, Columbus OH 43202. ▼

directory of ZINES

PLEASE OBSERVE SOME MINIMAL POLITENESS WHEN SENDING FOR A ZINE:
1) if you just want a catalog, send $1 & enclose a self-addressed stamped envelope or send 2-4 International Reply Coupons (IRCs, available from Post Office)
2) always send cash (not a check) plus 2-4 stamps (or IRCs) when ordering a zine
3) always write a hand-written letter (no computer letters, please)
4) always write a "positive feedback" letter after you've received a zine
5) be sure to print your name/address legibly on your letter

Daily, zines become unavailable and new zines are produced. This directory is best viewed as a "snapshot" of history rather than an eternal resource (warning: some addresses are defunct). Also, this is but a small fraction of all the zines in existence. For currently available zines, subscribe to *Factsheet Five*, POB 170099, San Francisco CA 94117-0099 ($5 single copy; sub. $20). Also, check their index for zine distributors' ads. A new zine guide is Doug Holland's *Zine World*, $3 (sub. $20) from 924 Valencia #203, San Francisco CA 94110.

SOME ZINE SOURCES [usually distribute mostly "slicker" zines; some retail only]:
QVIMBY'S-Steve Svymbersky, 1328 N. Damen Av, Chicago IL 60622 (312) 342-0910. $3 catalog/zine highly recommended: "How to Produce a Zine"
AK DISTRIBUTION, $2 catalog/guide to good books, from POB 40682, San Francisco CA 94140
WOW COOL, 48 Shattuck Sq, Box 149, Berkeley CA 94704 $3 catalog
ATOMIC BOOKS, 1018 N. Charles St, Baltimore MD 21201 TEL (410) 625-7955; FAX (410) 625-7945
WFMU catalog, POB 1568, Montclair NJ 07042 $3 cat
DESERT MOON, 1226A Calle de Comercio, Santa Fe NM 87505 (505) 474-6311 (zine distributor)
SEE HEAR-Ted, 59 E. 7th St, NYC 10003. (212) 982-6968 $3 catalog.
BOUND TOGETHER, 1369 Haight St, San Francisco CA 94117 Anarchist bookstore, zine retailer
FLATLAND-Jim Martin, POB 2420, Fort Bragg CA 95437-2420 (707) 964-8326 $3 book catalog, & zine $5
READING FRENZY, 1420 SE 37th, Portland, Oregon 97214
MIND OVER MATTER, 1710 Central Av, Albuq NM 87106
SUBTERRANEAN RECORDS, POB 2530, Berkeley CA 94702
TOWER RECORDS, 2605 Del Monte St, West Sacto, CA 95691 (send your zine for possible distribution to)
NAKED EYE-Steve, 533 Haight, San Francisco CA 94117
LEFT BANK, 1404 18th Av, Seattle WA 98122.
SUBWAY SISSY ZINE DISTRO-Witknee, 17337 Tramonto #306, Pacific Palisades CA 90272

General Zines:
11/12 DAVE-c/o Dave Matthews, POB 23483, Pittsburgh PA 15222 50¢
50/50 MAGAZINE-2336 Market St. #20, San Francisco CA 94114 $4.95
67 BOYFRIENDS-c/o Cindy, POB 1734,Asheville NC 28802
A PUNK WALKS INTO A BAR-c/o Barclay Mitchell, 720 Milton Rd. #L4, Rye NY 10580 50¢
AIN'T NOTHIN' LIKE FUCKIN' MOONSHINE-POB 6645, Portland OR 97228 $4
ALARM CLOCK-POB 1551, Royal Oak, MI 48068-1551
ALICE IN REALITY-1705 Glenmore Rd., Libertyville IL 60048 $2
AM I REALLY 24?-POB 3326, Hoboken NJ 07030
AMERICAN JOB-T.B.S. Productions, POB 2284, Portland OR 97208 $1.50
ANGRY YOUNG WOMAN-POB 50167, Fort Wayne IN 46805 $3 New Issue Out!
AORTA-c/o Petak, Postfach 778, A-1011 Wien, AUSTRIA
ARM'S EXTENT, THE-1463 E. Republican St. #112, Seattle WA 98112
ARTPIG INTERNATIONAL-c/o Robert L. Brown, HCR 67, Box OH39, Mifflin PA 17058-0801
AWOL-c/o CCCO, 655 Sutter #514, San Francisco CA 94102 $1
BAD NEWZ-P.O. Box 28, 2336 Market St., San Francisco CA 94114 $2.95
BAD TRIP-4325 John Wesley Dr., Dallas GA 30132
BAFFLER, THE-P.O. Box 378293, Chicago IL 60637
BASEMENT CHILDREN-1210 Gregory Pl., Downers Grove IL 60515. Also do Zine Distribution.
BATTERIES NOT INCLUDED-c/o Richard Freeman, 130 W. Limestone St., Yellow Springs OH 45387
BEER FRAME-160 St Johns Pl, Brooklyn NY 11217 $3
BEM CATALOG-POB 8619, Pittsburgh PA 15221-0619

BEN IS DEAD-POB 3166, Hollywood CA 90028 $4
BETTERDAYS-POB 14234, Santa Rosa CA 95402 $1
BI-GIRL WORLD-c/o Karen Friedland, 99 Newtonville Ave., Newton MA 02158
BIKINI GIRL-c/o Lisa B. Falour, 117, Boulevard Voltaire MBE 177, 75011 Paris FRANCE $10
BITCH-3128-16th St., Box 201, San Francisco CA 94103 $2.50
BITCHFIELD-1780 Wrightstown Rd., Newtown PA 18940 $2
BITCH RAG-1202 W. 2Nd St., Sanford FL 32771
BLACK CAT-4110 Roosevelt Wy. NE, Seattle WA 98105
BLACK DOG-224 Adelaide Pl., Munster IN 46321 $3
BLACK PUMPKIN-POB 4377, River Edge NJ 07661-4377
BLINKMOXY-P.O. Box 10532, Burke VA 22009 $1
BLOOD RED-c/o Adam Carr, 35 Grenadier Rd., Toronto, Ontario M6R-1R1 CANADA $2.50
BLOW JOB QUEEN-c/o Clara T., SU 2509, Williams College, Williamstown MA 01267
BOYS IN TROUBLE ON THE INTERSTATE-POB 8054, Austin TX 78713-8054
BOYS WHO WEAR GLASSES-c/o Mark Hain, Box 411, Bellefonte PA 16823 $1
BOY TROUBLE-POB 1450, Chicago IL 60690-1450 $3
BRASS TACKS-POB 69, Drewryville VA 23844-0069 $3
BROKEN PENCIL-POB 203, Station P, Toronto, Ontario M5S 2S7 CANADA $5, halpen@interlog.com Zine Guide!
BROOKLYN!-c/o Fred Argoff, 1204 Avenue U (#1290), Brooklyn NY 11229-4107
BUFFY & JODY'S GUIDE TO THE GALAXY-405 NE 5th Ave. #R, Pompano Beach, FL 33060
BUNNYHOP-POB 423930, SF CA 94142-3930. $6
BURNING THE ANCESTRAL CHI-1420 NW Gilman Blvd Ste. 2400, Issaquah WA 98027-7001
BURPING LULA-c/o Scott, POB 14738, Richmond VA 23221
BUST-POB 319, Ansonia Station, NYC NY 10023 $3
BYPASS-POB 148, Hove, BN3 3DQ ENGLAND $4
CANNOT BECOME OBSOLETE-POB 1232, Lorton VA 22199-1232 $2 [*Incredibly Strange Music* zine; great]
CAPITOL PUNISHMENT AND OTHER ORDEALS-c/o Lane Van Ham, 135 Bruce Dr., Lincoln NE 68510 $5
CARBON 14-POB 29247, Philadelphia PA 19124 $4
CASCADIA SALMON: A WILD SALMON FANZINE-An Ecofreak (Evil Twin) Publication, c/o Amber Gayle, POB 12124, Seattle WA 98102 $5
CAUGHT IN FLUX-POB 7088, NYC NY 10116-7088 $2
CDG DUNGEONER, THE-3023 N. Clark #806, Chicago IL 60657-5205 $5
CHAINSAW ENEMA-P.O. Box 1011, Russellville KY 42276
CHARACTER BUILDER-1317 Grant Ave. #516, San Francisco CA 94133
CHEROTIC REVOLUTIONARY, THE-c/o Frank Moore, POB 11445, Berkeley CA 94712 $5
CHEWING ASPIRINS DRY-5125 35th St., San Diego CA 92116 $2
CHICKFACTOR-245 E. 19th St. 12T, New York City, NY 10003 $3
CHRONICLES OF DISORDER-c/o Thomas Christian, POB 721, Schenectady NY 12301 $2.95
CHUCK-POB 10122, Berkeley CA 94709-5122
CHUM MAGAZINE-POB 148390, Chicago IL 60614 $2
CHUNKLET 10-POB 2814, Athens GA 30612-0814
CODE MAGAZINE-1412 Northwest 61st #2, Seattle WA 98107
COFFEE-POB 7591, Olympia WA 98507
COFFEE NO GIRL-c/o Carolyn, 6622 Tremont St., Oakland CA 94609
COLORADO ZINE POOL-c/o Brian Payne, 1801 East 112th Pl., Denver CO 80233 $2
COMETBUS-Aaron, POB 4279, Berkeley CA 94704 $3 ***
COMPULSION 2-c/o Tony Dickie, 10 Netherhill Rd., Gallowhill, Paisley, PA3 4RE, Scotland UK
CON(TRA)SCIENCE-POB 8344, Minneapolis MN 55408-0344
COOL AND STRANGE MUSIC!-c/o Dana Countryman, POB 8501, Everett WA 98201, coolstrge@aol.com
COOTIES-c/o Kate, 2504 Ravencroft Ct., Virginia Beach VA 23454
CRANK-POB 633, Prince Street Station, New York City NY 10012, www.crank.com
CRAP HOUND-POB 40373, Portland OR 97240-0373 $6
CREEPY MIKE'S OMNIBUS OF FUN-POB 983, Buffalo NY 14213-0983 $2
CREMECON-POB 37986, Milwaukee WI 53237
CRIMEWAVE USA-POB 675283, Marietta GA 30067-0013 $3
CRITIC, THE-c/o Hugo Kobayashi, 1391-8th Ave. #3, San Francisco CA 94122 $2
CUIR UNDERGROUND-3288-21st St. #19, San Francisco CA 94110
CULTURAL DEVIANCE-c/o Squid Soda, 540 Shrader St., San Francisco CA 94117

CUTIE PIE-2901 Parklawn Ct., Herndon VA 22071
DANGERFOX-310 Lexington St., San Francisco CA 94110 $1.50
DANGERS OF LIBEL-c/o Jenna, POB 1266, Venice FL 34284-1266
DANZINE-625 SW 10th Ave. #233B, Portland OR 97205
DAUGHTERS OF HOUDINI POB 40291, SF CA 94140 $2
DEAD MEN SITTING AT TYPEWRITERS PRESS-c/o Robert W. Howington, 4405 Bellaire Dr. S. #220, Fort Worth TX 76109
DELIRIOUS-c/o Steven R. Johnson, 1326 Cleveland Hts. Blvd., Cleveland Hts. OH 44121 $5
DELIRIUM-c/o Sophie Diamantis, 779 Riverside Dr. #A-11, NYC NY 10032 $4
DESIGN #816-POB 479081, Chicago IL 60647
DISASTER FANZINE-POB 215, Mission TX 78573 $1
DIVERSITY MAGAZINE-P.O. Box 47558, #1-1020 Austin Ave., Coquitlam BC V3K 6T3 CANADA
DIY: AN A-Z GUIDE TO DOING IT YOURSELF-POB 720716, San Jose CA 95172 $6
D.L.K. THE HELL KEY-c/o Marc Urselli-Scharer, Via Gorki 5, 74023 Grottaglie (TA) ITALY $2.50
DON-O'S ODDS & ENDS-POB 5681, Santa Monica CA 90409 $1
DON'T SAY UH-OH!-POB 5871, Kansas City MO 64171
DON'T SHOOT IT'S ONLY COMICS-140A Harvard Ave. #308, Allston MA 02134 $3
DORIS-Cindy, POB 1734, Asheville NC 28802 $1 (Great!)
DR. DUCKY DOOLITTLE-POB 1474 Sty. Stn. NYC 10009-1474
EAST TO CALI-c/o Keffo, POB 5184, Bethlehem PA 18015
ECCO:THE WORLD OF BIZARRE VIDEO-POB 65742, Washington DC 20035 $5.95
ELECTRIFYING TIMES-c/o Bruce Meland, Solarland, 63600 Deschutes Market Rd., Bend OR 97701, 102331.2166@compuserve.com
E.L.F.-POB 515, Spokane WA 99210-0515
EMPTY SPACES-c/o Kathy Robinson, POB 9238, Lyndhurst NJ 07071 $2
ENOUGH IS ENOUGH-c/o Dennis W. Brezina, POB 683, Chesapeake City MD 21915 $3
EROS ARCHIVES-5708 Cahuenga Blvd., N. Hollywood CA 91601-2191 $3
ERSATZ CULTURE-441 West 37th, 2nd Fl., NYC NY 10018-4015
ESCARGOT-1230 Market St. #224, San Francisco CA 94102
ESKHATOS-POB 961, Portland OR 97207 $4
ESOTERIC POPULAR CULTURE-c/o Robert Koenig, POB 1672, Mineola NY 11501
ETCH MAGAZINE-POB 10132, Lansing MI 48901-0132
EXEDRA-c/o Kim Carlyle, POB 53110, Washington DC 20009-9110 $1
EYE-153 E. Lindsay St. Ste. 108, Greensboro NC 27401-3007 $3.95
EYES-POB 303, NYC NY 10009 $3
EYEWASH-POB 20013, Dayton OH 45420-0013
FACTSHEET FIVE-POB 170099, San Francisco CA 94117-0099 $3.95
FAT GIRL-2215-R Market #197, SF CA 94114 $5; $20 sub.
FEH! THE JOURNAL OF ODIOUS POETRY-c/o Tony Arnold, 196 Alps Rd. #2-316, Athens GA 30606 $3
FEMME FLICKE-99 Hancock St. #4, Cambridge MA 02139 $2
FERN-c/o Kim Fern, POB 11496, Milwaukee WI 53211
FESTIVAL EYE-BCM 2002, London WC1 N 3XX ENGLAND
FISHWRAP-c/o Marty Wombacher, 2130 Broadway #915, NYC NY 10023-1722 $3, http://www.fishwrap.com
FIRST PERSON-c/o Tracey West, POB 416, Sparkill NY 10976 $1.99
FLAMES FROM THE INTERNET-POB 8131, Burlington VT 05402 $1.50
FLAMING JEWBOY-POB 20656, Seattle WA 98102 $3
FLAMING SIN-P.O. Box 726, University Station, Syracuse NY 13210
FLATTER-Jaina Davis, POB 40923 SF CA 94140-0923 $3
FLY-c/o Gargoyle Mechanique Lab, POB 1318, Cooper Station, New York City NY 10276
FOR THE LOVE OF . . . -c/o Kyle Hetrick, 743 State St., Lemoyne PA 17043 $1
FRANTIX 'ZINE-329 Main St. #4, Nashua NH 03060
FREAKS!-c/o Chris Fellner, 45 Taylors Wy., Holland PA 18966 $4
FREE THOUGHT CONCEPTIONS-POB 432, Glen Echo MD 20812-0432
FRINGE WARE REVIEW-POB 49921, Austin TX 78765 $3.95
FRISSON-c/o Scott H. Urban, 1012 Pleasant Dale Dr., Wilmington NC 28412 $1.25
FUCKTOOTH-Jen Angel, POB 3593, Columbus OH 43210 $2
FUEL MAGAZINE-POB 146640, Chicago IL 60614 $3
FULL MOON GIRL-c/o Henry, 13503 Clubside Dr., Tampa FL 33624

FUNK 'N GROOVE-c/o Ferris and Morgan, POB 471881, San Francisco CA 94147-1881 $3
FUNKY BUTT-c/o Dale Flattum, 805 Valencia St. #7, San Francisco CA 94110
GALA-c/o Karen Srebro, RR 4 Box 413, Tunkhannock PA 18657
GEARHEAD-Mike LaVella, POB 421219, San Francisco CA 94142-1219 $5.95 (A lot of Zine for the $$)
GEE-ZUZ-297-810 W. Broadway, Vancouver BC, CANADA V5Z 4C9 $4.50
GENERIC-POB 14201, Madison WI 53714-0201
GENETIC DISORDER-P.O. Box 151362, San Diego CA 92175 $2
GIANTS AND LITTLE PEOPLE IN FACT AND FICTION-c/o Bob Nelson, 75 Hale St. #1, Beverly MA 01915
GINGER'S RAG-117 E. Louisa #348, Seattle WA 98102 $1
GIRLFRENZY-POB 148, Hove BN3 3DQ ENGLAND $5
GIRLS DON'T LIKE IT-263 Bridle Run Ct., Alpine CA 91901
GIRLYHEAD-POB 423657, San Francisco CA 94142 $4
GLOBAL MAIL-c/o Ashley Parker Owens, Soapbox Junction, POB 410837, San Francisco CA 94141 $3, http://www.well.com/user/soapbox/eglob96a.html
GOGKORP-5221 Loop Rd., Dorsey IL 62021
GORILLA COOKIES-c/o Catherine Noel, 1200 Riordan Ranch Rd. #56, Flagstaff AZ 86001
GOSPEL-c/o Stefan Zachrisson, Fatburs Kvarngatan 18, 118 64 Stockholm SWEDEN
GRAND LARCENY-7712 Lexington Ave., W. Hollywood CA 90046 $5
GRAPHOMANIA BLUES-BEM, POB 8619, Pittsburg PA 15221-0619
HALO-Chasen W., 25800 Barnard St., Hayward CA 94545
HAPPY MAGAZINE-Anathema Enterprises, 2002-A Guadalupe St. #227, Austin TX 78705
HARDCORN-AK Press, POB 40682, San Francisco CA 94140
"HAVE YOU SEEN THE DOG LATELY?"-Permanent Swim Press, 495 Elwood Ave. #5, Oakland CA 94610-1947
HEADVEINS CATALOG-POB 4816, Seattle WA 98104
HEALING STONE-2502 N. Rockwell #B, Chicago IL 60647
HEROES FOR TODAY-c/o Seth Bogard, 2007 E. 3Rd St., Tucson AZ 85719
HEX-POB 989, Berkeley CA 94701 $1
HIGHLANDS LOWLIFE-POB 4964, Louisville KY 40204-0964
HIP-HOP HOUSEWIFE-Fran Liscio, TLR Pubs, 19 Bellgrove Dr., Upper Montclair NJ 07043 $1
HOLY BIBLE OF PUNK ROCK-POB 460760, San Francisco CA 94146-0760
HOMOTILLER-Box 460695, San Francisco CA 94146-0695
HUH!-POB 590104, San Francisco CA 94159-0104
HUNGRY FREAKS-P.O. Box 20835, Oakland CA 94620 $3.95
ICARUS WAS RIGHT-POB 191175, San Diego CA 92150 $2
ICE-9 MAGAZINE-c/o Daniel Broadhead, POB 6737, Fullerton CA 92834
IF YOU LIKE PINA COLADAS-POB 90282, Pittsburgh PA 15224 $2 (from Al Hoff of ThriftSCORE!; hilarious)
INCHWORM-53 W. Park Ave., Lindenwold NJ 08021 25¢
INDUSTRIAL NATION-114-1/2 E. College St., Iowa City IA 52240-4005 $2.95
INFORMATION SUPER HIGHWAY-1123 Hillcrest Loop, Lindsay CA 93247
INQUISITOR-POB 132, NYC NY 10024 $5
INSIGHT-POB 125, Farmington MI 48332 $2.95
INSOMNIA-c/o Sam Panico, POB 5937, Pittsburgh PA 15210 $3
INTERROBANG?!-3288 21st St., San Francisco CA 94110
INVINCIBLE STUDIOS-POB 421110, San Diego CA 92142-1110
IRON FEATHER [PHUN]-POB 1905, Boulder CO 80306 $6
IT'S ONLY A MOVIE-c/o Michael Flores, POB 14683, Chicago IL 60614 $3
JAMBALAYA-POB 9849, Berkeley CA 94709 $2
JAVA MONTHLY-119 E. 7th St. Ste. 2, Tempe AZ 85281
JOE MAYNARD-411 Kent Ave., Brooklyn NY 11211
JOURNAL OF UNCONVENTIONAL HISTORY-c/o Aline Hornaday, POB 459, Cardiff-by-the-Sea CA 92007-9900 $7.50
JOYBUZZER-POB 1609, Murray Hill Station, NYC NY 10156-1609
K-Box 7154, Olympia WA 98507
KARMA LAPEL-POB 5467, Evanston IL 60204 $2
KICK IT OVER-POB 5811, Station A, Toronto, Ontario CANADA M5W 1P2 $3
KILL 'EM ALL-c/o Nemo Unlimited, Ltd., POB 466, Wickliffe OH 44092-0466
KILL ROCK STARS-120 NE State Ave. #418, Olympia WA 98501
KITTENKORE-3710 S. Gaffey St., San Pedro CA 90731
KUKUNOR-Rautatienkatu 18, Tampere 33101 FINLAND
LACKLUSTER-c/o Amy Balkin & James Harbison, 456-14th St. #8, San Francisco CA 94103
LAST DECADE MINUS FOUR,THE-c/o Dave Matthews, POB 23483, Pittsburgh PA 15222 $3
LAST PROM, THE-137 S. San Fernando Blvd., Box 243, Burbank CA 91502
L.C.D. (LOWEST COMMON DENOMINATOR)-POB 1568, Montclair NJ 07042 $4
LIE-55 La Salle St. Staten Island NY 10303
LIES THEY TELL-POB 230079, Encinitas CA 92023-0079
LIFE DURING WARTIME AUDIO ZINE-POB 1113, Portland OR 97207 $3
LIFE SUCKS-c/o Justin, 5070 Canonsburg Rd., Bellmont MI 49306
LIL' RHINO GAZETTE, THE-POB 14139, Arlington TX 76094-1139
LIMOUSINE-c/o E. Lampert, POB 14715, San Luis Obispo CA 93406-4715 $2
LITERARY WHORE, THE-c/o Timothy Kane, POB 22161, San Diego CA 92192
LIZARD EYELID-POB 5627, Miami FL 33116
LOOKS YELLOW, TASTES RED-c/o Colette, POB 1275, Wellfleet MA 02667
LORD LOVES A WORKING MAN-POB 1764, New York City NY 10009
LOSERS ARE COOL-c/o Robert W. Howington, 4405 Bellaire Dr. South #220, Fort Worth TX 76109-5103
LOST TEQUILA WEEKEND-98 Western Ave. Ste. 102, Petaluma CA 94952 $5
LOU CHRISTIE OFFICIAL FAN CLUB-POB 748, Chicago IL 60690-0748
LOUNGE, 315 S. Willaman Dr Bungalow #1, Los Angeles CA 90048 $5 (the zine of lounge culture)
LOVE, JANE-c/o Jenna, 63 Bovet Rd. #224, San Mateo CA 94402 75¢
LUCID NATION-1015 N. Kings Rd. #313, Los Angeles CA 90069
LUMPY HEAD-c/o Ann K., 9118 Crest Hill Rd., Marshall VA 22115
MALCOLM AND MADAME X-65 E. Scott St., Chicago IL 60610 $3.95
MALEFACT-POB 464, Alexandria VA 22313-0464 $5
MAMASITA-2415 Fordham St., San Pablo CA 94806
MARK MAYNARD-POB 675283, Marietta GA 30067-0013
MATCH, THE: AN ANARCHIST JOURNAL-POB 3488, Tucson AZ 85722 $2.75
MAXINE-2025 W. Augusta, Chicago IL 60622 $3
MEN SPEAKING OUT ON MEN AND SEXISM-c/o M.A.S.S., Box 25, 52 Call Ln., Leeds LS1 6DT ENGLAND
MENACE-POB 82026, Columbus OH 453202 $2
MIGRAINE CATLOG-CHEAP INSPIRATION $3, SUPER BLACK BLACK $2.50, VELOUR $2.50, VAPID 75¢, POB 2337, Berkeley CA 94702
MILKCRATE DIGEST-c/o John Freeborn, POB 1412, Providence RI 20901 $1+2 stamps
MIND WORD-The 5th Wall, POB 22161, San Diego CA 92192-2161
MISCHA-c/o Natascha, P.O. Box 6844, San Carlos CA 94070-6844 $2 plus 2 stamps
MISS PRISS-c/o Kimberly, 4019 Little Finger Rd., Lake Havasu City AZ 86406
MOLLY KIELY COMICS-865 Mesa Ave., Palo Alto CA 94306
MONDOCINE-c/o Roger Leatherwood, P.O. Box 10597, Oakland CA 94610 $2.50
MONOZINE-c/o Todd, POB 598, Reisterstown MD 21136 $2
MOO JUICE-POB 11619, Chicago IL 60611-0619 $3
MOUTH-61 Brighton St., Rochester NY 14607-2656
MR DENSITY-c/o Generic Mike, POB 172, Westview Station, Binghampton NY 13905-0172 $2
MSRRT NEWSLETTER-4645 Columbus Ave. S., Minneapolis MN 55407
MUFFIN BONES-c/o Emily K. Larned, 178 Farms Rd., Stamford CT 06903-2721 $1 plus 2 stamps
MULTIBALL-POB 40005, Portland OR 97240-0005 $1
MY LITTLE BOX-c/o Corinne Thornton, Box #190, 2080 Tulpehocken Rd., Reading PA 19610
MY STRAIGHT-FACED TWIN-c/o Aren Rogal, 1092 Lyndhurst Dr., Pittsburgh PA 15206
MYSTERY DATE-POB 641592, SF CA 94164-1592 $3
NANCY'S MAGAZINE-POB 02108, Columbus OH 43202 $4
NAUGHTY NURSIE, POB 40291, SF CA 94140 $2 (Great)
NEAR MISS-c/o Brendan, POB 528, Bronx NY 10454
NEON VANILLA-c/o William G. Raley, POB 538, Sunset Beach CA 90742-0538, after.hours@genie.geis.com
NIMBLE FINGERS-300 Queen Anne Ave. N. Ste. 250, Seattle WA 98109-4599 $2
NOBODADDIES-POB 95094, Pittsburgh PA 15223-0694
NOISES FROM THE GARAGE-8811 Rue Riviera #3A, Indianapolis IN 46226
NO LONGER SILENT!-c/o Eliza Blackweb, POB 3582, Tucson AZ 85722 $3
NO ROOM FOR SQUARES-2240 SE Taylor, Portland OR 97214 $2
NOT BORED!-POB 1115, Stuyvesant Station, NYC NY 10009-9998
"NOT DEAD, BUT DREAMING..."-POB 442572, Lawrence KS 66044 $1
NOTHING'S PERSONAL-c/o Occupant, 2809 Rio Grande M, Austin TX 78705
NOT YOUR BITCH-c/o Christine Johnston, POB 2984, Denver CO 80201
NOUS SOMMES TOUS DES CASSEURS-POB 13515, Berkeley CA 94712
NOW MEET SATAN-323 Broadway Ave. E. #1002, Seattle WA 98102 $3
OBLONG-c/o Bruce Townley, 1732 Washington St. #8, San Francisco CA 94109-3625 $2 Funny, Witty, Sarcastic
OCTOJELLO-POB 42365, Portland OR 97242-0365
OCULUS MAGAZINE-POB 148, Hoboken NJ 07030
ODYSSEY MAGAZINE-584 Castro St. #302, San Francisco CA 94114-2500
OFFICIAL RIGHT REICHERS, THE-7841 Renton Wy., Sacramento CA 95828-4341
ONE STAR DISTRO-c/o Scout, POB 4526, Santa Rosa CA 95402-4526
ON THE RAG-OTR, PSC 3 Box 1024, APO AE 09021 $1
OPTIC NERVE-POB 4025, Berkeley CA 94704 $2
OUTPUNK-POB 17051, San Francisco CA 94117 $2
PANIC BUTTON-POB 62, Prospect Hts. IL 60070 $1
PANTY LINE FEVER-234 E. 7th St. #1FE, NYC NY 10009 $3
PARANOIA-P.O. Box 3570, Cranston RI 02910 $4
PASTY-c/o Sarah-Katherine, 6201-15th Ave. NW #P-549, Seattle WA 98107 $2
PAWHOLE MAGAZINE-c/o House of VILE Productions, POB 81202, Pittsburgh PA 15217 $4
PEARSHAPED-c/o Megan, 26 Third Ave., Bath BA2 3NY ENGLAND
PEDIATRICS FOR PARENTS-POB 1069, Bangor ME 04402-1069 $2.50
PINK LEMONADE-3344 Mission St., San Francisco CA 94110
PIT REPORT-POB 1605, Stuyvesant Station, NYC NY 10009
PIXIEBITCH-c/o Zoe, Rdl Box 37b, Montrose PA 18801
PLANET DEMENTED-c/o Laurel Wilson, 1927 Forestwood Dr., Richardson TX 75081 $2
PLASTIC ASS-c/o Mary Hackett, 118 N. Peoria St. #4, Chicago IL 60607 $1 plus 2 stamps
PLOTZ-P.O. Box 819, Stuyvesant Station, New York City NY 10009
PMS-POB 2563, Cambridge MA 02238
P.O.BOX-El Zine de Mail Art, Apartat 9242, 08080 Barcelona SPAIN
POISON PEN-c/o Nihilistik Survivalist Front, 1870 Schieffelin #5 E., Bronx NY 10466 $1.25
POLITICALLY INCORRECT JOURNAL, THE-POB 771, Grand Haven MI 49417
POP LIFE-c/o Timothy Friend, POB 34, Belton MO 64012-0034, jfriend@cctr.umkc.edu
POP SMEAR-105 Thompson St., NYC NY 10012 $3
PORTRAIT OF A YOUNG MAN TRYING TO EAT THE SUN-Beet Publications, c/o Maynard, 372-5th Ave., Brooklyn NY 11215 $1
POWER TOOT-c/o Brian Winters, 55 E. 10Th St. #608, NYC NY 10003
PRE-CUM-130 Barrow St., Athens GA 30601 $2
PREGNANT MUSE-POB 5112, Larkspur CA 94977 $3.33
PRETENTIOUS SHIT-Eclectic Enterprises, POB 22351, Indianapolis IN 46222 $1
PRIMAL CHAOS-c/o Wendy Van Dusen, 1072 Folsom St. #388, San Francisco CA 94103 $3.50
PRINTED MATTER, INC.-77 Wooster St., New York City NY 10012
PROBE, THE-c/o Aaron Muentz, POB 5068, Pleasanton CA 94566 $6
PROZAC & CORNFLAKES-c/o Kez Panel, POB 589, Moon PA 15108-0589 $3
PSYCHEDELIC ILLUMINATIONS-POB 3186, Fullerton CA 92634 $5
PSYCHOBITCH-c/o Kim Bright, 4655 SR 37 S, Martinsville IN 46151
PSYCHOHOLICS UNANIMOUS-c/o Joni Liebermann, 309 Quimby NE, Grand Rapids MI 49505
PTBH!-2440 E. Tudor Rd. #414, Anchorage AK 99507-1185
PUCKER UP-POB 4108, Grand Central Station, NYC NY 10163 $5
PUNK PLANET-POB 1711, Hoboken NJ 07030-9998 $2
PUPPIES AND KITTIES-c/o Alex, POB 461163, Los Angeles CA 90046 $1
QUEEN OF THE SCENE-POB 1910, BH CA 90213
QUITTER QUARTERLY-POB 20515, Tompkins Square Station, NYC NY 10009 25¢
RADIO RIOT-75 Nichols Ave., New Brunswick NJ 08903 $2
RAHAB'S PSALMS-850 SW 87th Terrace, Plantation FL 33324
RANK CULTURE-3425 NE Hancock, Portland OR 97212
RAVEN, THE-300 Lenora St., Ste. B251, Seattle WA 98121 $2.95
READING FRENZY CATALOG-POB 40373, Portland OR 97240-0373
REAL DEAL-POB 19129, Los Angeles CA 90019 $2
REAL GIRLS-POB 13947, Berkeley CA 94712-4947 $3
RED DAWG-POB 2192, Bloomington IN 47402 $2
REIGN OF TOADS-c/o Kyle Silfer, P.O. Box 66047, Albany NY 12206 $4
RELIGION OF THE MONTH CLUB-POB 2430, Santa Clara CA 95055-2430 $2
RESISTER-POB 1479, NYC NY 10276-1479 $4
REVOLUTIONARY PLEASURE OF THINKING FOR YOURSELF, THE-POB 1731, Tucson AZ 85702 $1.50
REVOLUTIONARY SELF-THEORY-Spectacular Times, Box 99, Freedom Press, 84B Whitechapel High St., London E1 7QX ENGLAND $1.50
RIOT NRRRD-c/o Jose Aumentado, Northwestern U, Dept. of Physics and Astronomy, 2145 Sheridan Rd., Evanston IL 60208 $1, http://pubweb.-acns.nwu.edu
ROCTOBER-1507 E. 53Rd St. #617, Chicago IL 60615 $3
RUBY SLIPPERS, THE-c/o Milly, POB 16-0963, Miami FL 33116-0963
SAD MAGAZINE-11693 San Vicente Blvd., Los Angeles CA 90049 $2.50
S.A.M. (SEARCHING FOR ALYSSA MILANO)-c/o Tony, POB 801145, Santa Clarita CA 91380-1145 $2
SAMIZDAT-POB 4296, Ann Arbor MI 48106 $1
SAPROPHILE-c/o Eric Landmark, 714 E. Johnson, Madison WI 53703 $1.50
SARASVATI-2025 Peachtree Rd. NE #511, Atlanta GA 30309 $3
SCIENCE HOLIDAY/OCCUPANT-POB 3891, Huntington Beach CA 92605
SCRAM-POB 461626, Hollywood CA 90046-1626 $4
SCREAM, THE-34 Short Hills Dr., Hilton NY 14468 $3 Cash
SCREAMS FROM INSIDE-POB 13044, Minneapolis MN 55414
SCREEN DUMP-c/o D.S. Black, 41 Sutter St. #1651, San Francisco CA 94104
SECOND GUESS-POB 9382, Reno NV 89507
SECONDS-24-5th Ave. Ste. 405, NYC NY 10011 $2.95
SEMIGLOSS-9 W. 8th St. #4, NYC NY 10011 $3
SEWER CUNT-S.H. Kristensen, Godthabsvej 18 A, DK-7400 Herning, DENMARK $4
SEXTIME LAFFS-c/o Dave Matthews, POB 23483, Pittsburgh PA 15222
SF EYE-POB 18539, Asheville NC 28814 $5
SHARK FEAR, SHARK AWARENESS-c/o Darin Johnson, Society of Shark Fear, 120 State Ave. NE Ste. #1414, Olympia WA 98501-8212
SHELF LIFE-POB 91260, Santa Barbara CA 93190
SHOCK CINEMA-c/o Steve Puchalski, POB 518, Stuyvesant Station, NYC NY 10009 $5
SHOCKED & AMAZED-POB 22262, Baltimore MD 21203
SHOCKING IMAGES-POB 601972, Sacramento CA 95860 $4
SHOELACE FANZINE-POB 7952, W. Trenton NJ 08628 $1.75
(SIC)TEEN-POB 1173, Green Bay WI 54305 24¢
SIDNEY SUPPEY'S QUARTERLY & CONFUSED PET MONTHLY-POB 515, Brisbane CA 94005-0515 $2
SIMBA-68 Maitland Ave., Manchester M21 7WH ENGLAND
SLANT-1809 Walnut St., Philadelphia PA 19103
SLOP HUT-POB 85510, Seattle WA 98145-1510 $1
SLUG & LETTUCE-c/o Christine Boarts, POB 492, W. Chester PA 19381
SLUG FEST, LTD.-POB 1238, Simpsonville SC 29681
SNAK FUD-2300 Market St Box 23, SF CA 94114 $1.50
SNIPER'S NEST-POB 2351, Galveston TX 77553-2351 25¢
SOCIAL SKILLS-c/o John Sulak, 535 Geary #604, San

Francisco CA 94102 $1
SOCIAL UNREST-Mail Box 138, 4001 Stockdale Hwy., Bakersfield CA 93309
SOCK MONKEY-c/o Alexandra Darch Stolarski, 25071 Calle Playa Unit J, Laguna Niguel CA 92677
SOFT SMOOTH BRAIN-POB 6645, Portland OR 97228
SOUND CHOICE-POB 1251, Ojai CA 93023 $3
SOUTH TO THE FUTURE-POB 191475 SF CA 94119-1475 $2 great! subscription $6 (Intelligent; no typos!)
SOUTHERN CALIFORNIA SCENE REPORT-c/o Tang, POB 17746, Anaheim CA 92817
SPAGHETTI DINNER & DANCING-POB 2536, Missoula MT 59806
SPECTACULAR TIMES-Aldgate Press, 84b Whitechapel High St., London E1 ENGLAND
SPECTRE MAGAZINE-c/o Jennifer, P.O. Box 474, Lexington KY 40585-0474 $5
SPLEEN-POB 8122, Las Vegas NV 89119 $1
SPOONFED-POB 21036, Washington DC 20009-1036
SQUEALWORM-c/o Freda, POB 7581, Fort Lauderdale FL 33338
STAIN FANZINE-POB 2501, Philadelphia PA 19147-2501 $3
STAY FREE!-341 Lafayette #558, NYC NY 10012 $3
STIFF & CRUSTY-POB 4816, Seattle WA 98104-0816 $3
STIFLED-c/o Jocelyn Rouseeau, POB 471, Allston MA 02134
STOREFRONT BAR-B-Q PERSONALITY MAGAZINE-POB 433, Portland OR 97207-0433
STORYVILLE-POB 642896, San Francisco CA 94164 $3
STY ZINE-300 N. Bryan, Bloomington IN 47408-4144 $1
SUBURBIA-c/o Ceci, 521 Golden Gate Ave., Point Richmond CA 94801
SUPER TINY-c/o JohnnyFuckerFaster, 2336 Market St., Studio 120, San Francisco CA 94114 ("The Penis")
SURREAL UNDERGROUND ENTERTAINMENT-POB 2105, Detroit MI 48231-9864 $4.95
SWING-Buskvagen 28, S-611 45 Nykoping SWEDEN
SWING TIME-30B Baker, San Francisco CA 94117 $5 YES!
TAB MAGAZINE-444 Lodi St., Akron OH 44305-3170
TAILSPIN-POB 5467, Evanston IL 60204 $3
TAPE OP MAGAZINE-POB 15189, Portland OR 97293 $2
TAPE WORM-POB 19351, Seattle WA 98109
TAYLOR'S DAUGHTER-POB 471, Allston MA 02134
TEENY TINY PRESS-P.O. Box 267953, Chicago IL 60626-7953 $2
TESTICLE PRESS-228 E. 10Th St. Ste. 810, NYC NY 10003 $4
THAT GIRL-c/o Kelli Williams, POB 170612, San Francisco CA 94117 $1
THAT WEIRD GUY MATT-POB 3388, Fairfield CA 94533
THEORYSLUT-POB 426965, San Francisco CA 94142 $3.50
THEY WON'T STAY DEAD!-11 Werner Rd., Greenville PA 16125-9434 $3
THRIFTSCORE-POB 90282, Pittsburgh PA 15224 $1
TIFF-POB 97011, 149 Roncevalles Ave., Toronto Ontario CANADA M6R 3B3 $3
TIME BOMB-POB 4964, Louisville KY 40204-0964 $4
TIME TO ORGANIZE-c/o Jane G., 80-50 Baxter Ave. #125, Elmhurst NY 11373
TOTALLY NORMAL-BM CRL, London WC1N 3XX ENGLAND $4
TOWARDS 2012-POB HP94, Leeds LS6 1YJ, ENGLAND
TRAILER TRASH-c/o Michelle Shute, POB 753086, Memphis TN 38175-3086 $1
TRANSEXUAL NEWS TELEGRAPH-41 Sutter St. #1124, San Francisco CA 94104-4903 $5
TWENTY BUS, POB 170612, San Francisco CA 94117 $2
TYPEWRITER-POB 460074, San Francisco CA 94146-0074 $3
ULTRA LATEX-12062 Moorpark St. #1, Studio City CA 91604
UNBEARABLE SEANCE, THE-c/o Joe Maynard, 372-5th Ave., Brooklyn NY 11215 $2
UNDERGROUND ZINE SCENE-c/o John Ridge, 316 E. Main St., Sebewaing MI 48759
UNDER TERRA-Predawn Productions, 9 Riverglen Dr., Keswick, Ontario L4P 2P9 CANADA
UNHAPPY PLANET-c/o Ross Taylor, 25351 Kay Ave., Hayward CA 94545
VAPID-c/o Ian Lynam, POB 2337, Berkeley CA 94702 75¢
VINEGAR-48 Carnarvon St., Glasgow G3 6HP ENGLAND
VIOLET POLYESTER-912 N. I St., Tacoma WA 98403 $1+2 stamps
WARCOM-POB 1175, San Jose CA 95108
WASTING THE DAWN-David Hurwitz, c/o Timothy Kane, POB 22161, San Diego CA 92192-2161
WAX MUSEUM-c/o T.C. Costulis, 909 McCoy Creek Ct., Suisun CA 94585-3775 $2
WEIRD FLOWER-P.O. Box 366, Station B, Toronto Ontario CANADA M5T 2W2 $4
WENDALL AND INC. CATALOG-c/o Robert Hewitt, 2610 W. Leland 2nd Fl., Chicago IL 60625
WHAT ARE YOU GOING TO DO ABOUT IT?-Black Swan Press, POB 6424, Evanston IL 60204
WHAT NOW-3691 Ontario E., Montreal PQ H1W 1S1 CANADA
WHITE BOY-c/o Paul Weinman, 79 Cottage Ave., Albany NY 12203
WHITE DOT, THE-POB 577257, Chicago IL 60657
WHOREZINE-2300 Market St. Ste. 19, San Francisco CA 94114 $3
WISHBONE-31921 Camino Capistrano #200, San Juan Capistrano CA 92675 $1.50
WORLDS OF ARTIFICE-47 Summer St., Nashua NH 03060 $5
WW3-POB 20271, Tompkins Sq. Station, NYC NY 10009
XEROMORPHIC-c/o Terrance Jennings Wharton, POB 481, Lancaster OH 43130
X-RAY-POB 170011, San Francisco CA 94117 $20; Rools!
YAWP!-c/o Johanna Novales, Box 752723, Dallas TX 75275-2723 $2
YEARS WITHOUT ART 1990-1993, THE-c/o S. Perkins, 1816 E. College, Iowa City IA 52245
YOB-c/o Craig Garrett, 917 E. Jefferson St., Seattle WA 98122
YOU COULD DO WORSE-POB 74647, Cedar Rapids IA 52407
ZAPRUDER HEADSNAP-537 Jones #207, San Francisco CA 94102
ZINE WORLD-924 Valencia St. #203, San Francisco CA 94110
ZONTAR-c/o Brian Curran, 29 Darling St. #2, Roxbury MA 02120 $2
Z MAGAZINE, 18 Milllfield, Boston MA 02115 $4 (political)

Zines by People of Color: (compiled by Robin Takayama)
ACHE-c/o Starr, 335 Shotwell, San Francisco CA 94110
ADVENTURES WITH YELLOW MAN LI/FOREST KIN-c/o Donna Han, 2850 21st St. San Francisco CA 94110
AMUSING YOURSELF TO DEATH-c/o Ruel Gaviola, POB 91934, Santa Barbara CA 93190
BAD AZZ MOFO-404 NE 63rd Ave., Portland OR 97213
BAMBOO GIRL-POB 2828, NYC NY 10185-2828 $2
BLACK HOLE LIPSTICK-POB 422, Great Falls VI 22066
CHICA LOCA-c/o Lala, 341 W. 11th St. #PHA, New York City NY 10014
CHI-TAVO-BUS-751 Laurel St. #518, San Carlos CA 94070 $3 (Title parodies COMETBUS)
CINERATOR-c/o Richard Akiyama, POB 240226, Honolulu HI 96824
COMET DEBRIS-c/o Koji, 308 Westwood Plaza #446, Los Angeles CA 90024
CROSSPATCH-c/o Racheal, POB 170130, San Francisco CA 94117
DA JUICE!-POB 156, Station P, Toronto, Ontario M5S2S7 CANADA
DISSENT-c/o Loi Calo, POB 12623 Ortigas Center, Post Office, Pasig PHILIPPINES
DOOCHSUCK-c/o Anne Yen, RRI Box 433A, Kula HI 96790
FROM FAR OFF-POB 6274, Minneapolis MN 55406
FUZZYHEADS ARE BETTER-c/o Patty Kim, Box 68568, 360A Bloor St., W. Toronto, Ontario N5S-1X1 $1
GEAN IS DEAD-c/o Anna Garza, 8326 Leather Market, Houston TX 77064
GIANT ROBOT-POB 2053, Los Angeles CA 90064 $4
GODZILLA WEST-POB 10421, Oakland CA 94610
GORDON YAMAMOTO AND THE KING OF GODS-c/o Gene Yang, 2550 Shattuck Ave. #113, Berkeley CA 94704
GUNK-c/o Ramdasha, 16 Lord Sterling Rd., Basking Ridge NJ 07920
HEY MEXICAN!-c/o Bianca Ortiz, 2415 Fordham St., San Pablo CA 94806
HIJINX-c/o Joanie Chen, POB 675, Walnut CA 91788-0675
K CHRONICLES-c/o Keith Knight, POB 591794, San Francisco CA 94159-1794
KITTUMS-c/o Mikel Delgado, POB 410312, San Francisco CA 94141
KREME KOOLERS-c/o Keyan, 110 Legion Way SE #403, Olympia WA 98501
KRONIKLE KOMIX-c/o Jennifer Gonzalez, 5 W. 8th St. #504, New York City NY 10011
LA MALA YERBA-c/o Carlos, POB 3051, Oakland CA 94609
LIMBO DEMONS-c/o Senzuri, 1 Riverdale Ave. Suite #474, Riverdale NY 10463-4912
LOST ID-c/o Claudia, 700 E. 9th St. #20, New York City NY 10009
L'OUVERTURE-c/o Kevin Campell, POB 8565, Atlanta GA 30306
MAKE YOUR OWN ZINE-c/o Gani Requizo, 815 Ialia St., Muzon, Taytay 1920 Rizal PHILIPPINES
MARKS IN TIME-c/o Iraya, POB 421912, San Francisco CA 94142
MAYBE (SHE SAID)-c/o Lisa Gonzalez, 5024 Hyde Park Dr., Fremont CA 94538
MENISCUS-c/o Yuan-Kwan Chan, 12793 Misty Creek Ln., Fairfax VA 22033
MONSOON JUNIOR-c/o Kevin Chan, Pacific News Service, 450 Mission St. #204, San Francisco CA 94105
MY BROKEN HALO-c/o Mesheyle, 15344 62nd Ave. S., Tukwila WA 98188-2503
MY LETTER TO THE WORLD-c/o Lily, POB 40082, Berkeley CA 94704
PLANET DRAG KING-c/o Olivia Edith, 3233 Juliet St., Pittsburgh PA 15213
POCHO MAGAZINE-c/o Esteban Zul and Lalo Lopez, POB 40021, Berkeley CA 94704
POODLE-POB 743, #161-6200 McKay Ave., Burnaby BC V5H4M0 CANADA
PURE TUNA FISH-c/o Rita Fatila, 16 Fairview Ave., St. Thomas, Ontario N5R4X4 CANADA
RIOT GRRL REVIEW-c/o Kristy Chan, POB 1791, Fort Meyers FL 33902
RUBBER BALLS & LIQUOR-c/o Apolinar, POB 48133, Niles IL 60714-0133
SAL, SI PUEDES-City Terrace, Box 376, 2168 S. Atlantic Blvd., Monterey Park CA 91754
SCAREDY-CAT STALKER-5535 NE Glisa #5, Portland OR 97213
SECRET ASIAN MAN-80 Edgecombe #41, New York City NY 10030
SKUNK-Girl-Trouble Publications, POB 20524, Tompkins Square Station, New York City NY 10009
SOME HOPE AND SOME DESPAIR-c/o Lance Hahn, POB 460346, San Francisco CA 94146. (J CHURCH)
STATIC-c/o Nono Girl and Squeaky, POB 420902, San Francisco CA 94142-0902 $3
STUFF-c/o Evan Lim, 85 Sequoia Dr., Pasadena CA 91105
THE WORLD IS YOURS: A ZINE BY AND ABOUT ASIANS AND OUR STRUGGLE IN AMERIKA-Buddhahead Productions, 11974 Idaho Ave., Los Angeles CA 90025
WE LIKE POO-c/o Tara Sin, 3128 16th St. #125, San Francisco CA 94103
ZUM-c/o Yvonne and George Chen, POB 4449, Berkeley CA 94704

ZINES RECOMMENDED BY OTHER ZINES
FROM *ZINE WORLD #1:*
J MAN TIMES-J. Rassoul, 655 Hidden Valley Dr #113, Ann Arbor MI 48104 $1
CRAWFISH-Stephanie Webb, 2701 University Ave. #404, Madison WI 53705. $1 pop culture satire smorgasboard
MEDIA DIET-POB 441915, Somerville MA 02144 $2
FILTH, 2336 Market St #104, San Francisco CA 94114 $2
MUSEA-4000 Hawthorne #5, Dallas TX 75219-2223 $1
BUMMERS & GUMMERS-POB 91, Lorane OR 97451 $2
A SHATTERED MIND-Jerianne, 220 S. McCombs St #2, Martin TN 38237 $1
GULP LIFE-Joe Gallo, 924 Valencia #157, SF CA 94110 $2
HIP MAMA (kid-raising)-POB 9097, Oakland CA 94613 $4
BLACKSHEETS-POB 31155, San Francisco CA 94131 $5
STATIC-POB 420902, SF CA 94142 $3 (about pranks)
FROM *GIANT ROBOT:*
ALBINO PECTARE-c/o Patti Kim, 293 Clinton St., Toronto, Ontario M6G2Y7 CANADA
ALLRIGHT-c/o Simon Murphy, Charlotte Cooper 8 Hanley Ct., Hanley Rd., London N43QB ENGLAND
APB-POB 1551, Royal Oak MI 48068
ASIAN EYE-c/o Colin Geddes, 253 College St. #108, Toronto, Ontario M5T 1R5 CANADA
BIGGER THAN YOUR ROBOT-16 Blenheim Dr., Brampton, Ontario L6Z1H9 CANADA $2, winnie@innuendoi.-tlug.org
BLOW MY COLON-c/o A. Vegue, POB 1881, Santa Ana CA 92702 $2
BROWBEAT-POB 11124, Oakland CA 94611-1124 $5
CHIKA QUARTERLY-3710 W. Nassau St., Tampa FL 33607
DO THE POP-101 Boren Ave. Ste. 114, Seattle WA 98104-1300, dothepop@netcom.com
DOUBLE NEGATIVE MAGAZINE-POB 59, Boston MA 02123-0059 $2, jwiesner@emerson.edu
EAT AND GET OUT!-POB 267953, Chicago IL 60626-7953 $2
ELECTRIC INK-16787 Beach Blvd. #636, Huntington Beach CA 92647
EXILE OSAKA-S. Kaufman 3115 Brighton 6th St. #6B, Brooklyn NY 11235. M. Kaufman, 2-7-304 Takabedai 3 chome, Tondabayashi, Osaka 584 JAPAN $3, exileosaka@aol.com
FIREBALL-c/o Brian Ralph, 2 College St., RISD Box 406, Providence RI 02903 $1+2 stamps
FIZZ-www.io.com/~fizz
GET OFF MY WAGON-c/o Imminent Rock, POB 16041, Oakland CA 94610-6041 $3.50
GIRL DETECTIVE-c/o A. Vegue, POB 584, Claremont CA 91711 $1
HELLO, SAILOR!-207 Sullivan St. #5, NYC NY 10012 $2.50
HOE-c/o Allan Horrocks, 189 Russ St., San Francisco CA 94103 $3, mool@sfnet.com
HOT MEXICAN LOVE COMICS-542 Los Robles, Pasadena CA 91101
INDY MAGAZINE-611 NW 34th Dr., Gainesville FL 32607
JACKIE CHAN FAN CLUB NEWSLETTER-USA, POB 2281, Portland OR 97208 $13.50
KAIJU REVIEW-c/o Dan Reed, 301 E. 64th St. NYC NY 10021 $3.50
KIT 'ZINE-c/o Kit, 27 E. Central Ave, Rt. 5, Paoli PA 19301-1358
KUNG-FU GIRL-1215 SW 4th Ave., Gainesville FL 32601 $3, FN08959@freenet.ufl.edu.
MILKCRATE DIGEST-Box 1560, 2 College St., Providence RI 02903
MOD FUCK EXPLOSION-c/o Jon Moritsugu, POB 210535, San Francisco CA 94121-0535 $1
NEW EXPATRIATE-c/o Chuck Eisenstein, No. 9, Lane 13, Chang Chun Rd., Hsintien TAIWAN, Chuck@Pristine.com.tw
NEW POMPAI-MJ Hind Fuji Flat #203, 4-18-23 Wakakusa-cho, Utsunomiya-shi T320 JAPAN
NEW POSITIVE SANCTIONS-103 Downey St., San Francisco CA 94117-4419
PARTY MANIA-c/o Tado, 2-24-14 Nishi Kunitachi-shi, Tokyo JAPAN
PERVERT'S CLUB-c/o A.M. Works, POB 49542, Austin TX 78765 $3.75
PRINCESS-863 Clayton St. #2, San Francisco CA 94117 $3, Prinsss@aol.com.
PRO-WRESTLING TORCH-POB 201844, Minneapolis MN 55420 $2
POP SCENE-10480 Imperial Ave., Cupertino CA 95014 $2
PSYCHO MOTO ZINE-c/o Ethan, 45 Ave. B #2, NYC NY 10009 $1
R2D2-c/o Jef Czekaj, 515 W. Buffalo St., Ithaca NY 14850-4013 $1.50
RED CALLOWAY'S BIG BANG-c/o Zoo Arsonist Press, POB 6322, San Pedro CA 90734 $3
RESTAURANT FUEL-POB 803, Greenbelt MD 20768 $3
ROOMMATE STORIES-1234 Tiegen, Hayward CA 94542 $1+2 stamps
SHAMAN JUMP-c/o Zero Hour Productions, 3217 Shelley St., Victoria, B.C., V8P 4A6 CANADA $2.50
SUSHI CONCEPTION-185 S. Whitney St., 3rd Fl., Hartford CT 06105
THUMB-c/o Eric Mast, 144 Woodlawn Saratoga Springs NY 12866 $3
TOP SHELF-c/o Primal Groove Press, POB 15125, Portland OR 97293-5125
VES: MOVIES AND WHATEVER-POB 319, Roselle NJ 07203 $3
WRESTLING OBSERVER NEWSLETTER-POB 1228, Campbell CA 95009-1228.
XENORAMA-c/o David McRobie, 4540 Maple Ave. #141, La Mesa CA 91941-6355 $2
YAKUZA-POB 26039, Wilmington DE 19899-6039

ZINES RECOMMENDED BY KYANNE BREDEN AND STACY WAKEFIELD:
BURN COLLECTOR-c/o Al Burian, 307 Blueridge Rd., Carrboro NC 27510 50
FAST CONNECTION-POB 54 Heaton, Newcastle-upon-tyne NE65YW ENGLAND
HOT PANTS-CP5756, Succ. C, Montreal, Quebec, CANADA $1
MEDUSA-POB 586, Accord NY 12404 50¢
MONS OF VENUS-3566 Walker, Box 1203, Memphis TN 03811 $1
WIVES TALES-Britton, POB 81332, San Diego CA 92138 $1

Catalog

From V. Vale, former
co-publisher of RE/Search

For the past 20 years V. Vale has brought uncompromising content and innovation to the staid, predictable world of publishing, beginning with *Search & Destroy*, 1976-1979. In 1980, wishing to expand beyond punk rock, he founded *RE/Search*, the cutting-edge compass of alternative cultural development. *RE/Search* has sparked trends and exerted a major influence disproportionate to numbers sold; e.g., *Incredibly Strange Music* (lounge music), *Modern Primitives* (tattoo/piercing), *Incredibly Strange Films*, *Angry Women*, *Industrial Culture Handbook*, *Freaks*, etc. Vale's newest publishing venture, V/Search, promises to continue the "tradition" of examining and illuminating the untraditional, without compromise.

ZINES! Vol. Two *Incendiary Interviews with Independent Publishers*

Zines! Vol. Two continues the investigation of the territory surveyed in *Zines! Vol. One*. In-depth interviews include Dishwasher Pete (chronicling his goal of washing dishes in every state in the USA); Keffo of *Temp Slave* (talking about pranks on the job and the resurgence of interest in the I.W.W. [International Workers of the World]); Revolutionary Knitting Circle (three feminist teenage anarchist-sympathizers discuss dreams of a better world); *Murder Can Be Fun* (John Marr discusses provocative crime and teen sex advice books that inspired his zine); Candi Strecker (who has produced fringe-pop-culture zines since 1979, spotlighting trends before they become trendy again); and much, much more! V/Search, continuing the legacy of RE/Search books, documents contemporary cutting-edge dissatisfaction with the status quo, providing inspiration and creative alternatives to mass media "information" that reinforces conformity. Zine reviews, directory of zines, index and over 200 photos and illustrations. 8½x11″. 148 pp. illus. **$14.99**

Due out in Summer '97   **NEW LOW PRICE!!**

Search & Destroy, Vol. 1 & 2

By the mid-'70s the Punk aesthetic had spread out from England to America. The American Punk scene soon developed an energy and talent of its own, which was documented in its own home-grown, heavily illustrated magazine, *Search & Destroy*, edited by V.Vale between 1976 and 1979. This complete facsimile reprint of all 11 issues captures the rage, riot and revelations of an extraordinary period. Innovators such as Devo, Iggy Pop, Dead Kennedys and Ramones are featured alongside William Burroughs, J.G. Ballard, John Waters, Russ Meyer and David Lynch. This is the *real thing*, written when punk was first inventing itself. JUMBO SIZE 10x15″, 150 pp, over 150 articles and 400 photos & illustrations per volume. **Vol.1: $19.95; Vol.2: $19.95.**

"Unsurpassed! The best punk rock documentation there will ever be. A library resource."–LAST GASP NEWSLETTER

Memoirs of a Sword Swallower *by Daniel P. Mannix*

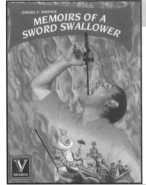

"I probably never would have become America's leading fire-eater if Flamo the Great hadn't happened to explode that night . . ." So begins this true story of life with a traveling carnival, peopled by amazing characters (the Human Ostrich, the Human Salamander, Jolly Daisy, etc.) who commit outrageous feats of wizardry. This is one of the only authentic narratives revealing the "tricks" (or more often, the lack thereof) and skills involved in a sideshow, and is invaluable to those aspiring to this profession. Having cultivated the desire to create real magic since early childhood, Mannix rose to become a top act within a season, and here is his inspiring tale. **NEW: RARE PHOTOS!** This is the first edition to include photos of the actual characters in the book, most of them taken by Mannix himself in the '30s. 8½x11″, 128 pp, 55 photos & illustrations. **$15.99.**
A few signed copies available at $30; author died 1/29/97.
"The beautiful world of outcasts and freaks banding together to form an alternate society is accurately and compassionately portrayed by an insider."–CIRCUS ARTS

ZINES! Vol. One *Incendiary Interviews with Independent Publishers*

In the past two decades a quiet revolution has gained force: over 50,000 "zines" (independent, not-for-profit self publications) have emerged and spread—mostly through the mail, with little publicity. Flaunting off-beat interests, extreme personal revelations and social activism, zines directly counter the *pseudo-communication* and glossy lies of the mainstream media monopoly. These interviews with a dozen zine creators capture all the excitement associated with uncensored freedom of expression, while offering insight, inspiration and delight. Includes: *Beer Frame, Crap Hound, Thrift SCORE, Bunny Hop, OUTPUNK, Fat Girl, Housewife Turned Assassin, Meat Hook, X-Ray, Mystery Date* and more! 8½x11″, 184 pp, over 200 illustrations & photos, quotations, zine directory, index. **$18.99**

" These fanzines represent an almost unprecedented breakthrough . . ."–ALTERNATIVE PRESS
"An excellent look at the history of the zine movement."–AMERICAN BOOKSELLER MAGAZINE
". . . a fascinating survey . . ."–PUBLISHERS WEEKLY

#16: RE/Search Guide to Bodily Fluids by Paul Spinrad

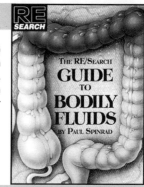

Table of Contents: Mucus, Menstruation, Saliva, Sweat, Vomit, Urine, Flatus, Feces, Earwax & more
This guide sparks a radical rethinking of our relationship with our bodies and Nature, humorously (and seriously) spanning the gamut of everything you ever wanted to know about bodily functions and excreta. Each bodily function is discussed from a variety of viewpoints: scientific, anthropological, historical, mythological, sociological, and artistic.
Topics include: constipation (such as its relationship to cornflakes and graham crackers!); the history and evolution of toilet paper; farting; urine (including little known facts about urinalysis); earwax; smegma as well as many other engrossing topics! 8½x11″, 148pp. **$15.99**

"A stunning new release . . . *The RE/Search Guide to Bodily Fluids* is a must buy."–BIKINI
"This is an important work that shouldn't be ignored, packed with fascinating facts on excreta."
–LOADED MAGAZINE

#15 & 14: Incredibly Strange Music, Vol. 1 & 2

Incredibly Strange Music surveys the territory of neglected "garage sale" records (mostly from the '50s–'70s), spotlighting genres, artists and one-of a-kind gems that will delight and surprise. **Genres examined include:** "easy listening," "exotica," and "celebrity" (massive categories in themselves) as well as more recordings by (singing) cops and (polka-playing) priests, undertakers, religious ventriloquists, astronauts, opera-singing parrots, beatnik and hippie records, and gospel by blind teenage girls with bouffant hairdos. Virtually every musical/lyrical boundary in the history of recorded sound has been breached; every sacred cow upturned. EACH 8½x11″, 208 pp, over 200 photos.
Vol. 1: $17.99, Vol. 2: $17.99, *SPECIAL: both for $32.00.*

"Fans of ambient music, acid jazz, ethno-techno, even industrial rock, will find the leap back to these genres an easy one to make."–ROLLING STONE

#13: Angry Women

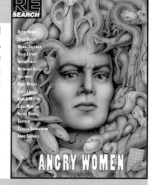

16 cutting-edge performance artists discuss critical questions such as: How can revolutionary feminism encompass wild sex, humor, beauty, spirituality *plus* radical politics? How can a powerful movement for social change be *inclusionary*? A wide range of topics is discussed *passionately*. Armed with contempt for dogma, stereotype & cliche, these creative visionaries probe deeply into our social foundation of taboos, beliefs and totalitarian linguistic contradictions from whence spring (as well as thwart) our theories, imaginings, behavior and dreams. 8½x11″, 240 pp, 135 illustrations. **$18.99**

◆ **Karen Finley** ◆ **Annie Sprinkle** ◆ **Diamanda Galás** ◆ **bell hooks** ◆ **Kathy Acker** ◆ **Avital Ronnell** ◆ **Lydia Lunch** ◆ **Sapphire** ◆ **Susie Bright** ◆ **Valie Export** ◆ **and many more . . .**

"The view here is largely pro-sex, pro-porn, and pro-choice . . . Art and activism are inseparable from life and being. This is the 13th step, beyond AA's 12: a healing rage."–THE VILLAGE VOICE
"This book is a Bible. . . it hails the dawn of a new era–the era of an inclusive, fun, sexy feminism. . . Every interview contains brilliant moments of wisdom."–AMERICAN BOOK REVIEW

#12: Modern Primitives

An eye-opening, startling investigation of the undercover world of body modifications: tattooing, piercing and scarification. **Articles & interviews:** *Fakir Musafar* (Silicon Valley ad executive who has practiced every known body modification); *Genesis & Paula P-Orridge* describing numerous ritual scarifications and symbolic tattoos; *Ed Hardy* (editor of *Tattootime*); *Capt. Don Leslie*; *Jim Ward*; *Anton LaVey* (founder of the Church of Satan); *Lyle Tuttle*; *Raelyn Gallina* (women's piercer) & others talking about body practices that develop identity and philosophic awareness and explore sexual sensation. 22 interviews, 2 essays, quotations, sources/bibliography & index. 8½x11″, 212 pp, 279 photos and illustrations. **$17.99**

"Through 'primitive' modifications, they are taking possession of the only thing that any of us will ever really own: our bodies."–WHOLE EARTH REVIEW
"The photographs and illustrations are both explicit and astounding . . . This is the ideal biker coffee table book, a conversation piece that provides fascinating food for thought."–IRON HORSE

#11: Pranks!

A prank is a "trick, a mischievous act, a ludicrous act." Although not regarded as poetic or artistic acts, pranks constitute an art form and genre in themselves. Here pranksters such as Timothy Leary, Abbie Hoffman, Monte Cazazza, Jello Biafra, Earth First!, Joe Coleman, Karen Finley, John Waters and Henry Rollins (and more) challenge the sovereign authority of words, images & behavioral convention. This iconoclastic compendium will dazzle and delight all lovers of humor, satire and irony. 8½x11″, 240 pp, 164 photos & illustrations. **$19.99**

"The definitive treatment of the subject, offering extensive interviews with 36 contemporary tricksters . . . from the Underground's answer to Studs Terkel."–WASHINGTON POST

"Men never do evil so completely and cheerfully as when they do it from religious conviction."–Pascal

RE/SEARCH BACKLIST

#10: Incredibly Strange Films

Spotlighting unhailed directors–*Herscell Gordon Lewis, Russ Meyer, Larry Cohen, Ray Dennis Steckler, Ted V. Mikels, Doris Wishman* and others–who have been critically consigned to the ghettos of gore and sexploitation films. In-depth interviews focus on philosophy, while anecdotes entertain as well as illuminate theory. 13 interviews, numerous essays, A-Z of film personalities, "Favorite Films" list, quotations, bibliography, filmography, film synopses, & index. 8½x11″, 224 pp, 157 photos & illustrations. **$17.99**

"Flicks like these are subversive alternatives to the mind control propagated by the mainstream media."–IRON HORSE

"Whether discussing the ethics of sex and violence on the screen, film censorship, or their personal motivations . . . the interviews are intelligent, enthusiastic and articulate."–SMALL PRESS

#8/9: J.G. Ballard

A comprehensive special on this supremely relevant writer, now famous for *Empire of the Sun* and *Crash*. 3 interviews, biography by David Pringle, fiction and non-fiction excerpts, essays, quotations, bibliography, sources, & index. 8½x11″, 176 pp, 76 photos & illustrations. **$17.99**

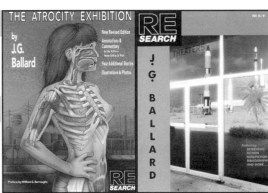

The Atrocity Exhibition *by Ballard*.

A large-format, illustrated edition, *Atrocity Exhibition* is widely regarded as Ballard's finest, most complex work. Withdrawn by E.P. Dutton after having been shredded by Doubleday, this outrageous work was finally printed in a small edition by Grove before lapsing out-of-print. With four additional fiction pieces, extensive annotations (a book in themselves). Illustrated. 8½x11″, 136 pp. **$13.99 Limited edition, signed, hardback $50.00.**

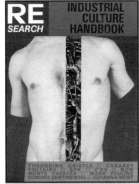

#6/7: Industrial Culture Handbook

Essential library reference guide to the deviant performance artists and musicians of the *Industrial Culture* movement: *Survival Research Laboratories, Throbbing Gristle, Cabaret Voltaire, SPK, Non, Monte Cazazza, Johanna Went, Sordide Sentimental, R&N,* and *Z'ev.* **Some topics discussed:** brain research, forbidden medical texts & films, creative crime & *interesting* criminals, modern warfare & weaponry, neglected gore films & their directors, psychotic lyrics in past pop songs, art brut, etc. 10 interviews, essays, quotations, chronologies, bibliographies, discographies, filmographies, sources, & index. 8½x11″, 140 pp, 179 photos & illustrations. **$15.99**

". . . focuses on post-punk 'industrial' performers whose work comprises a biting critique of contemporary culture . . . the book lists alone are worth the price of admission!"–SMALL PRESS

✳   ✳   ✳

#4/5: W.S. Burroughs, Brion Gysin, Throbbing Gristle

Interviews, scarce fiction, essays: this is a manual of ideas and insights. Strikingly designed, with rare photos, bibliographies, discographies, chronologies & illustrations. 7 interviews, essays, chronologies, bibliographies, discographies, sources. 8½x11″, 100 pp, 58 photos & illustrations. **Topics discussed** include self-defense, biological warfare, the possibility of Revolution, utopias, assassination, con men and politicians, lost inventions, turning points in history, the JFK killing, dreams, ideal education, Hassan I Sabbah, nuclear weaponry, cloning, the cut-up theory (and practice) for producing prophetic writing, Moroccan trance music, the Dream Machine, art forgeries, Manson, the media control process, prostitution, the possibilities of video, etc. **$15.99**

"Interviews with pioneering cut-up artists William S. Burroughs, Brion Gysin and Throbbing Gristle . . . proposes a ground-breaking, radical cultural agenda for the '80s and '90s." –Jon Savage, LONDON OBSERVER

RE/SEARCH #1, #2, #3—*the shocking tabloid issues*

Deep into the heart of the Control Process. Preoccupation: Creativity & Survival, past, present & future. These are the early tabloid issues, 11x17″, full of photos and innovative graphics.
◆ **#1:** J.G. Ballard ◆ Cabaret Voltaire ◆ Julio Cortazar ◆ Octavio Paz ◆ Sun Ra ◆ The Slits ◆ Robert K. Brown (editor *Soldier of Fortune*) ◆ Conspiracy Theory Guide ◆ Punk Prostitutes ◆ and more.
◆ **#2:** DNA ◆ James Blood Ulmer ◆ Z'ev ◆ Aboriginal Music ◆ West African Music Guide ◆ Surveillance Technology ◆ Monte Cazazza on poisons ◆ Diane Di Prima ◆ Seda ◆ German Electronic Music Chart ◆ Isabelle Eberhardt ◆ and more.
◆ **#3:** Fela ◆ New Brain Research ◆ The Rattlesnake Man ◆ Sordide Sentimental ◆ New Guinea ◆ Kathy Acker ◆ Sado-Masochism (interview with Pat Califia) ◆ Joe Dante ◆ Johanna Went ◆ SPK ◆ Flipper ◆ Physical Modification of Women (anticipated *Modern Primitives*) ◆ and more.
$8 each, full set for $20 WHILE THEY LAST!!

143

The Confessions of Wanda von Sacher-Masoch

Finally available in English: the racy and riveting *Confessions of Wanda von Sacher-Masoch*—married for ten years to Leopold von Sacher-Masoch (author of *Venus in Furs* and many other novels) whose whip-and-fur bedroom games spawned the term "masochism." In this feminist classic from 100 years ago, Wanda was forced to play "sadistic" roles in Leopold's fantasies to ensure the survival of herself and her 3 children—games which called into question who was the Master and who the Slave. Besides being a compelling story of a woman's search for her own identity, strength and ultimately, complete independence, this is a true-life adventure story—an odyssey through many lands peopled by amazing characters. Underneath its unforgettable poetic imagery and almost unbearable emotional cataclysms reigns a woman's consistent unblinking investigation of the limits of morality and the deepest meanings of love. Translated by Marian Phillips, Caroline Hébert & V. Vale. 8½x11", 136 pp, photo-illustrated. **$13.99**

"Extravagantly designed in an illustrated, oversized edition that is a pleasure to hold. It is also exquisitely written, engaging and literary and turns our preconceptions upside down."–LA READER

The Torture Garden *by Octave Mirbeau*

This book was once described as the "most sickening work of art of the nineteenth century!" Long out of print, Octave Mirbeau's macabre classic (1899) features a corrupt Frenchman and an insatiably cruel Englishwoman who meet and then frequent a fantastic 19th century Chinese garden where torture is practiced as an art form. The fascinating, horrific narrative slithers deep into the human spirit, uncovering murderous proclivities and demented desires. Lavish, loving detail of description. Introduction, biography & bibliography. 8½x11", 120 pp, 21 photos. **$15.95**

". . . sadistic spectacle as apocalyptic celebration of human potential. . . A work as chilling as it is seductive."–THE DAILY CALIFORNIAN

"Here is a novel that is hot with the fever of ecstatic, prohibited joys, as cruel as a thumbscrew and as luxuriant as an Oriental tapestry. This exotic story of Clara and her insatiable desire for the perverse and the forbidden has been hailed by the critics."—Charles Hanson Towne

". . . daydreams in which sexual images are mixed nightmarishly with images of horror."—Ed. Wilson

Freaks: We Who Are Not As Others *by Daniel P. Mannix*

Another long out-of-print classic book based on Mannix's personal acquaintance with sideshow stars such as the Alligator Man and the Monkey Woman. Read all about the notorious love affairs of midgets; the amazing story of the elephant boy; the unusual amours of Jolly Daisy, the fat woman; the famous pinhead who inspired Verdi's *Rigoletto*; the tragedy of Betty Lou Williams and her parasitic twin; the black midget, only 34 inches tall, who was happily married to a 264-pound wife; the human torso who could sew, crochet and type; and bizarre accounts of normal humans turned into freaks–either voluntarily or by evil design! 88 astounding photographs and additional material from the author's personal collection. 8½x11", 124 pp. **$15.95**

"RE/Search has provided us with a moving glimpse at the rarified world of physical deformity; a glimpse that ultimately succeeds in its goal of humanizing the inhuman, revealing the beauty that often lies behind the grotesque and in dramatically illustrating the triumph of the human spirit in the face of overwhelming debility."–SPECTRUM WEEKLY

Bob Flanagan, Super-Masochist

Bob Flanagan, 1952-1996, was born in New York City, grew up with Cystic Fibrosis (a genetically inherited, nearly-always fatal disease) and lived longer than any other person with CF. The physical pain of his childhood suffering was principally alleviated by masturbation, wherein pain and pleasure became linked, resulting in his lifelong practice of extreme masochism. In deeply confessional interviews, Bob details his sexual practices and his relationship with long-term partner and Mistress, Sheree Rose. He tells how frequent near-death encounters modified his concepts of gratification and abstinence, reward and punishment, and intensified his masochistic drive. Through his insider's perspective on the Sado-Masochistic community, we learn about branding, piercing, whipping, bondage and endurance trials. Includes photos by L.A. artist Sheree Rose. 8½x11", 128 pp, 125 photos & illustrations. **$14.99**

". . . an eloquent tour through the psychic terrain of SM, discussing the most severe sexual diversions with the humorous detachment of a shy, clean living nerd. I came away from the book wanting to know this man."–DETAILS MAGAZINE

TWO by Charles Willeford: High Priest of California *and* Wild Wives

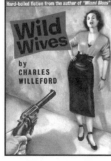

A classic of hard-boiled fiction, Charles Willeford's *Wild Wives* is amoral, sexy, and brutal. Written in a sleazy San Francisco hotel in the early 1950's while on leave from the Army, Willeford creates a tale of deception featuring the crooked detective Jacob C. Blake and his nemesis–a beautiful, insane young woman who is the wife of a socially prominent San Francisco architect. Blake becomes entangled in a web of deceit, intrigue and multiple murders in this exciting period tale. 5x7", 108pp. **$10.99**

Russell Haxby is a ruthless used car salesman obsessed with manipulating and cavorting with a married woman. In this classic of Hard-boiled fiction, Charles Willeford crafts a wry, sardonic tale of hypocrisy, intrigue and lust. Set in San Francisco in the early fifties–every sentence masks innuendo, every detail hides a clue, and every used car sale is an outrageous con job. 5x7", 148 pp. **$10.99**

"A tempo so relentless, words practically fly off the page."–VILLAGE VOICE

ALSO AVAILABLE

Incredibly Strange Music, Vol. 1

CD $16; (cassette only $10!) This is an amazing anthology of outstanding, hard-to-find musical/spoken word gems from LPs that are as scarce as hen's teeth. *Vol. One* contains "Up, Up & Away" played on an unbelievably out-of-tune sitar, "The Will to Fail" (hilarious) and "A Cosmic Telephone Call," etc. These tracks must be heard to be believed!

Incredibly Strange Music, Vol. 2

CD $16 Lucia Pamela's barnyard frenzy "Walking on the Moon'; "How to Speak Hip" by Del Close & John Brent; "Join the Gospel Express" by singing ventriloquist doll Little Marcy; "Bumble Bee Bolero," "Terror" by Bas Sheva; "Billy Mure's "Chopsticks Guitar"; "The Letter" by the Nirvana Sitar & String Group, and many more musical gems. Full liner notes.

Ken Nordine COLORS CD $16 A kaleidoscope of riotous sound and imagery. The pioneer of "Word Jazz" delivers "good lines" which are as smooth as water, inviting the listener to embark upon a musical fantasy evoking ethereal images of every poetic hue. An essential addition to the musical library of the hip connoisseur. Contains extra tracks not on original vinyl record.

Eden Ahbez EDEN'S ISLAND CD $16 Released in 1960 on Del-Fi records, it "is a bizarre cross between exotica, '50's pop, and Beat-Era lyricism, whose genius was probably unintentional." In *Incredibly Strange Music, Vol. I*, Mickey McGowan calls *Eden's Island* "one of the truly strange masterpieces on record." Contains additional tracks not on the original, rare LP. Hard-to-find and probably already out-of-print.

THE ESSENTIAL PERREY & KINGSLEY CD $ 16 Two fantastic, classic LPs (*The In Sound from Way Out* and *Kaleidoscopic Vibrations*) combined on one hard-to-find, currently out-of-print CD available exclusively from RE/Search mail orders. This CD contains *all* the tracks recorded by the Perrey-Kingsley duo. Recordings were painstakingly spliced together by hand in a labor of love. Sounds as fresh as tomorrow!

SEARCH & DESTROY original tabloids: Incomplete Set, #1-2, 4-11 $5 each; **$39** for incomplete set. "Living the punk life, 1976-1979." Incendiary interviews, passionate photographs, art brutal. Corrosive minimalist documentation of the only youth rebellion of the seventies.. Crammed with information and inspiration. *The real thing, not some doddering sensational rehash.* #1) Nuns, Crime #2) Devo, Clash, Ramones, Iggy, Weirdos, Patti Smith, Avengers, Dils #4) Iggy, Dead Boys, Bobby Death, Jordan & the Ants, Mumps, Helen Wheels, Patti Smith #5) Sex Pistols, Nico, Screamers, Crisis, Crime, Talking Heads #6) Throbbing Gristle, Clash, Nico, Pere Ubu, UXA, Negative Trend, Sleepers, Buzzcocks #7) John Waters, Devo, DNA, Cabaret Voltaire, Roky Erickson #8) Mutants, Cramps, Siouxsie, Chrome #9) Dead Kennedys, X, David Lynch, Pere Ubu, DOA #10) WSB, JGB, Plugz, X, #11: All-photo supplement. Tabloid format, 11x17."

Louder Faster Shorter *Punk Video*

San Francisco, March 21, 1978. In the intense, original punk rock scene at the Mabuhay Gardens (the only club in town which would allow it), the AVENGERS, DILS, MUTANTS, SLEEPERS and UXA played a benefit for striking Kentucky coal miners ("Punks Against Oppression!"), raising $3,300. The check was actually mailed and received. One of the only surviving 16mm color documents of this short-lived era, *LOUDER FASTER SHORTER* captured the spirit and excitement of "punk rock" before revolt became mere style. The filmmaker was Mindaugis Bagdon, a member of *Search & Destroy*, the publication which chronicled and catalyzed the punk rock "youth culture" rebellion of the late '70s. "Exceptionally fine color photography, graphic design and editing" (S.F. International Film Festival review, 1980). by Mindaugis Bagdon. 20 minute video in **US NTSC VHS Format** only. **$15**

Tattoo Time *edited by Don Ed Hardy*

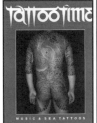

♦ **#1: NEW TRIBALISM** This classic issue feature OUT OF PRINT attooing renaissance started by Cliff Raven, Ed Hardy, Leo Zulueta & others. **$10**
♦ **#2: TATTOO MAGIC** This issue examines all facets of Magic & the Occult. Tattooed Charms, Sacred Calligraphy, Dragons, and Christian Tattoos. **$10**
♦ **#3: MUSIC & SEA TATTOOS** Deluxe double book issue with over 300 photos. Mermaids, pirates, fish, punk rock tattoos, etc. **$15**
♦ **#4: LIFE & DEATH** Deluxe double book issue w OUT OF PRINT os, examining trademarks, architectural and mechanical tattoos, the Eternal Spirit, a Tattoo Museum, plus the gamut of Death imagery. **$15**
♦ **#5: ART FROM THE HEART** All *NEW* issue that's bigger than ever before (128 pp) with hundreds of color photographs. Featuring in-depth articles on tattooers, contemporary tattooing in Samoa, a survey of the new weirdo monster tattoos, and much more! **$20**

Halloween
by Ken Werner

A classic photo book. Startling shots from the "Mardi Gras of the West," San Francisco's *adult* Halloween festivities in the Castro district. Beautiful 9x12" hardback bound in black boards. 72 pp. Black glossy paper stock. This shocking hardcover photo book is an absolute steal at this price; when stocks are exhausted that will be it! **$15**

Sidetripping
by Charles Gatewood

Unforgettable, deviant fringe photographs by Charles Gatewood. Deep focus commentary by William S. Burroughs. A classic photo book, long out of print. Available here in a *limited offering,* as-is condition. As intense as Larry Clark's *Tulsa,* and equally as rare. 9x12". Warning: *perfume de molde.* For persons possessing an iron constitution and a steel stomach. **Only $10 while they last!**

✍ ✍ SPECIAL DISCOUNTS ☎ ☎

Just The RE/Search Library: (Save $36!) All RE/Search serials

Offer includes the *RE/Search #1, 2 & 3 tabloids, #4/5: Burroughs/Gysin/Throbbing Gristle, #6/7: Industrial Culture Handbook, #8/9: J.G. Ballard, #10: Incredibly Strange Films, #11: Pranks!, #12: Modern Primitives, #13: Angry Women, #14: Incredibly Strange Music, Vol. 1, #15: Incredibly Strange Music, Vol. 2,* and *#16: RE/Search Guide to Bodily Fluids* by Paul Spinrad.
Special Discount Offer Only: $175 ppd. Seamail/Canada: $190.

The Classic RE/Search Library: (Save $19!) All RE/Search classic reprints

Offer includes *Freaks: We Who Are Not As Others, The Torture Garden, The Atrocity Exhibition, The Confessions of Wanda von Sacher-Masoch, High Priest of California* and *Wild Wives.* **Special Discount Offer: $68 ppd.** Seamail/Canada: $74.

The Complete Library: (Save $100!)

Includes all issues of RE/Search (both offers above), PLUS the first 5 issues of V/Search
Special Discount Offer Only: $332 ppd. Seamail/Canada: $365.

Incredibly Strange Library: (Save $13!)

Includes *Incredibly Strange Music Vol. One, Incredibly Strange Music Vol. Two* and *Incredibly Strange Films.*
Special Discount Offer Only: $49 ppd. Seamail/Canada: $55.

The Music Library: (Save $19!)

Offer includes *Incredibly Strange Music* CDs Vol. One & Two; *The Essential Perrey & Kingsley;* Ken Nordine's *Colors;* and Eden Ahbez's *Eden's Island.*
Normally $84 with shipping and handling; NOW: all CDs only $65 postpaid! ($75 postpaid Air Mail Overseas)

S&M Library: (Save $16!)

Offer includes *RE/Search #12: Modern Primitives* , *Bob Flanagan: Super-Masochist*, *The Confessions of Wanda von Sacher-Masoch*, and ***The Torture Garden***. Special Discount Offer: $52 ppd. **Seamail/Canada: $58.**

Subscriptions to V/Search

Receive the next three books published by V/Search, either our numbered interview format serials or *WHATEVER!* **$40.** Overseas/Canada: **$50.** *Please state which issue you would like your subscription to begin with (i.e., next, most recent, etc).* *Sorry no library or university subscriptions. Libraries and universities please place individual orders from this catalog.*
NEW: **Retro subscription: any 3 backlist paperbacks $40.**   *NOTE: Subscriptions sent surface mail only! No airmail.

✍ ✍ ORDERING INFORMATION ☎ ☎

MAIL: V/SEARCH Publications
20 ROMOLO #B
SAN FRANCISCO, CA 94133

OR

PHONE: Orders may be placed Monday through Friday: 10 AM to 6 PM PST, fax any time
TEL (415) 362-1465, FAX (415) 362-0742

Cash, Check or Money Order Payable to V/Search Publications **OR** Charge to Credit Card: VISA or MASTERCARD Only

SHIPPING & HANDLING CHARGES

DOMESTIC CUSTOMERS: first item $4; add $1 per additional item; for priority mail add $1 per order.
INTERNATIONAL CUSTOMERS: SEAMAIL: first item $6; add $2 per each additional item;
  AIRMAIL: first item $15; add $12 per additional item.

PAYMENT IN U.S. DOLLARS ONLY

ATTENTION CANADIAN CUSTOMERS: We *do not* accept personal checks even from a U.S. dollar account! Send Cash or International Money Orders Only! (available from the post office)

SAVE YOUR CATALOG! (SEE BACK OF THIS PAGE) XEROX THIS FORM OR JUST WRITE INFO ON A SEPARATE SHEET!!!

TITLE	#	TOTAL	
			NAME
			ADDRESS
			CITY, STATE, ZIP
			VISA/MASTERCARD #
SUBTOTAL			**EXPIRATION DATE and SIGNATURE**
CA residents add 8½% sales tax			
Shipping and handling (see above)			**PHONE NUMBER**
TOTAL			**SEND SASE FOR CATALOG (or 4 IRCs for OVERSEAS)**

index

Adams, Neal 105
Albers, Josef 96,101
Aldrich, Thomas Bailey 118
Alfred Hitchcock's (magazine) 119
American Splendor 109
Apollinaire 88
Arman 100
art cars 34-35
Asbury, Herbert 119
Asian Male Underground 64
Asimov, Isaac 115
Ask Beth 128
Auld, Sam 71,74
B-52s 69
Bagdikian, Ben 61
Ballard, J.G. 105
Barbie dolls 47
Baxter, Les 82
Beginner's Guide to Group Sex 128
Benatar, Pat 62
Berry, Jeff 84,85
Bikini Girl 111,113-114
"Black Hair/Style Politics" 64
Black Panthers 64
Blank, Harrod 35
Bloodiest Sex Crimes in History 131
Bloodlust 128
Blume, Judy 62
Board, Mykel 62
Body Parts 128
Bon Jovi 125
"Born to Wash Dishes," 17
Bosko (Hrnjak) 84,85
Boston Molasses Flood 130
Brady, James & Sarah 32-33
Brady Bunch 113
Brand, Stewart 115
Braudel, Fernand 127
Brecht, George 96
Brewton, Johnny 38
Breiding, G. Sutton 110
Bridges, Harry 21
Brown, Fredric 120
Brunner, John 105
Buck, Joan Juliet 115
Buda, Max 82
Buffet-Picabia, Gabrielle 89
Bukowski, Charles 123
Bummers & Gummers 31
Bunch, David R. 105
Bundy, Ted 132
Burroughs, William 89
Busch, Wilhelm 116
Cacophony Society 85
Caen, Herb 21,129
Cage, John 89,96,98
Cage, Nicolas 85
Camp Pendleton 57,58
Cannon, Harold 124
Cantsin, Monty 101
Caro, Marc 92
Cazazza, Monte 100
CB radio 113
Celine, Louis-Ferdinand 90
Chandler, Raymond 120
Chekhov, Anton 49
Chomsky, Noam 61
Christianity 47
Chronicle, San Francisco 7,124,129
Cibo Matto 57
Cline, Cheryl 110-112
Clinton, Chelsea 12
Clinton, Hillary 12
CNN 15
Coad, Rich 112
Combustible Edison 85
Conroy, Jack 21
Cramps 132
Crass 47
Cunningham, Merce 96
Dada 89,96
Davis, Angela 62
Dead Kennedys 61,121
Dead Ringer 120
Dear Abby 128
DeBord, Guy 88
Deisler, Guillermo 100

Delany, Samuel R. 105,107
Denny, Martin 66,82,85
Depeche Mode 59
Der Strummelpeter 116
DEVO 69,105,112,121
Dhalgren 107
Diamond, Leo 66
Dick, Philip K. 105
Diet Or Die 124
Dimples, Dolly 124
Disch, Thomas 105
Dish Rag, The 12
"The Dishwasher" 20
Dishwasher's Quarterly 12
Disinherited, The 21
Disneyland 94-95,116,123-125,127
Dixon, Jeanne 109
Doc Savage (by Kenneth Robeson) 132
Doctor Strange 105
Don the Beachcomber's 80
Douglas, Alan 110
Down and Out in Paris and London 4,8
Dracula 118
Dream Time Talking Village 31
Duchamp, Marcel 86-89,98,99
Duchamp, Suzanne 98
Dylan, Bob 110
Edison, Thomas 72
Exoticism 56-57
e-zines 18-19,86-88
Ellery Queen's (magazine) 119
Ellison, Harlan 120
Epicenter Zone 54
Factsheet Five 25,35,109,122,127
Family, The 130
Fantastic Four 105
Fleener, Mary 82
Flipside 122
Fluxus 96,99-101
Flying Machine Boys 118
Forbes 103
48 Hours 23
Frazetta, Frank 105
Freak Show Murders, The 121
Freddy the Pig 118
Friedman, Milton 77
Gangs of New York 119
garbage barges 49
gas shortage 113
General Strike (San Francisco) 21
Gingrich, Newt 12
Gold, Michael 21
Garbage People, The 130
Grand Funk Railroad 77
Grandma Moses 111
Green Day 46
Groening, Matt 94
Grosz, George 93
Gunderloy, Mike 109
Hammett, Dashiell 120
Harpers 103
Hayes, Isaac 69
Helter-Skelter 130
Higgins, Dick 96,101
High School Boys 118
Hilliard, Jess 15-16,18
Hinz, Colin 100
Hitchcock, Alfred 120
Hite Report 48
Hitler, Adolf 50
Ho Chi Minh 57
Hoffman, Dr Heinrich 116
Holmes, Sherlock 118
Home, Stewart 101
hooks, bell 57
Hot Buttered Soul 69
Hottentot Venus 63
Human Animal, The 43
Humboldt House 41-42,53
Iacocca, Lee 28
Illuminatus Trilogy 107
Indiana Torture Slaying 132
Interior, Lux 132
International Workers of the World (I.W.W.) 20, 21, 24
Internet 18
Iron Maiden 48

Jews Without Money 21
Johnson, Jack 88
Johnson, Ray 96-100
Journey 121
Kaprow, Allan 96
Kelbos 80,82
Killer in Drag 131
King, Margaret 124
Kroc, Ray (Museum) 66
Kromer, Tom 21
Labor Notes 25
Lear, John 75
Lear, William 71-72
Leave It To Beaver 119
Led Zeppelin 70,72
Leger, Fernand 100
LeGuin, Ursula K 105
Letterman, David 4,14-16,18,72
Liars, The 121
Little Rascals 119
Lorde, Audre 62
Lyman, Arthur 82
Lynch, David 115
Maciunas, George 96,101
Madame Butterfly 56
Madball 120
Magnum, P.I. 58
Maintenant 88
Mannix, Daniel P. 119,123
Manson, Charles 130
Marines, U.S. 13
Mariscal 94
Martians Go Home 120
Marvel comics 104-105
masturbation 47-48,126-127
Match, The 30
Mathematical Reviews 102
Mattachine Society 110
Max and Moritz 116
Maximumrock'n'roll 61-63,122
Mayhew, Henry 131
McGuff, Luke 106-107,112
McVeigh, Timothy 58
Media Monopoly, The 61
Memoirs of a Sword Swallower 119, 122
Mercer, Kobena 64
mimeography 104
Miss Saigon 56
Moderan 105
Modern Plastics 106
Monzan, Carlos 129
Morris, Desmond 43
Moss, Kate 46
Motherwell, Robert 88
Motor Boys 118
MTV 52
Muntz, Earl 71
My Lai massacre 59
Mystery Date 114,126
Mystery Scene 119
National Restaurant Association 12-13
Nelson, Bob 28
Neoism 101
New York Times 127
Norb, Rev. 62-64
Norris, Chuck 58
Nouveau Realism 96
Oceanic Arts (Leroy & Bob) 85
Oklahoma bombing 58
1001 Ways to Reward Employees 28
Ono, Yoko 101
Oregon Restaurant Association 11
Orwell, George 4,8
Pablo Cruise 121
Padin, Clemente 99
Page, Bettie 114
Paik, Nam June 101
Panter, Gary 92,94
Partridge Family 113
Paul, Les 72
Pekar, Harvey 109
People's Park 54-55
Peril, Lynn 114,126
Petasz, P. 101
Phantom Surfers 85
Pink Floyd 68
Pinocchio 118
Plastics, Tokyo 106
Plath, Sylvia 51
Playboy 15
Pomeroy, Jesse 130
Pop, Iggy 66,74
Pore, Jerod 127
P-Orridge, Genesis 99-100
Post Office 123
post office shootings 116,123
"PT" 86
pulp fiction 132

Purcell, David 84
Rambo 58
Ramones 121
Rancid 46,51
Rauschenberg, Robert 96,98
Reader's Digest 106,118,128
Reed, Lou 69
Remington, Frederic 98
Retail Clerks Union 8
Rich, Charlie 69
Riot Grrrl 52,61-62
Rivethead 21
Rosaldo, Renato 57
Rosebud 54-55
Roswell 39
Rowe, Chip 15
Rule, Ann 132
Rush 72
Russ, Joanna 105
Sabotage in the Workplace 29
Said, Tina 110
Sandburg, Carl 66
San Francisco earthquake, 1906 130
Saturday Night Live 28
Saunders, Pharoah 66
Scholastic Book Services 119
Schneider, Charles 82
Schwitters, Kurt 100
Sehee, Joey 80
Selleck, Tom 58
Seymour, Jim 20
Shonen Knife 57
Simpson, O.J. 129
Sinatra, Frank 72
Siouxsie 59
Slash magazine 92
Slattery, Desmond 110
Slattery's Review 109
Smile magazine 100-101
Smith, Barry 105
Sniffin' Glue 103
Sound of Music, The 75
So Wrong They're Right 66
Spelling, Tori 122
Spiderman 105
Spock, Mr 104
sports deaths 129-130
Stand On Zanzibar 105
Star Trek 104
Steele, Danielle 132
Stooges, The 74
Story of a Bad Boy 118
streaking 113
talent scouts 52
Tamimant Library (NYU) 21
Thomas, Roy 105
Thompson, Jim 120,132
Three Sisters 49
Three Stooges 119
Thrift Score 131
Titanic 131
Tolstoy, Count Lev 49
Trader Vic's 80
TV Guide 111
Twain, Mark 118
UFOs 37,39
Unabomber 18
unions 26
Van Gogh, Vincent 98
Vapors, The 63
Vernon, Florida 79*
Vibrators 69
Viet Minh 57
Vonnegut, Kurt 105
Wagner Act 26
Waiting for Nothing 21
Warhol, Andy 100,114
Wayne State Library 21
Wells, H.G. 118
Where Will You Be In 1984? 109
White Zombie 73
Wild Wheels 35,79
Wilde, Oscar 88-89
Wilder, Laura Ingalls 115
Wilson, Donald Roller 106
Wilson, Robert Anton 107
Wolfe, Gene 105
Wolfe, Tom 105
Wong, Anna May 57
Wood, Ed 131
Woolrich, Cornell 117,119-120
Woodward, Fred 30
X-Men 105
X-Ray 38
Zappa, Frank 115
Zelazny, Roger 105
Zeros 121
zoo deaths 123-124
◆ ◆ ◆

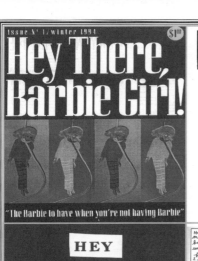

Issue N° 1/winter 1994 $1⁰⁰

Hey There, Barbie Girl!

"The Barbie to have when you're not having Barbie"

PLOTZ
Issue #3

CASHIERS DU CINEMART
2ND LUCKY #7

JERRY LEWIS
vs
DOLEMITE
BILL THE MILL
ON A RAMPAGE
GEORGE LUCAS
EXPOSED
WITCHBLADE SISTERS

WE LIKE POO

HEY

MEXICAN!

Number 11

Ain't Nothin' Like Fuckin'

MOONSHINE!

AOCHI SINGLE INSIDE(¹)

Chi-Tavo-Bus
The Renaissance Issue

JUST WHERE WE WANT YOU...

Life is a Joke

libel #16

One day she's your girlfriend. The next day she's introducing you to hers.

FLATTER!
NUMBER SIX

$3

THE JAPANESE JEWISH ISSUE

flaming jewboy

A STYLE ALL HER OWN

«NOUS SOMMES TOUS DES CASSEUR

Youth Revolt in France, March 1994

PARTY APPROVED!

FASCIST
SWIMSUIT ISSUE

The production of images furnishes a ruling ideology.

fascist HITS the Beach!

YOUR FASCIST FAVE DOFFS HIS BROWNSHIRT FOR SOME SUN 'N' FUN!

.slop hut.
issue two $1.00

HUNGRY FREAKS

2

black panthers
bigfoot   charles mingus
mexican horror films   jack hill
advice comics records & more

$3.00 cash

ZINE #1
Freedom of the pre Is for everyone
WORLD

CENSOR THIS!

Daughters of Youthn Musical Fine

Naughty Nursie

MY BLOODY SISTER #3

PATHETIC LIFE
DIARY OF A FAT SLOB
20

two bucks in stores
three bucks by mail

Zacklaster
JOBS
ALL KINDS
$2.99

THE SEX ISSUE   VOLUME 1 NO. 4 SUMMER/FALL 199

BOS+

SEX
WHAT IS IT GOOD FOR?
PUPPY LUST
PETTING THE KITTY
a job that sucks
porn stars, virgins
and swingers
lush